CHRISTIAN DENOMINATIONS

THEIR FAITH AND HISTORY

REV. DR. SALATIEL SIDHU

AuthorHouse™
1663 Liberty Drive
Bloomington, IN 47403
www.authorhouse.com
Phone: 1 (800) 839-8640

© 2015 Rev. Dr. Salatiel Sidhu. All rights reserved.

No part of this book may be reproduced, stored in a retrieval system, or transmitted by any means without the written permission of the author.

Published by AuthorHouse   04/14/2015

ISBN: 978-1-4969-6675-9 (sc)
ISBN: 978-1-4969-6676-6 (e)

Print information available on the last page.

Any people depicted in stock imagery provided by Thinkstock are models, and such images are being used for illustrative purposes only.
Certain stock imagery © Thinkstock.

This book is printed on acid-free paper.

Because of the dynamic nature of the Internet, any web addresses or links contained in this book may have changed since publication and may no longer be valid. The views expressed in this work are solely those of the author and do not necessarily reflect the views of the publisher, and the publisher hereby disclaims any responsibility for them.

Contents

About this Attempt /An introduction xiii

1. The Beginning of Christianity 1
    St. Paul and the Gentiles 7
    Catholic Christians 8
    Spreading of Christianity 10
    Persecution of Christians 14
    Downfall of Roman Empire 18
    Eastern Orthodox Church 21
2. Light of Reformation 30
    John Wycliffe 31
    John Huss 33
    Martin Luther 34
    John Calvin (1509-1564) 38
    Reformed Churches 39
3. The Lutheran Church 44
    Modern day Lutherans 46
4. Presbyterian Church 49
    John Knox and Ulrich Zwingli 49
    Presbyterians Today 50
    Evangelism in other countries 52
    William Carey 52
5. Roman Catholic Church 59
    Reformed Roman Catholic Church 59
    Faith of Roman Catholic Church 60
    God's arrangement of Salvation 61

	Religious sacraments	65
	Pope John Paul II	73
	Pope Francis	74
	Pope Benedict XVI	75
	Making sign of Cross	76
6.	Anglican Church	80
	Henry (VIll)	81
	Beginning Of Anglicanism	81
	Cranmer's Achievements and his Death	83
	Anglican Church in Present Times	85
7.	Methodists	90
	United Methodist Church	95
	Faith of the United Methodist Church	98
	John Wesley	99
8.	Quakers	104
	George Fox	104
	James Naylor's Campaign	105
	Persecution of Quakers	106
	William Penn's Holy experiment	107
	Quakers Beliefs	108
	Splinter Groups	111
9.	Baptists	115
	Hubmeier Balthasar and his wife	116
	John Bunyan	116
10.	Mennonites (Ana-Baptists) and Swiss Brethren	120
	Mennonite Beliefs	124
	Worship Services	126
	Families Values	128
11.	Amish (The simple people)	130
	Professions	132
	Family Life	134
	Amish Dress	135
	Worship Services	136
	Amish Wedding	136
12.	Seventh Day Adventist	139
	William Miller	139
	What do they believe?	142
	Who Are Seventh Day Adventists?	147

13. The Church of Christ, the Scientist..150
    Mary Baker...151
    Their Faith..153
    Healing and Medication 154
    What They Do...155
    Controversial Things of the Church 156
14. Jehovah Witnesses..161
    History of Jehovah Witnesses...161
    Charles Taze Russell 161
    What do the Jehovah Witness Publish? 163
    What do they believe?.. 164
    Misinterpretation of the word of God......................................167
15. Unification Church..171
    Faith of Unification Church..174
    First Adam..174
    Second Adam..176
    Lord and Messiah of the Second Advent 177
16. Mormons 183
    Church of Jesus Christ of Latter Day Saints.............................183
    Joseph Smith Jr 184
    Angel and the Book of Mormons..185
    Baptism of Joseph Smith and Oliver Cowdrey 188
    Book of Mormons and the Bible scholars 190
    Structure of the Church-..191
    Views about Jehovah God...192
    Opposition of Mormon Church..194
    Restoration Branch Movement...197
17. The Salvation Army 201
    William Booth the Founder.. 202
    Faith of Salvation Army.. 203
    What they do not believe 204
    Their Work 204
    Salvation Army Structure... 205
18. Congregationalists 208
    Their Faith and Beliefs...210
19. Worldwide Church of God 215
20. Unitarian Universalists.. 223
    Worship and Symbol... 226

21. Pentecostals 227
    Charles Parham 228
    Pentecostal Beliefs 229
    Pentecostal Worship 231
    Sacraments/Ordinances 233
    American Pentecostal Church 234
    Ceylon Pentecostals 235

The Last Word 239
Catholic Daily Prayer 241
(Courtesy Roman Catholic Church)

This book is dedicated to my Parents, my beloved family and to all those believers who believe in the Lord God and the living Messiah the savior of the world.

"The scripture quotations contained herein are from the New Revised Standard Version Bible, copyright,1989, by the Division of Christian Education of the National Council of the Churches of Christ in the U.S.A. Used by permission. All rights reserved."

Scripture quotations marked NKJV are taken from the New King James Version. Copyright © 1982 by Thomas Nelson, Inc. Used by permission. All rights reserved.

About this Attempt

An Introduction

This dissertation is about the causes and reasons regarding formation of religious groups or denominations. At the time of building tower of Babel, God created confusion among the people by changing their spoken tongues to many. They could not understand each other and thus got scattered into different groups. Likewise when the difference comes in understanding the word of God and peoples have different opinions about God and His word they split up into different groups and denominations. While writing and discussing about the History and faith of these denominations I have tried to be above prejudice and so I have not criticized any denomination on purpose, rather I have tried to write about each sect whatever I got through my study of various sources. I have tried to be honest in writing about the faith and history of each denomination. The denominations I chose are split away groups from one denomination or the other.

Originally the group of believers that Jesus founded they had one Christian faith based upon the teaching of Jesus Christ. It was real Catholic faith but when it turned out to be Roman Catholic Church it was no longer a Catholic faith. This Roman Catholic faith started eroding and cracks started appearing in the Roman Catholic Church. Pope's human factor created hatred in the minds of many believers and they started looking for alternate groups. After this the process of splitting did not stop. This process of formation of different groups is not only in Christianity but also in all the major religions of the world. In Hinduism, Islam and Sikhism there are hundreds of denominations and cults.

Sikhism itself is a split away group from Hinduism and it has many split away sects. That is why there are certain things common between Sikhism and Hinduism. In Islam the different groups believe in the same holy book 'Quran' and same prophet 'Mohammad' yet the various denominations not only hate each other but fight against each other. I have limited my dissertation to the Christian denomination only. People these days believe more in denominations than the supreme savior Jesus Christ. World famous evangelist Dr. Billigrahm said in his book, 'The Reason for my Hope' "Professing faith in Christ is clearly not the same as professing Christ". Then he further states that in the case of America, our country is moving in the direction of "310 million people with 310 religions" and that is very true. People have divided Christ the Supreme Savior in more than 400 denominations and sub-denominations.

Wherever I have given my comments about their faith I have based my opinion on the word of God and tried to justify the reason and the cause for the split in the already existing religious group and formation of new denomination. The books I consulted, for my dissertation, their names and the names of their authors are given at the end of each chapter. The name cult for any group is a controversial issue, because no religious group wants itself to be called a 'Cult'. However strongly they may oppose biblical facts even then they try to justify themselves and claim to be right. I have not tried to go into all the minute details about religious groups. I have written enough to justify my point regarding the cause and the reasons behind the formation of a denomination.

The purpose of writing this book is not to appease or displease any person or to compare the denominations to point out which is good or bad but to tell the reader about the beliefs and historical background of the different denominations. People all over the world eat different meals according to their food habits to satisfy their hunger and no one can say which food is good or bad, it is simply a meal. Likewise all over the world people have different faiths to satisfy their spiritual hunger. A meal is a meal whether it is American, Indian, Spanish, Chinese, Italian, and they eat to satisfy their hunger, but it may not apply to the spiritual hunger of the human soul, because soul belong to God. You can feed your mortal body with any kind of food you like and feel satisfied, but this is not true with your soul. Your soul is imperishable and it belongs to God. You cannot feed your soul with any kind of food. Religious leaders of different religions have told many ways to save your soul from the dire consequences it may face. Since human soul is God given and imperishable so Psalmist tells the way how to feed your soul and save it from going into the eternal fire. "My soul thirsts for the living God" Psalm 42:2, and that is why Jesus said, "I am the bread of life. Whoever comes to me will never be hungry, and whoever believes in me will never be thirsty" John 6:35. "I am the bread that came from heaven. John 6:41, 48. "This is the bread that comes down from heaven, so that one may eat of it and not die. I am the living bread that came down from heaven. Whosoever eats of this bread will live forever". John 6: 50, 51. Here Jesus is not talking about the perishable body, but about the human soul. So that is the only food which human soul needs to live forever and escape the torment in the eternal lake of fire. Can your religion (or the religious leader) save your soul? No religious leader claimed to be God and promised to save your soul. Since your soul belongs to God only He can save, that is why He sent His son Jesus Christ to pay the price of your sins on the cross and through His resurrection save your soul from the eternal fire and give it eternal life. Every faith has various sects and denominations and they like to worship the same God in different ways and that gives rise to the different denominations. Faith is a personal matter and every person has the right to choose his faith. Since there is only one creator God, He has to decide between wrong and right. Even the atheism is a faith and they are responsible for their faith and answerable to God their creator.

Since Jesus was not rigid like Pharisees and Sadducees rather He was above narrow mindedness and stood for the poor, helpless, hated, oppressed people and he loved the sinners. Ultimately He laid down His life for these people. So based upon the ministry of Jesus several Christian thinkers thought of social challenge in their faith. Christ said, "I was hungry and you gave me food, I was thirsty and you gave me something to drink. I was naked and you gave me clothing, I was sick you took care of me, I was in prison you visited me….. Truly I tell you, just as you did to one of the least of these who are members of my family, you did it to me". Based upon this teaching of Jesus Christ He is considered to be socialist. So many Christian denominations like the Salvation Army, Methodists, Jehovah Witnesses, Roman Catholics, Presbyterians, and Baptists are involved in social service to the people suffering because of natural calamities and disasters all over the world. Salvation Army (founded by William Booth 1829-1912) and other denominations have established hospitals, orphanages, homeless shelters, and food kitchens to help the suffering humanity.

Some of the denominations believe in 'Liberation' theology. These denominations stress upon radical social change to eliminate poverty and liberation of the oppressed. They think Jesus was the chief liberator. A section of the Roman Catholic Church opposes this idea on the ground that this is Marxist idea. Some of the denominations have stressed for equality for women and on account of that protestant denomination like Anglicans, Methodists, and Presbyterians have started ordaining women as priests, but Roman Catholics still oppose it. The main aim of feminist theologians is to eliminate the oppression of women based upon gender and race and grant them equal rights in the service of the Lord. This has given birth to wonderful feminist priests and preachers.

This book is a door through which you can see how the different groups who claim to be Christians worship the Lord God. How they interpret Jesus Christ the son of God, His birth and works. How they look on Virgin Mary the mother of Jesus Christ and God the creator of the universe. How they interpret Trinity, sacrificial death of Jesus Christ and the gift of salvation through the boundless love and grace of God. This book does not assert the supremacy of any faith over the other. Once a Presbyterian pastor asked me why have I joined Methodist Church when you have a Presbyterian background? I asked him can you tell me which denomination Jesus Christ belonged to. Was He a Presbyterian, Methodist, Anglican, Lutheran, Jehovah Witness, Mormon, or Roman Catholic? Some of these sects and denominations have done a great harm to the true Christianity preached by His disciples.

These days in the human society we find followers of one faith terrorizing and killing the people from the other faith. Even the sects having same religious leader and same religious book are killing each other and bombing their religious places, because they think the way they worship their religion is the only right way and rest of the world is wrong. Such people do not realize that as long as the people from the other faith do not do any harm to you, you do not have any right to kill or terrorize them by bombing their religious places.

The tragedy of man has been because of his free will which God has given him. So it is the free will which makes every person to think in his own way and have his own explanation and interpretation of the word of God and hence so many sects and denominations of human race. If there would have been no free will then all human beings would have been like mechanical or remote controlled toys and even that would have given joy neither to God nor to human beings. In this modern world people like everything designer. Latest designer clothes, latest electronic gadgets and not only those they want designer religion and designer God. People want religion tailored according to their own choices and taste and so want a God that can fulfill their desires and ambitions that is a designer religion and designer God. That is why in some religions there are many gods and goddesses which gives option to the individual to choose any god which he or she likes and fits their choice and requirement. In doing so they forget the Almighty God the creator and sustainer of this universe who sent His son Jesus Christ to pay the price of their sins and one day they have to face that living God to whom they are accountable for every action of theirs and will be judged on His own terms by the man Jesus Christ whom He has appointed.

A major part of this book is based upon the dissertation submitted to Freedom Bible College and Seminary Rogers Arkansas U.S.A. for my doctoral degree in Theology. I planned to publish this dissertation by expanding and making it more comprehensive by adding some more important denominations. Since I have been a student of science and theology and I am not an English major, so the language used herein is very simple and explicit. How far have I been successful in my attempt I leave it to the reader to decide? I hope this book will be more helpful to those readers who do not know about all these denominations. To include my dissertation in this book a written permission has been granted by the president of Freedom Bible College and Seminary Rogers Arkansas. I am grateful to my grandson Ankur Arora for helping me in organizing the manuscript and also thankful to my son Sandeep Sidhu senior Marketing Officer in Startec/Impact Global Communications for correcting and fixing the manuscript. Last of all but not the least I am beholden to Pastor Lee A. Brewer Ph.D for his valuable suggestions and guidance in writing this book. I am also grateful to Author House Publishers who gladly accepted to publish this dissertation and have already published my two

Rev. Dr. Salatiel Sidhu

books, "A man from the Dusty Streets" and "Holidays and Rituals of Jews and Christians".

Salatiel Sidhu
12901 Flack Street
Silver Spring Maryland U.S.A.20906

Chapter One

The Beginning of Christianity

Why different groups?

Different interpretations of the word of God have been the cause of dissensions among the different groups of believers and hence we have different denominations. Though all the major groups among the Christian believers claim that Christ is the Savior, He died for the salvation of sinners. He is the foundation and corner stone of the Christian Church, yet different groups of believers and denominations interpret the word of God differently, and so they have differences with other denominations. Sometimes they criticize other believers and try to convince the believers from other denominations that their faith is not right. Their baptism is wrong. To be saved they need to get baptized second time. Such denominations are Jehovah Witnesses, Pentecostals, Mormons and Baptists. There are other groups who doubt and reject the lordship of Jesus Christ. They refute the claim that Christ is God. They say Christ is a created being like the angels and the Adam. He by His obedience became like the Son of God. All human beings by obedience can achieve the same status as that of Christ. Such groups are Jehovah Witnesses, Mormons. Yet another group who say Christ was ordinary human being born like other human beings. He was not perfect because he did not marry and had not children, which is important for a man to be perfect. Then they believe Christ did not rise from the dead bodily. His body changed into gases and disappeared from the grave. It was ghost of Jesus Christ who appeared to the disciples after his crucifixion and resurrection on the third day. That ghost could have a body that you could touch and feel. These are some of the conceptions or misconceptions, which give birth to different denominations.

The Beginning of Christianity:

The foundation of Christianity was laid upon the unshakable rock Jesus Christ, the Son of God. After the crucifixion and resurrection of Jesus Christ on the third day of His death and His appearance to more than 500 people for 40 days, He strengthened the foundations of Christian Church. Disciples acted upon the commandment of their Lord before He was taken into heaven. He said, "Go therefore and make disciples of all the nations, baptizing them in the name of the Father and of the Son and of the Holy Spirit, teaching them to observe all things that I have commanded you; and lo, I am with you always even to the end of the age". (Matthew 28: 19, 20). On the day of Pentecost, the promise made by Jesus in John 14, was fulfilled and so Holy Spirit came with power upon every believer gathered in the Upper Room. They were filled with power and courage as they received the Holy Spirit. The same moment fear, which had gripped them, was gone. They started speaking in tongues and everyone marveled at them. They started preaching with courage before the people gathered there from different countries. Peter did first miracle by healing the paralyzed man who was sitting at the entrance of Jewish temple. People were surprised at this miracle done in the name of Jesus. Then Peter full of excitement and courage declared that the man you crucified and third day he rose from the dead, He was the Messiah. After victory over death He is sitting at the right hand of God. Without believing in Jesus Christ, His crucifixion and resurrection there are no salvation and no Christian Church, because this is the foundation of Christian faith and the Church and with this is the plan of God for salvation completed. So to the whole crowd, which was there, Peter declared, "repent, and let every one of you be baptized in the name of Jesus Christ for the remission of sins and you shall receive the gift of Holy Spirit". Acts 2:38

After hearing to Peter more than 3,000 people accepted Jesus Christ and got baptized. So every day the number of believers was increasing more and more people were added to the believers group. Even the Stephan's martyrdom bore fruit and proved a great witness for the work of the Lord. Day of Pentecost was the beginning of the Lord's work and number of believers kept increasing every day. During the first forty years Christianity had spread its roots in all the big cities of the Roman Empire. Those who accepted Christianity, most of them were Jews. Out of these main figures were Mary the mother of Jesus, four half brothers of Christ (sons of Mary and Joseph), their relatives, disciples of Jesus Christ that is Peter; James; John; Andrew brother of Peter; Philip; Thomas; Bartholomew; Matthew; James the son of Alpheus; Simon Zealots; Judas the son of James. After the death of Judas Iscariot, they elected Matthias in his place. As all the disciples and believers were mostly Jews so they kept observing all the Jewish teachings and customs and in addition they accepted Jesus Christ as the promised Messiah and savior of the world, who died for the sinners. They believed that there is no salvation through anyone else except Jesus Christ. They were called 'Ekklesia' which meant a gathering of God's people, Jewish religious leaders openly opposed new believers. After the Pentecost when disciples started preaching openly about the resurrection of Jesus and declaring Him to be the Messiah, that proved to be irritant for the Jews. To stop them from preaching and projecting Jesus as the Messiah, they arrested disciples along with Peter(1.1). Since all the disciples were Jews and they were going to the Jewish temple, attended services regularly, observed Jewish laws and rituals, so they had all respect for the Jewish faith. So they had to release them the next day and warned them not to preach in the name of Jesus. The first group of Christians believed that death of Jesus on the Cross, His burial and resurrection on the third day were unique events. Then the receiving of Holy Spirit on the Pentecost was fulfillment of the promise of Jesus made in John 14. All these divine events made them strong in faith and courageous to witness for the Lord under all circumstances. Celebrating the Lord's Supper made them realize that Jesus was the Son of God and Savior of the whole world. Drinking from the same cup and eating from the same bread cemented their unity together and all these things renewed their covenant with God and their relation with one another.

Hellenistic Jews:

Christians with Jewish background were conservative and hesitated to eat and mix up with the gentiles. The disciples like Peter with Jewish background considered themselves superior and hesitated to eat with the gentiles. Hellenistic Jews (1.2) were not so conservative. They were very faithful Christians. Since Hellenistic Jews were more liberal, so many converts came from this class of Jews. As more and more people from the Jewish community accepted Christianity, this aroused new fears in the

Jewish authorities and created new tensions between Jewish community and the Christianity. These Hellenistic Jews were scattered all over Egypt, Asia Minor, and Europe. They had Greek Cultural background and mixed easily with the gentiles. These Hellenistic Jews who believed in Jesus were very zealous workers for the Lord. It was this group of Hellenistic Jews who complained that their widows are being neglected. So they chose a group of seven believers including Stephan and Philip to oversee the welfare of their widows. These assistants in Greek were called 'Diakonoi' which we now call 'Deacons' (1.3).

In addition Stephan was doing preaching work as well. When he was preaching in Hellenist's synagogue, there was riot over his preaching and he was dragged out of the city and stoned to death (Acts 6:8-15). That was the beginning of persecution of Christians. Jewish temple authorities started to arrest and imprison those who preached about Jesus. One of the most violent and active persecutors of Christians was Saul working for the Jewish authorities. He was very zealous Pharisee. These actions widened the gap between Judaism and Christianity. Because of the persecutions, disciples were compelled to flee Jerusalem. They fled to Samaria and different places, like Antioch in Syria. These loyal believers planted churches in Damascus, Antioch, Tarsus in Syria and in Egypt and Islands like Cyprus. When Church leaders like Peter and John heard the news of these newly founded Churches they felt the need of strengthening these churches in faith and establish contacts with them so Philip and Barnabas and some other converts visited these Churches. Not only that, many newly converted zealous Christians did the revolutionary work in evangelizing the Gentiles.

After Rome and Alexandria, Antioch was the largest city with a population of more than 500,000. Antioch was the capital city of Roman province of Syria, where they had administrative offices. Majority of the population was gentiles and second largest was Jewish community. It was here in Antioch where people accepted Christianity. It was in Antioch where converts were first called 'Christians'. Actually opponents of Christianity used a derogatory word in Greek 'Christianoi' but later on Christians adopted this name. After the martyrdom of Stephan, Saul was witness to the stoning of Stephan and took the lead in persecuting Christians. Afterwards the same Jesus, whom he was persecuting, caught him while he was traveling to Damascus to arrest and put the Christians believers in

Jails. He fell to the ground blind when Jesus called him, "Saul, Saul why are you persecuting me". Then he recognized and understood why Stephan died in the name of Jesus. Saul then surrendered to the Lord as His most obedient servant. Lord told him, "It is hard to kick back against the goads". Jesus promised him to deliver from the Jewish people, as well as from the gentiles to whom he will be preaching the good news of living Messiah. Jesus appointed him to open their eyes blinded by the sin and turn them from darkness to light and from power of Satan to God, so that they may receive the forgiveness of sins and inherit the kingdom of God with those who are sanctified in the name of Jesus by faith in Him (Acts 26: 12-18).

After that, the persecutor of Christians felt happy to be persecuted for Jesus. The one, who was advocate of the Jewish law, termed as curse on everyone who failed to keep it. He advocated that there is an escape from the curse of the law. He wrote in Galatians 3:10-14 "Christ redeemed us from the curse of the law, having become a curse for us, for it is written, "Cursed is everyone who hangs on a tree". So St. Paul spent his whole life in the service of the Lord and was an instrument in spreading Christianity in Rome, Asia Minor (1.4), and in the distant places in Greece and Europe. He was faithful to the Lord till his death at the hands of Roman emperor Nero. Romans were not happy with the Jews. They started persecuting Jews. Paul was evangelizing the gentiles and disciples in Jerusalem were toeing along different lines. Paul did not stress upon adherence to the Jewish law, like circumcision and other Jewish sacraments, while the Christians in Jerusalem with Jewish background toed the Jewish line of orthodoxy. With the fear of rebellion from both the Christians and Jewish sectors, Roman authorities started laying hands on Christian leaders too. James the son of Zebedee and brother of John was murdered by the order of Herod Agrippa-I (king of Palestine). Peter also escaped and left Jerusalem. He faced martyrdom with Paul at the hands of Nero, the enemy of Christians. James half brother of Jesus stayed in Jerusalem, but around 62 AD he too was murdered at the command of Jewish high priests. So these deaths and persecutions demoralized the Church leadership. Romans considered their king Caesar as god and they had ordered Jews to perform daily sacrifices for the king. Jews did not perform sacrifices for anyone except for their Jehovah God. So they revolted against this order. Many Jews lost their lives in this conflict, which continued for four years. Finally emperor Vespasian's forces under the command of Titus attacked

Jerusalem, they looted and killed Jews. They burned the Jewish temple. Holy city was devastated and destroyed. All' Jewish temples in Palestine were razed to the ground. This was the fulfillment of prophecy of Jesus, in which had said to the disciples, "Do you see these great buildings? Not one stone shall be left upon another that shall not be thrown down" (Mark 13:2 NKV). As the city was looted, burned and their temple was destroyed, Jews doubted the Christians to be behind this mischief. It made difficult for the Church to get along with the Jewish majority community. Jewish leaders decided not to allow the Christian Jews to worship in the temple. They declared that any person who wants to remain faithful to the Jewish faith couldn't be a Christian.

According to Jews, Christianity was a gentile faith. That brought end to the apostolic age. Though most of the original apostles had died, yet they had left behind indelible mark on the pages of Christian history. Church in the Mediterranean region was founded on the strong foundation. The message written on the hearts of believers made them strong to endure persecution and opposition and when St. Paul jumped in the field of preaching and evangelism, Christianity was the dominant faith in the Roman Empire.

St. Paul and the Gentiles:

When St. Paul who was earlier known as Saul was caught by the Lord to be His Apostle, while going to, Damascus, he totally surrendered to Jesus. He became blind, so that he could not see with his physical eyes, but Jesus opened his spiritual eyes. He was taken to Damascus where Ananias with Lord's guidance prayed for him and scales of sins, which he had committed in ignorance, fell from his eyes and he opened his eyes in the presence of the Lord and he became chosen one of the Lord. He had got his education in the strictest Jewish tradition at the feet of famous Hebrew Rabbi Gamaliel. Paul was well versed in Greek and knew about the Greek culture and literature. Not only had that he had Roman citizenship. This made easy for him to express Old Testament beliefs to the gentiles. Knowing Hebrew and Greek was a great advantage for him. Paul mainly worked among the gentiles who had Greek background, so his converts were a mixed group of believers. They were not all with pious background that is why in 1Cor 6:9-11, he reminds them that they were sexually immoral, Idolaters, Adulterers, Male Prostitutes, Slanderers and

Swindlers, but you were sanctified and washed by the holy and precious blood of Jesus and were justified in the name of Jesus Christ. St. Paul remained unmarried throughout his life and spent his life in the service of the Lord by spreading His word in countries like Spain, Yugoslavia, Macedonia, Thessalonica, Athens, Corinth, Caesarea, Judea, Rome and many more places. He planted many Churches, St. Paul is considered to be leader in evangelizing the gentiles. He did so much work which none of the other disciples could do. He spent two years in jail. He had hope that he will be released. He was released because the persecution did not come to Rome, but he was caught again while preaching. He appealed to be judged by the king of Rome but he was unaware of the fate at the hands of Nero. So when he came to Rome second time he was murdered by the order of Nero, then Emperor and enemy of Christians.

Catholic Christians:

First century church was spiritual because the believers had heard the message directly from the disciples like John, Peter, Philip, James and others who had been with Jesus for three and half years. They had traveled with Jesus on the dusty roads of Palestine. They had heard Jesus telling them about the kingdom of God. They were witnesses to all the miracles, which Jesus had done. They had seen Jesus feeding more than 5,000 and 4,000 peoples with food which was just enough for one person. They were witnesses to the raising of Lazarus after four days of his death and also they had seen raising of daughter of Jairus, the leader of Jewish synagogue and the son of widow of Nain. They were strengthened in faith when they had seen Jesus casting out demons and they themselves did the same thing in the name of Jesus. With the power of Holy Spirit they had healed the sick. The same Jesus worked in their lives. Closed iron gates were opened for them, so they were delivered. Their prison foundations were shaken, iron gates fell open and the fetters in their feet got unfastened. There were innumerable miracles and incidents, which had made them strong in faith on the unshakable rock, which is Jesus Christ. Above all they had seen the suffering, torture and insulting death of their Lord on the cross and His resurrection on the third day. How they could deny all these happenings and incidents that proved Jesus to be the Son of God. For this reason after the Pentecost when they were filled with the power of Holy Spirit Peter preached and said, "God of Abraham, the God of Isaac and the God of

Jacob, the God of our ancestors has glorified this servant Jesus whom you handed over and rejected in the presence of Pilot, though he decided to release him, but you rejected the holy and the righteous one and asked to have murderer given to you, and you killed the author of life whom God raised from the dead and to this we are witness" Acts 3: 12-15. And when they had arrested Peter and John and then they released them with the warning that they should not preach in the name of Jesus, then Peter and John said, "Whether is it right in God's sight to listen to you rather than to God, you must judge; for we cannot keep from speaking about what we have seen and heard" Acts 4: 18-20. Then John writes in his first Epistle, "We declare to you what was from the beginning, what we have heard, what we have seen with our eyes what we have looked at and touched with our hands, concerning the word of life. This life was revealed and we have seen it and testify to it, and declare to you the eternal life that was with the father and was revealed to us. We declare to you what we have seen and heard so that you also may have fellowship with us ..." So the first century Christianity was founded on the hard facts and that is why it was truly spiritual and spread rapidly. The people who were fed up with the double standards and hypocrisy of the Jewish religious leaders accepted this new faith. As we recite the Apostles creed and say that I believe in the Catholic Church it does not mean the Roman Catholic Church. Actually Catholic faith was based on the faith of the apostles and Jesus was the foundation of that faith. The other meaning of Catholic Church is the Universal Church. St. Paul, Peter and John raised the structure of Christianity on the solid faith, which they had in Christ and the living God. St. Paul spent his whole life in raising the Church on this faith and for this faith he sacrificed himself at the hands of Nero the Roman Emperor. From 70 C.E to 312 C.E. Christian Church was truly Catholic and it spread through the Roman Empire. In 52 A.D Thomas disciple of Christ took the good news to India. This rapidly expanding faith was called Catholic. Catholic Christianity was based on the plans and commandments of Jesus. St. Paul and other disciples spread this new faith with their efforts. We can call this period from 70 A.D. to 312 A.D. of Catholic Christianity it was the Bishop Ignatius of Antioch who used this word in the second century, when he said, "Where ever Jesus Christ is, there is Catholic Church". So Catholic Church was both universal and orthodox. No one can deny that Christianity has come out of Judaism. The founder was poor carpenter of Nazareth. Three centuries after the resurrection of Jesus it became the most popular religion in the Roman Empire. In spite of all the efforts by adversaries of Christianity like Emperor Nero it survived and flourished and spread to far off places like Britain, Carthage, Persia, Asia Minor (Turkey), Yugoslavia, even up to Asia.

Jesus came for Jews as the promised Messiah. He tried to correct the drawbacks, which had crept into Judaism, but Jewish leaders rejected Him. But Jesus and His believers did not reject the Jewish religion. So, Christianity emerged as a new faith. Even today a true Christian considers Jews as the chosen nation of God. The Messiah, for whom they are waiting and the one who was born of Virgin Mary, died for sinners on the cross and rose from the dead on the third day. And after paying the price of sins of humanity, He ascended into heaven and is seated at the right hand of God, is the same Messiah. Even though three centuries after the Christ adversaries like Emperor Nero tried to finish Christianity, yet it flourished and was the most popular religion in the Roman Empire. During the rule of Emperor Constantine (312-337) there were big Christian groups in every big city of Roman Empire. Constantine himself became Christian and this resulted in the spreading of Christianity through missionaries up to Britain, Carthage, and Persia, where churches were established. Even some missionaries from Edessa traveled to India and strengthened the Christian Church in south India whose foundation was laid by the Christ's disciple Thomas in 52 A.D.

Spreading of Christianity:

What was the most inspiring characteristic of Christian faith, which made Christianity most popular religion far and wide? Disciples started evangelizing from the Jews, because the Jews knew the Old Testament and disciples presented the new faith wrapped in the pages of Old Testament, because of this except the orthodox Jews, others did not have the problem in understanding the good news. Rather those who were fed up with the everyday sacrifices, the hypocrisy of the Pharisees, they turned to Christ. Among the gentiles who were not happy with the idol worship, hollowness of the beliefs with no hope in future, they gladly accepted Christianity. Secondly descendants of Abraham that were fed up with the torturing action of Romans had scattered into other countries. So whenever and wherever they heard good news of Christianity they accepted it gladly.

Also St. Paul made it easy for the gentiles that they don't have to go for circumcision. Though Paul was circumcised, yet he himself, the Greeks and Romans hated circumcision. Because of the criticism by the Jews some Christian converts, from the gentiles got themselves circumcised. Majority of the converts believed that circumcision is not a condition for salvation; rather they believed what St. Paul preached that their salvation depended on their faith in Jesus Christ and their obedience to the commandments of Jesus Christ. So majority of the converts were those, who wanted to get rid of circumcision and every day sacrifices. For this reason Greeks and Romans accepted Christ. Specially those, who knew the Old Testament, they did not have problem in understanding the prophecies about Jesus and recognizing Him as the promised Messiah. Believers of Jesus did not have different groups based upon the different interpretations and thinking neither they had inferior or superior concept on the basis of their ancestral background. Jews had different groups, specially the Samaritans and Jews who did not get along together, because Jews hated Samaritan and gentiles. Among Christians, there were no differences on the basis of caste and creed, rich or poor. There was uniformity of faith and this Church was really a Catholic Church. After the destruction of Jerusalem in 70 A.D. Christianity's evangelism center moved to North and West. Antioch in Syria became the hub of Christianity. In the fourth century there were about 50 percent Christian converts in the total population of 500,000 in Antioch. Out of 70 disciples of Jesus many went to Melitene in Mesopotamia (1.5) and they established churches there. Edessa Christians were full of grace, power and enthusiasm for Christ. Adoi was a leading Christian among them. When missionaries from Edessa reached south India, they met Thomas Christians. They accepted them gladly, because the locals were poor and considered as low caste people. They were fed up with the treatment from the so-called high caste communities. So the south Indians accepted Christianity gladly, because in Christianity there were no high or low caste Christians, all were equal and all were Christians. Even today if you go to India (Madras City, Chennai) you will see a Catholic Church on the St. Thomas Hill. It is believed that when St. Thomas visited south India, adversaries of Christianity stoned him to death and his remains are still there.

From Antioch many missionaries traveled to the west and because of that Christianity spread rapidly in Ephesus, Bethonia, and in the neighboring cities. Being upset from the rapidly spreading Christianity, the Roman governor of that area wrote to Emperor Trojan, that in the towns and villages of this area Christianity is spreading rapidly and I fear that temples of Roman gods and goddesses will become desolated. I may please be advised what I should do to halt the spreading of Christianity. Due to the influence of Christianity in the sixth century Emperor Justinian had started a movement against the idol worshippers in Asia Minor (Turkey). In Rome where Christianity had reached in the first century, there were about 30,000 Christians living in Rome in 250 A.D. Most of the Christians among them were poor and belonged to the community of slaves. These people normally spoke Greek. People belonging to the rich community, did not like to speak Greek, rather they spoke Latin. The Jews who lived in North Africa visited Jerusalem quite often. Most of the Jews had migrated to North Africa in the times of Solomon and David and were living in Sudan, Ethiopia, Cyrene, Tunisia, Algiers (Carthage). One proof of this was the visit of the Court Official of queen of Candace to Jerusalem and Philip baptized him when he was going back. Secondly the Simon of Cyrene who carried the cross of Jesus to Calvary, and the Jews living in North African countries, when heard about Jesus, they accepted Jesus as their savior. This was how the Christianity reached North Africa in the first century. Some biblical scholars feel John Mark (Mark who is known as John) preached Christianity in North Africa. He specially preached in Alexandria where Greek Jews were entangled in social and political problems. When John Mark preached the Good News to them they accepted it gladly.

Why the Worthless and Rejected are Chosen?

If we study the history of Christianity, we find right from the first century to the 21st century majority of the people who accepted Christianity were so called worthless people, hated and rejected by the rich and so called high caste people who dominated the society. When the young plant of Christian faith started growing it was exactly according to the parable of mustard seed. "It is smallest of all seeds, but when it is grown, it is the greatest of all shrubs and becomes a tree, so that birds of the air come and make nests in its branches" Mathew 13:31,32.

In the first three centuries as many accepted Christianity, majority of them were simple, poor people, slaves and women, some businessmen, tax collectors and police officials hated by the society. One adversary and critic of Christianity was Celsus, who at that time said, "These Nazarene evangelists have only one aim to befool the worthless, poor, rejected, foolish slaves, poor women and Children and convert them to Christianity. They can convert such foolish and worthless people only". I think this critic did not know, what St. Paul had already written in 1 Cor. 1:26-31 "for you see your calling brethren, that not many wise according to the flesh, not many mighty, not many noble are called, but God has chosen the foolish things of the world to put to shame the wise, and God has chosen the weak things of the world to put to shame which are mighty, and the base things of the world and the things which are despised, God has chosen and the things which are not, to bring to nothing the things that are ...." It was done so that no one may boast before God. That's why word of God says, "let the one who boasts, boast in the Lord" When we read these words of St. Paul, we conclude that Celsus was right in his uttering and criticism, because Christian community did not reject the poor and the so called worthless people of the society but they embraced them. In today's society, so-called religious leaders like Rajneesh accepted and honored only the millionaires and billionaires. Many Christian scholars replied to the criticism of the adversaries like Celsus but the most famous out of these was Bishop Irenaeus of France "Gaul". He wrote five books based upon the Bible the impact of these books was so great on the church and the critics that it helped in the spread of Christianity. Tertullian who was born and brought up in Carthage and is considered to be father of Latin Theology. In 150 CE he wrote many books in Greek and most of them are not available now, because they are lost. Only 31 books in Latin are available.

In 185 CE a philosopher Pentius was teaching Christianity and with the purpose of Preaching he visited India too because the people who were considered untouchables and worthless were accepting Christianity because they enjoyed respect, honor and equality among Christians. Even today when poor people or anyone else accepts Christianity, baseless charges are laid against the Pastors and people preaching the word of God. They are being charged that they are converting the people by force or by offering money. Neither in the first three centuries nor now in the 21st century money is being offered. The poor pastors and missionaries living from hand to mouth have nothing to offer except the precious and living word of God. God works through simple, humble and pure hearts. Word of God is like a two edged sword which pierces through the heart of a person and that person realizes that there is no salvation except the name of Jesus and he or she accept Jesus as their personal Savior. Right from the 1st to the 21st century the spirit of God touched the grieving and empty hearts and they accepted the Lord. They understood that there is no salvation except through Jesus Christ. In the olden times non-Christian saints and sages preached that by suppressing out human desires we could achieve real happiness. Did they offer money to the people that they might follow them? Did Jesus offer money to the disciples and His followers so that they may follow him? Was it because of the money offered to them that people sacrificed their lives because of their faith in Jesus Christ? Christ did not have anything except one bag and long cloak. He did not have any place of His own to lay His head. Christ preached that God loves everyone. Only by trusting and believing in Him one can achieve true peace by His grace.

Secondly the love, respect and honor given by Christian believers to the dejected and so-called worthless poor people were a big attraction. Every Christian loved and respected his Christian brother. There was no discrimination on the basis of cast and creed. There was a time when curse of untouchability was prevalent in India. Even now in south India there are high casts and low casts people in the same religion. There used to be separate water sources for the superior and the inferior. Low cast was not allowed to touch the high cast. Low castes were not permitted to listen to the reading of the religious scriptures. Before 1947 there were separate water pots for Hindus and Muslims with the signs Hindu water and Muslim water and there was no water for the low caste. This was because of the pride of high caste people. This was also one of the reasons for the partition of India into 3 parts. Yet Christianity tried to get rid of this baseless pride and hatred for each other and they offered love, respect and equality to everyone.

Persecution of Christians:

For Jews and Christians the first two commandments of Moses were as important as rest of the eight. True Christian and a true Jew will not worship any other god, except the Jehovah God. In Islam they claim to worship one God but they worship and bow down at the graves of Muslim saints and sages. They offer sacrifices and sheets of flowers on their graves to get their demands fulfilled and their prayers granted. They believe in black magic and use Amulets to keep away demons and to be safe from black magic. Their so called saints like Ajmeri Baba, Peer Sayed Sahib, Peer Kazim Ali Shah and Pandit Ji Maharaj sitting in London give big ads on TV for the public to get rid of demons, solve their social, family and financial problems within 72 hours with a guarantee. They charge heavy amounts from their clients in dollars and pounds and are thus making a lot of money in the name of God. Does God demand pounds and dollars to answer the prayers of His believers and solve their problems? Till the rule of Christian ruler, Christians and Jews suffered at the hands of the Roman authorities. Roman wanted that Jews and Christians should worship Roman gods and goddesses as they worship their Jehovah God and Jesus Christ as their Lord and Savior. Romans regarded Caesar equal to God. When in Asia minor (Turkey) Bishop Polycarp of Symrna was asked by the governor of that day to swear in the name of Caesar, he replied firmly that, "I am Christian and I can't swear in the name of Caesar" Governor answered, "I will throw you before the wild animals". Bishop said, "I accept the challenge, bring the beast" If wild animals do not eat you, I will burn you in a furnace of fire. Polycarp replied, "I am not afraid of dying in a furnace of fire for one hour. You should know for you a furnace of eternal fire is ready which will never go out". Then the governor let the crowd free and asked the crowd to kill him because he is destroyer of our Roman gods and goddesses and so Bishop Polycarp met the martyrdom. Before the end of 2nd century, many Christians sacrificed their lives and because of this Christianity progressed more rapidly. Romans and Greeks had gods for different occasions, at the time of sowing seeds, for harvesting, rain, storms, rivers and volcanoes. They sacrificed separately for each god and goddesses. They used to invite Christians for such functions but every time Christians refused to go to such gatherings. For Romans it was insulting so they decided to finish the Christian community and decided to burn all the Christian religious books. They named hospitals after the names of their gods and goddesses. Christian workers were compelled to make idols of their gods and goddesses. Christians were forced to make temples for their gods and goddesses. In Roman and Greek society, women were considered inferior, girls were killed at the time of their birth and boys were kept alive. Slaves were treated like animals but Christian community opposed all these things. It was for this reason that many people got converted. As in the times of Nebuchadnezzar people were asked to bow down before his image and same thing was happening in Rome. Because Roman Empire was spread far and wide so, Roma was designated goddess of Rome. Romans were made to understand that goddess Roma lives in Caesar; therefore Caesar needs to be worshiped. So the first time temple for Caesars worship was built in 29BC in Pergmum. By the 3rd century Roman Empire was spread into Germany, North Africa, Spain and Britain and Caesar was worshipped throughout the empire. Christians refused to worship Caesar on the plea that worshipping a human being like Caesar is denying Jehovah God. Roman authorities argued that whosoever does not worship Caesar is not faithful to Caesar so these were the reasons for which Christians were persecuted and killed.

Appointing Bishops and their Authority:

From the epistles of St. Paul it is evident that wherever he planted churches there he appointed bishops and deacons as well. For the appointments of Bishops, Deacons and Pastors he stated some rules. Keeping in view such rules these people were appointed, but gradually with the passing. of time there appeared drawbacks in these appointments. Certain questions started cropping up.

- • Why only men should be appointed for this work?
- • Are not the women fit for God's service?

In the time of St. Paul, the thinking of the government and the society was different and that was male dominated society but now with the change of time people demanded that church should also change and position of elders should also be given to the women.

Some Christians were of the view that for certain things for which word of God is silent the church leaders should decide regarding the things which are beneficial for the church and God's name is glorified. It is possible in those times political system may not have certain things, but these days when there is no political pressure, church should change according to its needs. Some people believe whatever changes occurred in the first 3 or 4 centuries were under the guidance of the Holy Spirit. Now some Christians think, has the Holy Spirit stopped working among the believers? Faith and character of Christians in the early church was really catholic.

When governor Palini wrote to the Emperor Trojan, he wrote, "I have not seen anything in the Christians for whom they should be punished." In 220 AD the signs started appearing which proved that spiritual element is vanishing from the lives of Bishops and the church leaders. In the first 2 centuries it was thought that while getting baptized all the sins are washed away provided the believer repented and sought forgiveness of God. These sins were murder, adultery and refusing Christ, but church punished such people. Punishment for these was suspending his membership and refusal of Holy Communion. People believed that for God's grace Holy Communion is a must. Not partaking in the Holy Communion can endanger his salvation. In the 3rd century Bishop had the right to suspend the membership of any member at fault and to forgive any Christian and accept him into the church. Bishop Callistus (217-222 AD) accepted many adulterers into the church. His view was that church is like Noah's Ark in which there are righteous and unrighteous people. He also argued that Church of Rome is the custodian of St. Peters Church and Christ has entrusted the keys of this church to Peter. Christ has given authority to the earthly church to bind or loose in the name of Christ and it will be bound or loosed in heaven. So Bishop Callistus was the first Bishop who made use of this authority. This is when human interpretation of the word of God started. To this human interpretation different people had different views. In the rule of Emperor Decious of Rome in 250 AD, an order was issued throughout the Roman Empire that sacrifices should be offered to the Roman gods and goddesses. Those who obey this order will be awarded with certificate of loyalty to the Roman Empire and who do not obey this order will not be given such credit. Anyone not having such a certificate will not be counted faithful to the Roman Empire. Some Christians out of fear obeyed this order to save their skin. Those who did not obey this order were punished with torture, imprisonment, and some faced martyrdom. Because of disobedience to this order Bishops of Rome, Antioch and Jerusalem faced death. In 251 AD during the war with Goths (1.7) Emperor Decious was killed.

Cyprian the Bishop of Carthage said, "those Christians who denied Christian faith will be thrown out of the church membership. They have sinned against The Holy Spirit and there is no forgiveness for them and for them there is no salvation out of the church." If those who deny the Christian faith can be forgiven then any sin can be forgiven. In Hebrew 10:26-29 it is written, "for if we willfully persist in sin after having received the knowledge of the truth, there no longer remains a sacrifice for sins, but a fearful prospect of judgment and fury of fire that will consume the adversaries. Anyone who violated the Law of Moses dies without mercy on the testimony of 2 or 3 witnesses. How much worse punishment will be deserved by those who have spurned the Son of God, profaned the blood of covenant by which they were sanctified and outraged the spirit of grace". Gradually Bishop Cyprian realized that some of these people are ready to repent and they were forgiven only after undergoing punishment. So after the repentant Christians had undergone severe punishment, they were forgiven and accepted back into the church. Cyprian told them that, even after repentance and undergoing severe punishment only those would be forgiven who come before the congregation in sack clothes and with ashes on their heads. Then Bishop will lay his hands on their heads and pray for them, only after that they will be accepted back into the church membership. Yet one pastor of the church Novatian objected to this action of Bishop Cyprian and said, "no human being has the right to forgive sins like murder, adultery and refusal to Christian faith". These sins come under the judgment to be done by Jesus on the last day. Another Pastor Cornelius, who disagreed with Novatian said, "man of God like bishop has even more power than this, he can forgive sins even greater than that." Those agreed with Novatian and followed him were called society of saints, but those who supported Cornelius were called the school of sinners. Cornelius because of his liberal policies was elected the bishop of Rome and Novatian faced defeat. He made small groups of his followers everywhere and thus there was difference of opinion because of different interpretations and the church broke up into two major groups. This way difference of opinion and different interpretations started cropping up resulting in the breakup of church.

Downfall of Roman Empire:

Any political system who opposes God, persecutes His people does not last longer and does not survive long, because the creator of this universe is living God. His eyes and ears are always open and watching his believers.

He listens to their prayers and answers them. The persecutor may be one person or the whole society or the whole nation they can't escape the judgment of God. Dictators like Hitler and others are no more. Over every government there is another ruler called God who watches every good and bad government and he keeps account of every good and bad ruler. Roman Empire was one of such government who persecuted Jewish nation of God and the new Israel of God the Christian Nation. Foundations of Roman Empire had started shaking quite before this but even then it had not faced enemy for the last 620 years. But when a curse of God was let loose then in 410 AD Alaric Gothic (German) leader with its Aryan army attacked Rome. His attack was so severe that destruction of Rome was certain. Roman ruler sent the message for peace and asked the Gothic leader for terms and conditions for this as it happened in the Old Testament. Alaric who was Christian replied all your gold and silver is mine. As he was German and his army was Aryan he demanded freedom for all German slaves, but they could not reach an agreement. Gothic (1.7) army looted the whole city and demolished every temple, and every good building and palace. Alaric examined every item his army had looted. All that including utensils, gold and silver looted from the churches was returned back to the churches. He did not say anything to the Christians and Bishops but he dealt strictly with the Romans and their rulers.

After defeating and looting Rome Vizzi Goth and his army left Rome but destruction of Rome was such that glory of Rome was brought down to ashes. The Rome who ruled major part of the world and was considered to be powerful empire was in shambles and people were crying over its destruction. Roman gods and goddesses were all broken and lying in streets and were all trampled under feet. Romans were proud of their gods and goddesses but none of these lifeless images of gods and goddesses saved Rome from destruction. Even gods and goddesses could not save themselves. Some people thought that Constantine has converted to Christianity that is why goddess Roma and other gods became angry and Rome met its fate. Roman refugees fled Rome. In Hippo the port of North Africa lived bishop Aurelius Augustinus. When refugees reached this port he heard the problems of the refugees. No one had the answer that why Rome was destroyed. People started thinking that with the destruction of Rome, will the future of Christianity be in danger but Augustinus proved to be strong leader of Catholic Church. Today's Roman Catholic Church owes much to Augustinus. Protestant churches were watching closely the drawbacks and the shortcomings of the Roman Catholic Church. Protestant churches and leaders were aware not to repeat those mistakes. Augustine did many things, which were against the word of God. To oppose these drawbacks and shortcomings, a wave of Donatism(1.6) started. Many evils had crept into Catholic faith long before and to oppose these evils Donatism had already started. When Augustine became leader of Catholic Church, Donatism was already one hundred years old. Movement of Donatism advocated for the Purity, Holiness and Discipline in the church. The other purpose of Donatism was to keep away bad character people from the position of being Bishops because Catholic Church was ordaining such people as the priests and bishops. Confrontation between Augustine and Donatists continued. Finally Augustine died on August 28, 430AD. Hippo port was attacked by barbarians and was taken over by the enemy forces in August 431 AD.

Because of the controversy between the Catholics and the Donatists, those people who did not like fights and criticism chose the path of Asceticism. They wanted to serve the Lord with purity of heart. Egyptian citizen Anthony became the first monk. Before this also people used to live in forests and lead lonely life in mountains. Anthony was the first person who left the worldly pleasures and started leading saintly life. In the beginning monasticism became popular way of leading spiritual life. Both men and women started joining this movement. Then both Catholics and Protestants had disagreement over the various aspects of monasticism. This movement spread rapidly, the Christian believers to lead spiritual life founded these monasteries all over the world. Men and women who left worldly pleasures, started living in these monasteries. They not only lived there, but also took care of the sick, suffering people, helpless and the poor, whom no body looked after. They were also given religious education and for this reason they had preserved the old writings about the religion. People contributed huge amounts of money to these monasteries. So the people living there had enough resources and funds to take care of the sick and the suffering people. They were considered ordinary people. They prepared hand written manuscripts of religious books. By the end of fifth century their financial position was very sound. Since they were not attached to the Catholic Church, they wrote to the Pope to attach these monasteries with the Catholic Church. As the Pope was head of the Catholic Church and without his patronage they had no security and respect. When Pope realized that by attaching these monasteries, Catholic Church has nothing to lose, also there is no other problem, so Pope accepted them into his fold. So all men and women leading life of celibacy enjoyed security and honor. Due to the destruction of Rome and weaknesses in the Catholic Church and the different interpretations of the word of God, Church also got divided into two main sections, that is Eastern and Western Church, which meant Greek Catholics and Roman Catholics. They disagreed on certain issues regarding purity and discipline in the Church. The main cause was the abuse of power by the Catholic Bishops and priests. The gulf between the two Churches widened day by day.

Eastern Orthodox Church:

As already has been told that because of the drawbacks in the lives of Popes and Bishops the Church got bifurcated into Western (Roman Catholic) and the Eastern Catholic Church (Greek Orthodox). Greek orthodox or Eastern Orthodox Church claimed to live by the true teachings of Jesus Christ. Later on this Church also got partitioned and from it came out the Syrian Orthodox Church. In south India there are many Syrian orthodox Churches and about more than 20 churches are found in the Eastern Europe. The faith and background of these churches is the same. Orthodox Churches are recognized from those pictures of saints whom they honor and worship. On the heads of these pictures there is halo of light, which is symbol of their righteousness and being saint. Orthodox Christians bow down before these pictures and worship them. When a member of the Orthodox Church enters the Church, he first bows down his head before the pictures. These pictures are hung on a wall after the entrance and this place is separated from the main sanctuary. Before going for worship in the main sanctuary, orthodox member will kiss these pictures and then enter the sanctuary. If any visitor goes to the house of an Orthodox believer, he will find pictures of Christ and His disciples on the eastern wall of the living room. If the guest or the visitor is an Orthodox believer, he will pay respect to these pictures by bowing his head and then he will meet head of the house. Orthodox believers not only think these as pictures, rather they consider these personalities as the medium to meet God. Orthodox Christians believe that it is through these saints; God meets and talks with the believers and worshippers. Orthodox Christians believe that God made man in his own image and it is through these saints, God reveals himself to the believers. Whereas the Roman Catholic Church believes that to meet God, forgiveness of sins is very essential. If any Catholic member sins then Catholic priest has the right to listen to the confession of the member and then forgive his sins and his sins will be forgiven. But the protestant group believes that without God nobody can forgive the sins. Protestants believe if a Christian confesses his sins before God and repents from those sins then God will forgive his sins through Jesus Christ, because Christ has already paid the price of sins of the repentant believer by shedding His holy blood. Roman Catholics also believe, if while being in this world we do not repent and our sins are not forgiven then we have one more chance. Before the Day of Judgment when our soul goes to Purgatory, the resting place for the souls, there we have an opportunity to repent of our sins committed in this world. Since Roman Catholic Church is founded on St. Peters' faith and Pope is the head of this Church, so pope has the authority to make decisions, which will be supported by the Lord. Orthodox feel, God Himself came as Jesus Christ in this world, so human being can once again regain that state of purity, which Adam had in the Garden of Eden. By sinning a person hurts God and injures that image in which, he was created by God. A human being is completely saved when image of God is completely reflected in the life of a believer. Jesus came to save the sinning man and restore his purity and righteousness, so that God's picture and characteristics are revealed in the personality of a believer. Orthodox Christians believe that after the new creation of man he becomes like Christ. They believe church is not the formal group of believers; rather it is body of Christ, which keeps changing every day and is renewed through the Holy Spirit. When he or she becomes one with Christ the person changes to God's image and character. The founder of this thought was actually Constantine. Roman Catholic Church had a viewpoint that this thought is a rebellion against Roman rulers and the Roman Catholic Church. Roman ruler was considered like a shining sun. Worship of images in the Catholic Church and the worship of pictures of saints in the Orthodox Church were against the word of God. So the true picture and image of real Catholic Church started changing. In the seventh century there were many Jews and Catholic Christians in Mecca (Saudi Arabia). The disputes between the Catholics and Jews were very common. These conflicts between the two major faiths had effect on the locals. Idol worship by the Roman Catholics was against the Bible and the Law of Moses. At that time Khadijah a Christian religious woman with Jewish background and her husband a rich businessman were there in Mecca. After her husbands' death she stayed in Mecca, because of her business. Drawbacks in Roman Catholic faith and their differences with Jews, inspired prophet Mohammad to lay the foundation of Islam on the basis of Law of Moses. As some Moslems believe that prophet Mohammad started preaching Islam at the age of 40 years. He told people to stop fighting, total submission to God (Allah) and accept him as the prophet of Allah. But the people of Mecca refused to accept him as their prophet. From there he moved to Medina. Since people of Medina did not know him, they accepted him as Allah's prophet. He collected the army there and attacked Mecca and conquered it. He compelled all the people there to accept Islam. After this with the aim of establishing a Moslem Empire and root out the curse of Idol worship his attacks spread far and wide. As the tribal people were strong and good fighters, he ran through Israel and devastating spree went to Syria, Turkey, and Spain for the purpose of establishing Moslem Empire.

Pope Gregory (1073-1085)

In 1073 Hildebrand was made Pope of the Roman Catholic Church. Roman Catholic Church realized that Catholic Church could only flourish throughout the world if kings and Emperors are brought under the control of Catholic Church. That way pope will be the ruler over the whole world and catholic faith will flourish under the kings and rulers. Hildebrand was named as Gregory seventh. He had many power hungry plans. He had a plan to establish Catholic Empire and Pope to be ruler over this. Pope banned all those things, which could be hurdles in the implementation of his plans. He banned Catholic priests not to marry. Because of this order many Catholic priests got trapped in many worldly temptations and sexual Scandals. Many restrictions were imposed upon the kings, and Emperors and they were asked to obey the orders of the Pope without any opposition and resistance. But Henry (iv), ruler of Germany opposed this order. He rejected many things, which Pope asked to obey. Pope became furious and felt insulted, because of this refusal. So Pope issued summons to Henry to appear in his court, but Henry refused to accept those summons. Because of this refusal Pope's anger touched the third sky and Henry's membership from the Roman Catholic Church was terminated and his

Rule was taken from him. His ministers were asked not to obey Henry as the ruler. Henry was not a person to digest this easily. He called meeting of the German bishops. All the Bishops opposed Pope's order with one voice. They ruled that this order of Pope Gregory is unjust and devouring. Because of this people got divided and civil war started. His ministers rebelled against Henry. On the Pope's orders Henry was imprisoned. Henry under compulsion had to appear before Pope on the mountains of Kenosa on January 1077. Henry the German ruler waited for three days bare foot during the snow days. He wore sack clothes and kept beseeching pope for forgiveness all these three days. Finally Pope forgave Henry with these sarcastic remarks, "I the Pope take away chain of curse from his neck and I accept him back into the mother Church. By insulting and degrading German ruler bitterness did not vanish but Pope's grip became strong on kings and rulers. Pope used to compel officials and ordinary people to seek forgiveness publicly. Pope Gregory said, "I am the head of the Church founded on the Peter's faith whom Jesus authorized. Therefore all kings, Emperors, Rulers, Officials and general public is subordinate to him. Secondly unity of families can be in Christ to obey the commandments of God. The Bishops as weapons misused the Laws and Ordinances, which the Pope Gregory issued. This weapon was used frequently and to the maximum in Europe. Pope's rule was in fact a powerful worldly government, which circled around pope, and Pope was holding the strings. All the Bishops had sworn before Pope for loyalty and obedience. No one could dare to speak or raise head against the Pope.

In the celebrations of religious sacraments no one could make a change without Pope's permission. All the religious matters were presented to Pope in his court and everyone had his eyes fixed on Pope. No one could challenge pope's decision because it was binding on every one and must be accepted whether he liked it or not. Pope's rule could only be strengthened under the hands of strong, powerful, dominating and asserting leader and can be like a shadow over kings and emperors. Such a leader was Pope Innocent (III) (1198-1216). Pope Innocent and the Popes to come in the 12th and 13th centuries were less religious, but more experts like an advocate in Church rules and the Pope's government. Out of them only Pope Innocent was like Gregory (VII). He declared that pope is the custodian of St. Peter's Church and he is the chief priest of Christ's Church. Pope is the medium or the broker between Christ and the man and without Pope it is impossible to reach God. Pope is under God and human beings are under Pope. Pope can handle and judge all the cases of human beings. He can penalize a person after passing judgment, but no one can point a finger on Pope nor can anyone find fault with him. Innocent (III) declared to all European rulers that Pope is like a Sun and all kings and Emperors like moons around him. They shine by taking light from the Sun, so all the Bishops under Pope draw their energy from Pope. Anyone who does not obey Pope, his membership will be terminated from the Roman Catholic Church. And he won't be able to enter the kingdom of God. Since all Catholics believed in Paradise and Hell, so nobody wanted to go to hell by annoying Pope. Pope's order was binding on every Catholic because anyone disobeying pope could be punished with the termination of his membership from the Catholic Church and he could not get salvation without the mercy and forgiveness granted by the Pope. When any Bishop read the Pope's order for terminating membership of a member, then a special type of bell was sounded which resembled the bell sounded at the funeral of a person. Open Bible was closed and lighted candle was put out which meant spiritual death of a person. If a person with a suspended membership came to the mass, he was asked to leave the Church and was turned out by force and the worship service stopped. Any member with a terminated membership could not work as a judge, jury member, witness or an advocate. If such a member died no Catholic priest would perform the rites of his funeral. Third powerful and killing weapon was banning all religious rites or sacraments except baptism and Holy Communion. No public worship could be held. Wherever the ruler will not obey pope's order there all religious ceremonies will be banned. Pope Innocent (Ill), used this weapon 85 times against the rulers who were found guilty of disobedience to the Pope or his orders. Out of these one criminal was John the ruler of Britain. At the recommendation of some influential people, he felt sorry before the Pope Innocent and he had to pay heavy amount of money to pope every year as a punishment tax. Because of power, glory, and worldly privileges he enjoyed, everybody wanted to be the Pope, because all rulers were under him. When pope appeared before the public numbering hundreds of thousands, all people would pay their obeisance and respects by kneeling down on the ground and bowing their heads. Whenever Pope Boniface (1294- 1303) appeared before public he used to announce, "I am Caesar and I am the Emperor". In Pope's crown there were 48 red diamonds (Rubies), 72 sapphires, 45 emeralds, and 66 other most precious pearls and gems. Whenever there was big gathering Pope used to grant forgiveness to those who felt sorry for their sins. In return he asked people to pay huge amounts of money. At that time so much money was collected that it wasn't possible to gather it with hands, rather they used rakes or other devices to gather that money.

In 1378 when Pope Gregory died, a council of College of Cardinals was convened. They being under the pressure of Roman people they elected Italian Cardinal Urban (VI) as the new Pope. Due to the dictatorial attitude of this Pope every Cardinal got upset. So they decided to send the message to all the European people that pope Urban (VI) has grabbed the Papal chair by force, so all the actions by which he became Pope are held null and void. Pope Urban (VI), who was installed on April 18, was dethroned in August. After one month the new College of Cardinals was constituted. The number of French Cardinals was more, so they elected French cardinal Clement (VII) as the new pope and this massage was conveyed to all the civil and Church authorities about the election of new Pope. Clement visited Italy and went back to France, but pope Urban did not vacate the papal chair and he remained stuck to that position. That way Urban (VI) from Rome and Clement Avignon kept ruling from France. Roman government sided with Pope Urban (VI) and European people supported Clement Avignon. Thus two popes kept ruling the Roman Catholic Church for 39 years. Both Popes had two separate Colleges of Cardinals. Both the Popes claimed to be the true representatives of chief priest Jesus Christ. They had full rights of terminating membership of any member who did not obey the Pope.

The effect of this caused the whole Catholic Church to be divided into two main camps. France and Scotland supported Pope Clement. Rome and England came to support Pope Urban (VI). In every country there were people who did not support this split and they did not agree with the decisions of either Pope. So an environment of rebellion was created in these countries. People started damaging properties and setting the properties on fire. Rebellious people made groups and started attacking those with whom they did not agree and supported the two Popes. Finally in 1395 prominent professors from Paris University decided to call a meeting of the Church representatives from all over the country. The two groups came together and decided that this split should come to an end.

As a rule Pope could convene the meeting who has authority over the whole Church. In 1409 cardinals from both sides agreed to convene the meeting in Pisa Italy. They decided to dismiss both the Popes and they elected Alexander (V), the new Pope. But in spite of their dismissal the two Popes Urban (VI) and Clement remained stuck to their positions, and they were not ready to vacate the papal chairs. This way there were three Popes now instead of two and they claimed to be heirs to St. Peter's seat of Roman Catholic Church. In 1414 Roman Emperor came on a visit to the city Constance of Germany. He gathered all the people of the city, and representatives from the Greek Orthodox Church also participated. Representatives from Italy, France, Britain, Scotland, and Spain were also invited in this meeting. After consultations with the representatives, it was decided to have one Pope only. So one Pope vacated his seat. The other two were dismissed and a new Pope resident of Avignon of France, Benedict (XIII) was elected as the new Pope. So this way the big split in the Roman Catholic Church came to an end. The greed for the seat of Peter in the Catholic Church and the Church politics resulted in adultery and corruption during the reign of Pope Alexander (VI) (1492-1503). He being a person of weak character started gathering wealth for his family and appointed his children on high positions of profit.

This caused the honest church members to think of an alternative. They got fed up with the corrupt deeds of the Pope and dishonest Church officials. People got fed up with the corrupt papal system and started thinking of Churches which are not under the Pope rather those Churches should be controlled and led by the honest and local spiritual people. This opened the door for reformation in the church. In this chapter we find number of reasons for the split in the Roman Catholic Church and emergence of new groups or denominations, which broke away from the Roman Catholic Church which should have been real Catholic Church founded on the apostolic faith in Jesus Christ our supreme savior.

Notes:

1.1: Jews who had spread the false news that body of Christ was stolen by his disciples, did not like any such thing which proved that Christ has risen from the dead and He was the real Messiah.

1.2: Hellenist Jews. The Jews with Greek background and were faithful to their religion. They mixed more easily with Gentiles and were more responsive to the new ideas than the Palestinian Jews.

1.3: Diakonai (Modem day Deacons) means servant or minister

1.4: Asia Minor; Today's Turkey.

1.5: Melitene and Edessa were places in Mesopotamia, where Christianity reached through the disciples and it was the first place where Christianity was made the official religion of the state. (Reference: Atlas of the Bible-spread of Christianity-Published by Reader's Digest).

1.6: The name Donatism is from Donatus, who was the Bishop of Carthage (313-355). He led the opposition to Catholic practices. Donatists had this charge against certain Catholic Bishops, who had handed over scriptures to be burned during the persecution of Christians under Diocletian. Donatists argued that this is a serious sin of apostasy. Donatists claimed to be the true Church of Christ, but Augustine rejected their view and said, "Catholic Church is a mixed multitude of good and bad people. To support his argument he quoted Christ's parable of wheat and Tares.

1.7: Goths: The German army that ran over the Roman Empire in 251 C.E. Gothic means relating to or resembling the Goths, their civilization or their language. Relating to an architectural style, reflecting the influence of the medieval Gothic.

References:

1. Church History Bruce L. Shelly-Word Publishing
2. History and culture of the New Testament- Eric Lessing-Herder and Herder
3. The Bible and History by William Ed. Barclay-Nashville Abingdon
4. The spreading Flame- The rise and progress of Christianity by Frederick F. Bruce Grand Rapids Eerdmans.
5. The early Christian Church -A History of its first five centuries- J.G.Davies-Garden City Double day.
6. Persecution of Early Church-Herber B. Workman.

Chapter Two

Light of Reformation

Whenever People in authority misused their power, there was division in the society. Countries have been partitioned on the basis of caste, creed and religious dissentions and differences, because they cannot get along together. Why U.S.S.R. broke into fragments? The simple reason difference of ideology and people did not like Communism. Why India was partitioned in 1947, the simple reason being hatred between Hindus and Moslems because of the religion. Why there was genocide in the reign of ldi Amin of Uganda, because he differed with the people he killed. Why Hundreds of thousands of People were butchered in the reign of Saddam Hussain, because he differed with people of communities other than Sunnis. He even did not spare his sons-in-law, he got them killed, because they opposed his dictatorial ideology. He got killed their mothers and other family members, so that none of their family members may raise his head against him. Why there are so many denominations in every religion, just the difference of opinion regarding the faith. Whenever one group in a country dominated or discriminated against the other minority group on the basis of religious faith, language or political affiliations, country's unity was endangered, and country was partitioned. Why Texas is part of United States, which used to be a part of Mexico, because of the religious and political repression of the affected people. Likewise in the Church, whenever there have been differences of opinion on the interpretations of the word of God or there have been misuse of power by the ruling group or individual, splitting of church took place and gave birth to more groups called, 'Denominations'.

John Wycliffe:

Same thing happened because of excesses by the pope on the innocent Christians, his dictatorial attitude, torturing and murdering of true Christian believers. Being fed up with all these undesirable and cruel activities of Pope, Self-respecting Christian believers had to raise their head. They decided to fight against such excesses under all odds and circumstances; however high cost they may have to pay for that. John Wycliffe was the first warrior in this fight. He is known as the first bright star of dawn of reformation. Not much is known about his early life, but it is sure that he was brought up in northern England and got his education from the Oxford University. He was appointed professor in the Oxford University after completing his doctorate degree from the same university in 1372. Because of chaos in the Catholic Church people started thinking, who is the Head of the Church, Pope or Jesus Christ. Godly powers and characteristics originate from God. How far it is true that a human being may declare himself priest of Jesus Christ and rule the Church like a tyrant political ruler? Is it right for a human being to rule the Church and the world simultaneously? One of the Wycliffe's professors Richard said, "We cannot expect God's grace from a human being. Do the religious men leading a sinful life have the right to rule the religion and the general public". Wycliffe got the direction from this thought and he said, "English government has the right to root out all the evils that have crept into the Christian faith and all those people who are responsible should be dismissed from the Church. Government also has the right that a strict action should be taken against the corrupt and dishonest church officials." Pope strongly opposed this thought put forward by John Wycliffe. Even some rigid Roman Catholic Church members opposed this move by Wycliffe. Yet he did not turn back. He declared a true believer must have religious freedom. God does not give this authority to any human being that he may rule the world and the religion like God. May be he is Pope, Bishop, priest or common person, all are equal before God. Most humble person is the most beloved person of God. And this is what God declared about Moses. Human being's personal relation with God is most important. Worldly and spiritually human character should be acceptable to God. Wycliffe also said, "No middle man is needed between man and Jesus Christ nor there is need for any kind of sacrifice or expensive offerings before God for the forgiveness of sins". In that way, he supported the views of Martin Luther before he came into the picture. His view is based on Romans 3:30 where St. Paul writes that human beings are justified righteous only through faith in Jesus Christ. This way both Wycliffe and Martin Luther brought down the barriers raised by the Roman Catholic Church between God and human beings. On the other side the conflict between Popes of Rome and France gave strength to Wycliffe's views. Wycliffe stated that St. Peter, St. Paul and other apostles of Christ were poor, but were rich spiritually. So this Custodian of St. Peter's seat has become bankrupt spiritually and cannot become Custodian of St. Peter's seat, by putting on crown of gold, silver and precious stones. Christ's disciples were poor in worldly riches and before God they were humble. But custodians of St. Peter's seat wanted to reign over the kings and Emperors of the world and want to hold the reins of worldly power in their hands. Pope should be shepherd of Jesus' sheep. He should be messenger of God and Jesus Christ, who should bring the lost and stray sheep to Jesus Christ. Wycliffe strongly criticized the Pope's excesses on the people and his princely way of life. Dismissal of both the Popes by each other was a symbol of bankruptcy of their spiritual life. If two Popes do mudslinging on each other then it is symbol of un-holiness of their positions. Wycliffe even started thinking that Pope is that Anti-Christ, who is mentioned in the book of Revelation. He said where Christ is righteous; there Pope is a way of big fraud. Christ lived a life of utter poverty. He did not have a place to lay his head. On the other side Pope is struggling for the worldly glory and honor. Christ declined the worldly kingdom and said, "My kingdom is not of this world", whereas Pope wants to rule over the kings and emperors of this world. Only Christ is the foundation and head of the Church, whereas papal system is full of deadly venom. Wycliffe also condemned and rejected Roman Catholic Church's view that bread and wine served at the time of Lord's Supper (Holy Communion) actually change into Christ's flesh and blood. He said it does not happen really. Christ is present in those elements spiritually, but not in a material way. Because of these statements intelligentsia of Oxford University and Archbishop of Canterbury (England) turned against him, because Church of England was under the influence of Roman Catholic Church. He was barred from delivering such speeches in the Oxford University. After this defeat in 1382, he started preaching on the countryside and to the farm workers. Some highly educated professors of Oxford University, who supported his views, came with him and they translated the Bible from Latin to English. After his expulsion from the

Oxford University he prepared a group of poor preachers and sent them for preaching. Even those who followed Wycliffe were expelled from the church. They were beaten and tortured. Finally in 1384 while he was serving in Lutter Worth he died, but his ideology and the movement he started did not die with him.

John Huss:

This movement started by Wycliffe did not die completely, but continued at a slow pace. In 1383 when princess Anne of Boehemia was married to Prince Richard -II of England, then the path to Boehemia was opened for the people of England. Now the people who supported and followed Wycliffe went to Boehemia and started preaching about the new thought, which was called protestant movement. Exchange of students between the Oxford and Prague University started at a rapid rate. So Wycliffe's ideology and movement met a great success and John Huss the leader of National Party did a lot of work for the protestant movement. John Huss did M.A. in 1396. He was well qualified and supported the reformation in the Roman Catholic Church. He was very much impressed by the Wycliffe thought. He got a golden chance for passing on Wycliffe teachings to the people in Bethlehem Chapel near the Prague University. He told the people about the misuse of Papal authority. There were pictures displayed on the walls of the Chapel, which displayed the works of Pope and the Christ. Pope used horse while going from one place to the other whereas Jesus Christ walked bare foot on the dusty streets of Palestine. Jesus set an example of service by washing feet of His disciples before His crucifixion, whereas Pope compelled the people to kiss his feet. So John Huss touched the hearts of the people to the extent that there were fights between the followers and opponents of Wycliffe. Archbishop of Prague sent a message to the Pope about this. So Pope ordered to crush this movement with an Iron hand. So the Archbishop of Prague suspended the membership of John Huss. Therefore the government expelled him from there and he moved to south Bohemia.

Constance Church Council was very near so Sygsmund ruler of Germany compelled John Huss to participate in the Church Council and put his view before the participants. When he reached there, he found his enemies outnumbering his friends. This Church Council was a testing time for him.

If he had more witnesses against him, he will have to confess his mistakes and quit his stand. If he is not ready to confess then he will have to lose his life by burning in fire. If he confesses mistakes then instead of burning he will have to face imprisonment. When council started there were more votes against him. So he was punished to be burnt in fire. His enemies filed baseless charges against him. False witnesses said those things, which he had never said or preached. He denied all those baseless charges. He was held in jail for 8 months. During this time the letters he wrote were quite encouraging and quality literature for the believers. He prayed, "Holy and righteous Jesus, I am without any virtue and weak, please accept me in your presence. If you do not accept me I cannot walk after you. Grant me spiritual strength, so that I may follow you and I may not be scared from physical death. Grant me a fearless heart, right faith, firm hope and gift of thy love, so that with patience and joy I may sacrifice my life for you and for this gift of thy grace is sufficient for me". On July 6, 1415 when he was being taken for burning in fire, he saw a pile of his books being burnt in a church compound. With a smile on his face, he said to the people, standing over there, "Do not believe this false propaganda done against me". When he was brought to the place called 'Satan's place' and he was about to be burnt in fire, he knelt down and prayed. Government official once again asked him, even now you have a chance to admit your mistakes and save your life, but John Huss said, "God Almighty is my witness, out of all the charges against me none of these is true. All these witnesses are baseless and false. I have won the people not for me, but for Christ. Keeping in mind the truth in the gospel, I have written, taught and preached". Bohemian revolution did not die with him; rather it prepared the way for another warrior Martin Luther.

Martin Luther:

Struggle started by Wycliffe and John Huss against the misdeeds and misinterpretations of the word of God did not slow down with their death, rather it picked up speed and Church was divided into two major groups, that is Catholics and Protestants. Protestant group was further divided into four sub-groups. All this happened because of different interpretations of the word of God and the different views. Whatever Roman Catholic Church was practicing and preaching, the Protestants did not like and they opposed it. Whatever the breakaway protestant group did, certain groups did not like. So they further split up. Thus divisions and splits took place on the basis of understanding of the word of God and its implementation. The four sub-groups of Protestants were Lutherans, Reformed Church, Ana-Baptists and Anglicans. The confrontation and conflicts between Catholics and Protestants widened the ditch between these major groups. After that divisions continued in the Christianity.

Martin Luther was born in 1483 in the family of mine worker. Luther and his parents wanted him to be a lawyer. One day while he was returning home, he got stuck in a heavy Thunder Storm. When lightning struck nearby with a loud sound, he fell to the ground. His family was catholic and his father was a Mine Worker and most of them believed in St. Anne. All of a sudden Luther uttered, "Saint Anne protect me. After this I will become a Monk for Christ". After two weeks he joined Erfurt Augustinian monastery and became a Monk. Luther's decision of becoming a monk disappointed his parents. After joining monastery he dedicated his life and kept all the rules of the monastery. One time he recalled and said, "If anyone goes to heaven after joining the monastery then I will be the first person. Martin Luther also said, "If I continued abiding by the hard rules of the monastery, like keeping awake at night, reciting long catholic prayers and doing other activities in the monastery, I may have killed myself soon". He used to fast continuously for three days without eating anything. He used to sleep with blanket in severe winter to do penance. At the time of first mass he said, "I am without any virtue and am scared. I cannot dare to lift up my eyes and my hands toward the living God, because I am dust and a sinner". He was so much obsessed with his sins that one day he also screamed and said, "I do not love God rather I hate Him". After that he started Bible study and the heavenly love, which he was seeking, got from the Bible. He was appointed head of the Bible study department in Wittenberg University. Words of Jesus on the Cross, "My God, my God why have you forsaken me" touched his heart to such a depth, that he declared, how can God leave His son Jesus Christ. I am sinner. Then he understood the meaning of Christ's words. Jesus took place of sinners and because of sins of the world God had forsaken Jesus for a short while. The second verse, which had great influence on him, was from Romans 1:17; 3:30. "Righteousness of God is revealed from faith to faith as it is written, Just shall live by faith. God justifies everyone by faith". He kept thinking day and night about these words. He realized that judgment of God is mainly based upon the believer's faith on God and his son Jesus Christ. Judgment of God is that truth which a believer receives through His grace and mercy. I realized that I got new life in Christ and He has opened the gates of heaven for me. He started preaching that human beings can be saved only through faith in Jesus Christ, and His death on the cross. Cross is the way of salvation and following this way only one can get rid of Satan. His views did not match with the views of the Pope and Roman Catholic Church rules. If salvation is only through faith in Jesus Christ, then there is no need for the recommendation of the Pope, Bishop and the priests. The faith that flourishes on the word of God does not need the prayers offered in the Catholic Mass and to the Catholic Saints. Salvation does not require favors from Pope and Bishops, their forgiveness letters. Going to holy places has nothing to do with the forgiveness of sins. When Luther was opposing pope, at the same time Pope's representative John Tenzel was collecting funds to build a big Cathedral in honor of St. Peter. He was preaching that whosoever contributed large sums of money for this cause, his soul instead of going to Purgatory will straight way go to heaven. If he gives money in the name of dead person then as soon as money falls into the treasure chest, his soul will be saved and go to heaven immediately.

For Luther John Tenzel's propaganda, for collecting money was baseless and false. With the donations neither the sins are forgiven nor souls from Purgatory go to heaven. After some time Dominican (2.1) Christians turned against Luther, they declared Luther's preaching is a dangerous doctrine. Pope's spokesman issued an order that anyone speaking against Pope will be guilty of heresy. This order did not move Luther. Then another spokesman of Pope John Eck declared Luther a mad man and likened him to John Huss.

Yet Luther presented his case before the general public and the rulers and declared that Pope and his satellite bishops are collecting money to lead a luxurious life. Public should take away their wealth and worldly glory for which they are working. He brought revival in the public through News Papers and pamphlets. In 1520 Pope issued a statement saying that a boar has entered in the vineyard. He talks against catholic faith. He must be opposed at every front with full force. He was handed over a copy of this order and he was asked to reply to this order within sixty days. But Luther on the other hand set fire to all the books pertaining to the laws of Roman

Catholic faith and also he threw copy of the letter that Pope had sent to him. He saved the scriptures and readings about the Lord's Supper and the Baptism. He declared that believer's group is the true Church of Christ.

According to the order of Pope Leo (X), Luther was declared blasphemer and his membership from the Roman Catholic Church was terminated in January 1521. As the king Charles had swore to be loyal to the Pope, so he called Luther and asked him about his writings and statements. Luther replied and declared, "My conscience is clear. I am slave to the word of God. I will not say anything against the word of God nor I will do anything against it. God is my helper". Charles (V) expelled him from the country with the order saying, "He is a devil in the garb of a Monk". Luther was given 21 days time to go to Saxony (Germany) to escape punishment. Ruler of Saxony saved him from punishment. Duke Frederick gave place to live in his palace in Wartberg. He started living there under the name of George Junker. Within one year he translated New Testament into German language. Martin Luther's preaching created an environment of rebellion in the Roman Catholic Church. Most of the priests and city councils threw out the images of Christ and Mary from their Churches. Also the princes, rulers and the wealthy influential people supported Luther and rebelled against the Roman Catholic Church. In 1522 Luther returned back to Wittenberg and became leader of protestant Christians. He abolished the position of bishop. Many people started supporting him and the protestant movement. Roman Catholic fathers and nuns also rebelled and got married.

Luther himself married a nun named Katherine. Luther changed the liturgy and translated all books used in Churches from Latin to German. Freedom from Pope's slavery also had effect on farmers. They also rebelled against the Land Lords. They demanded freedom from slavery of the Land Lords. They demanded that extra work, which the Land Lords imposed on them, should be finished. In the beginning Luther supported their demand but when he saw that Land Lords were turning against him, he backed out and opposed farm worker's demand. Luther told the princely rulers and Land Lords to crush this movement with iron hand. In 1525 this movement was badly defeated and crushed. Poor farm workers lost jobs and were punished. They were helpless and the movement came to an end. About 100,000 farm workers were killed. Those who survived turned against Luther. They called Luther a big fraud and a false prophet and they went back to Roman Catholic Church. Luther tried to clarify his position and said, "He believes that in religious matters all human beings are equal before God, yet in worldly matters all are not equal.

Because of this statement Land Lords and Princes were very happy, so they got an excuse to collect wealth and keep supremacy over the poor. So the whole rich and wealthy community followed Luther and they got an opportunity to control the power and the wealth. Whole rich community followed Luther and Luther's followers were called 'Lutherans'. All Lutheran princes formed a league. Due to difference in Ideology a civil war started between people loyal to Charles (V) and the Lutheran rulers. As all Lutheran rulers were in sound position and had a big following, Charles (V) signed an agreement with them. According to this agreement, princely rulers got the right to make decisions regarding the state religion under their jurisdiction. Also there will be no denomination other than the Lutherans. Catholic bishop will transfer their Church property to Lutheran Churches. So major faith in Germany was the Lutheran. Lutheranism spread from Germany to Scandinavia. Princely rulers could decide whether their state religion will be Catholicism or Lutheran. Lutheran movement put the Protestantism on firm footing. He assured the people that salvation of a Christian is through faith in Jesus Christ and abiding by His commandments. Their salvation does not depend on the slavery to Pope and Roman Catholic bishops nor does it depend upon their mercy.

John Calvin (1509-1564)

John Calvin who was very impressed by Luther and John Huss's ideologies, wanted to go to Strasburg for higher education, but a war was going on between Spain and France, so he could not go to Strasburg directly. He decided to go through Geneva (Switzerland). He had a plan to stop in Geneva for a month and then go to Strasburg. He did not want to stay in Geneva longer, because Switzerland people had rejected ruler of Savoy and the Pope. Therefore there was chaos among the people of Switzerland in general and Geneva in particular. There was an evangelist by the name William Farel who continued preaching against the Roman Catholic Pope and because of this people of Geneva left Pope and accepted protestant Christianity, but they did not have an able leader, who could lead them in this new protestant movement. William Farel had already heard about John Calvin and his protestant movement. When John Calvin arrived in Geneva William Farel met him. Farel told him that people of Geneva need him, so you stay here and hold the reins of the Church, but Calvin refused and said, I have to go to Strasburg and finish my education. Therefore I cannot stay here. Farel told him, "your education is not important than the God's work. If you refuse to serve the Lord, then He may punish you". Calvin got scared after hearing these words; also he thought refusing Lord's work is rebellion against God. He gave a second thought to Farel's words and said, "Temperamentally I am a shy person and I have been avoiding mixing with the people, but God kept me so entangled in his work that I was never alone. He always kept me in the Fore Front in His service". So Calvin stayed there and put the protestant movement on firm footing. His followers were called Calvinists. They included Dutch and German reformed Churches; Presbyterians, Baptists and Congregationalists.

Reformed Churches:

Luther and Calvin were born in different countries. Their ways of living and early years of life were different, yet they had different views and different interpretation about the Christian faith. According to Luther salvation of human beings is totally based upon the faith in Jesus Christ and His sacrificial death on the cross. Calvin said, "God is almighty, Powerful and capable of doing everything. According to Luther God is the only one who can forgive sins. Calvin understood that God is firm in his purpose and no one can stop. Luther was the son of a mineworker; He was a Monk and a professor. Calvin was highly educated with a Master's degree in arts and a capable lawyer. Both based their faith and views on the word of God. John Calvin went to the University at the age of 14 and finished his degree in Master of Arts in 1528. He started studying law because his father wished him to be a lawyer, but his father died in 1531 and he became free. He came to Paris and started reformation movement in Christianity. He started spending more time in Bible study. He left the scholarly work in classics and started playing a leading role in protestant movement. In 1533 Nicholas Cop, who was the chancellor of the University delivered a powerful speech against the Catholic faith, which created turmoil not only in the University rather in whole of Paris. Everyone doubted that Calvin is behind this speech, so Paris University authorities turned against Calvin. To save his life Calvin left Paris and came to Basel (Switzerland). There he wrote his famous book 'Institutes of Christian religion'. He wrote all his views about Protestantism and the byelaws. Even to-day Protestantism is based upon those views. In the beginning of this book he wrote a letter to Francis (I) the ruler of France. In this letter he stated Protestantism to be the right faith and requested him to listen to his view with patience. With this Calvin became prominent and established leader of the protestant movement. It became difficult for him to live in France, so he stayed in Geneva (Switzerland), where he was appointed by the city council as professor of Biblical studies and other writings and they compelled him to stay in Switzerland. He formulated many rules and regulations for protestant faith and also made rules to excommunicate those whose life and faith was not according to the word of God and Protestantism. He prepared Code of conduct for Christian people. There was a dispute on the authority that who will expel the people from the Church, Church Officials or the city Magistrates. After one year's struggle Calvin and his companion Farel had to face defeat and as a result both of them were expelled from Geneva in 1538. After that he spent three years in Strasburg (France), which are considered to be the happiest years of his life. There he was appointed a pastor of a Church. He was a successful pastor and predominant religious teacher. He enjoyed respect in the whole city. He used to visit Germany as well in connection with the preaching of Protestantism. He married a widow, a mother of two children, who was his great helper till her death in 1549. In September 1541, when supporters of Calvin came to power in Geneva, they invited him to come back to Geneva. Geneva church accepted his views, so he went back to Geneva. There the Church officials were pastors, teachers, elders, and deacons. He suggested four crimes on the basis of which a person could be expelled from the church. These crimes were drinking alcohol, adultery, gambling, and dancing. But there was no consensus on these issues, so Calvin's opposition continued. Since in Geneva protestant Church was strong and powerful, so those who were persecuted in France came to Geneva for protection. From all over the Europe people started coming to Geneva for training, so John Knox termed Geneva as the training center for Christian education. Protestantism got stronger in Scotland and England. John Knox who was supporter and a preacher of Protestantism in Scotland and England faced opposition from the Catholicism and because of the strong opposition he had to run away from there.

When John Calvin died in 1564, Protestantism was already an established faith on firm footing in England, Scotland, and Europe, but soon after it spread its roots in America, India and third world countries. After the death of Calvin there were different views and interpretations, which gave birth to many denominations other than the Catholic Church. Main denominations were Eastern Orthodox, Lutherans, Reformed Churches, Anglicans, Baptists, and Calvinists. After that as the people's views differed about the word of God many more denominations came into existence.

We find here though majority of the reformists wanted to get away from the Pope and the Catholic Church, because of the wrong policies and interpretations of the word of God, yet they had different views. Zwingli, John Wycliffe, John Huss, Martin Luther, Farel and John Knox differed on certain points, which gave birth to so many protestant groups.

Notes:

2.1 Dominican-A member of a mendicant order of Friars (A certain order of Roman Catholic Church) founded by St. Dominic in 1215 and dedicated especially to preaching.

References:

1. The reformation of sixteenth century. Rolan H. Bainton-Abingdon Press 1950. 2. "The reformation" Owen Chadwick Penguin Books Ltd.1964.
2. 'Reformation Era' revised edition The Macmillan Company N.Y
3. The Church across the street by Reginald D. Manwell and Sophia L. Fahns, John Calvin pp. 36-50
4. Religions in America -Simon & Schuster
5. 'Religions of Man' Huston Smith Pp. 310-316
6. Encyclopedia of Religion and Religions, Calvin p 77-78, John Knox p- 224, Luther P-237
7. Church History by Bruce L. shelly
8. Our Religions and our Neighbors M.G. Miller and S.D. Schwartzman

Chapter Three

The Lutheran Church

(Protestant)

Martin Luther was against those things in Catholicism, which were against the word of God. Before his death in 1546, many Catholics who were fed up with the excesses of the Pope and unwanted restrictions imposed upon the people, they all deserted Roman Catholic faith and came after Luther. They realized that Luther's thinking and faith is based upon the word of God. All those who deserted Catholicism and followed Luther in his faith were called 'Lutherans'. In the early years he was friendly with the Jews and he shared his views with them. He thought that he may be able to convince Jews and they may follow him. When the Jews did not show any interest in his faith and did not care for him he was disappointed, and he turned against them. He had different views from Catholics on the following issues:

Authority:

Luther was of the view that no Church is under any person's authority. Church is the group of Christian believers and Jesus is the head of this group. Regarding the faith and their way of life, neither the Roman Catholic Church nor the Pope or any other priest can decide about these matters. Rather all rules, and commandments should be based upon the word of God. Christian Bible is the word of God and it should be taken as the light of our life. Under the guidance of Holy Spirit Bible is the final authority regarding the solution of religious questions.

Salvation:

Regarding the issue of salvation Luther criticized Roman Catholic Church, according to which salvation can be obtained only by obeying the rules and commandments of the Pope. This is totally baseless and misleading the Christian people. Salvation is the free gift of God to His believers. Neither any Church nor a priest can grant salvation to any sinner. No one can make any claim of salvation for its members. No one can be saved by his own human efforts or by abiding the rules of the Pope and living by the rules of the Church. It is enough for a human being to admit that he is a sinner and should believe in Jesus Christ, who died on the cross for the sinners. Only faith in Jesus Christ can provide access to God, and his sins washed away by the Holy Blood of Jesus Christ.

Priest Sector:

Luther Advocated that no priest should be forced upon the Church or Congregation by the Pope or the Bishop, rather congregation should have the right to choose their own pastor. He was not in favor monasteries and the unmarried life of monks. He wanted that to keep away from adultery and other temptations, the priest should get married. He himself left the monastery and the life of celibacy and married a nun Katherine Von Bora.

Worship:

Luther wanted that all Christians should participate in worship. For this he prepared liturgy and translated Bible from Latin to German language. He reduced the five sacraments celebrated in the Roman Catholic Church to two and these were Baptism and the Lord's Supper. He did not agree the opinion that bread and wine actually change into Lord's flesh and His blood.

Religion and Government:

Luther was of the view that though religion and the government are both from God, yet their functions are different therefore should be kept separate and should not be mixed with each other. Neither the religion should interfere in the political matters of the country nor should country's government meddle in the religious matters of the Church. There should be no political pressure of any kind on the religion. Religion is a personal matter of every person and freedom of faith is birth right of every person. Every citizen should be faithful to his country and should honestly obey the laws of that country. There should be political freedom for every citizen, so that he may practice his faith without any fear and may preach his faith freely. Even though Lutherans broke away from the Roman Catholic Church, yet lighting of candles, Crucifix and pictures of religious people still continued in the Church. In 1555 under the Ausburg agreement, ruler of Germany did not have the right to interfere in the internal matters of the Roman Catholic or the protestant churches, rather it was obligatory on his part to make it sure that people of both faiths can live with freedom and they do not criticize or throw mud on each other. They should not be allowed to interfere in each other's religious affairs.

Modern day Lutherans:

To-day Lutheran Church is one of the important and main denominations. Today the number of Lutherans is about 800 millions. Their Churches are found mainly in Germany, Finland, Sweden, Norway and Iceland. In United States their population is about 10 million. They took active part in politics. When people were immigrating to United States in the eighteenth century, the first immigrants were Dutch Lutherans. German Lutheran pastor, Henry Melcoir Mulanburg was the first Lutheran, who led Lutheran Church in the right direction. One of his sons fought for U.S. armies in the independence war and the second son served as the speaker of the first elected assembly. Though it is protestant Church and separated from the Roman Catholic Church, yet you will see the same objects on the altar in the Lutheran Church as in the Roman Catholic Church. The worship takes place in the people's spoken language, as in India the worship is conducted either in Hindi or locally spoken language. In North America the service is conducted in English, German or Swedish language depending upon the congregation of the Church. Sacrament of baptism is done either by sprinkling of water or by dipping hand in water and then keeping on the head of the believer or the child. They believe that at the time of celebration of Lord's Supper Jesus is actually present in the bread and the wine. Participants go to the front and take bread and wine by kneeling on the railing of the pulpit. To take into full membership or to take Lord's Supper for the first time initial formalities are completed on the Palm Sunday. Lutheran Church believes that human beings are born sinners and their salvation is only through faith in Jesus Christ. No human being can achieve salvation by his good works or fulfilling the Church laws and the sacraments. Any believer can talk or pray to God directly and all believers are priests of God. Jesus will judge everyone on the Day of Judgment. His true believers will live with Him, but those who are disobedient and deny God and His son Jesus Christ will be punished. So on the last day true and faithful believers of Christ will achieve victory over death. Lutherans believe in the Trinity that is God the father, Son Jesus Christ and the Holy Spirit. For the Lutherans Bible is the only true guide in religious matters of Christian faith. Even though they consider the Lutheran faith the right faith, yet they feel there are true Christians in other denominations as well. Every believer who believes in Jesus Christ is a part of bigger universal Church. It is responsibility of the Lutheran Church that it should be member of the Lutheran Synod or Council, who make rules for them. Every Church has the freedom to choose its own Pastor. Lutheran pastors can marry. In Europe they can be elected as Bishop, but in America it is not permitted.

Lutheran Church pays special attention to the true family life of their members. They have established Orphanages, Hospitals and Educational institutions. Special attention is paid to the education of Lutheran children. To attract people into Lutheran faith they use Radio and other media for preaching. They are no longer under the Pope, and their Church is independent and claims to be Protestant.

Lutheran Crosses:

Modern day Lutherans use different types of crosses as symbol of their faith without crucifix. One famous cross is 'Constantine's Labarum' also known as Christogram or Chrismon, a monogram of the name of Jesus Christ. It consists of the superimposed Greek letters rho (P) and chi (X) (read as Ki) often embroided on the altar paraments and priests' vestments. Often this symbol is referred Chi-Rho which are Greek letters in Christ's name.

References:

1. 'Lutheranism' Church History in plain Language by Bruce L. Shell World Publishing Pp 255-264; 295-296; 459-460.
2. "Reformation of the Sixteenth Century" by Ronald H. Bainton -Beacon Press Boston 1952.
3. "Reformation Era" 1500-1650 by Harold J. Grimm Revised Edition Macmillan Company
4. "Our Religions and Our Neighbors" By Milton G. Miller and sylvan D. Schwartzman Pp 116-119; 112-118.
5. "Encyclopedia of Religion and Religions' by Pike, E Royston Pp 237,238.
6. "The story of America's Religions" by Hartzell Spence Ch. Pp 39-58.
7. "World religions" B. Y. Landis
8. "Religions in America" Leo Rosten
9. "What is a Lutheran" by G. Elson Ruff Pp 112-120.

Chapter Four

Presbyterian Church

(Protestant)

Presbyterian Church is basically a protestant Church. The founders of this Church are considered to be Wycliffe, Martin Luther, John Calvin and Zwingli. There was not much difference in their thinking, yet their effort was to oppose the excesses done by the Pope and to make the Christian faith according to the Bible and teachings of Jesus Christ and confess Jesus as the head of the Christian Church. All these warriors for Christ had one thing common in their minds that salvation is only through faith in Jesus Christ and His grace is essential for this. In founding Presbyterian Church the names of John Calvin and Ulrich Zwingli are on the top. I have already mentioned about John Calvin in detail. Ulrich Zwingli was pastor of Catholic Church, but afterward when he saw the drawbacks in the Roman Catholic Church then this Switzerlander became leader of protestant movement and he tried to mould the Christianity according to the word of God. As every person's views can differ from views of other people, like wise in certain matters he differed from Martin Luther. His views were accepted by many people and won their hearts. His views got support not only in Geneva but he earned support in France, Germany and in far off lands. Those who accepted his views they were called 'Presbyterians' (4.1). The word Presbyterian has been taken from the Greek word, which means the elected one. Calvin believed that, Church be run by the locally elected people. John Knox a Scottish believer, who followed, the footsteps of Calvin, founded the Presbyterian Church in Scotland and England.

Afterwards John Knox carried the Presbyterian movement to America. As for as the views of Luther and Calvin are concerned they were identical regarding Roman Catholic Church, regarding the protestant Church they had minor differences. They both favored baptism and Lord's Supper, but Luther believed that at the time of Lord's Supper Jesus is actually present there, but Calvin stressed that Jesus is present there only spiritually. Luther permitted the display of pictures of saints, the Holy people and pictures of Jesus and Mary at the place of worship. He also allowed the use of candles, and use of Crucifix. On the other hand Calvin had different views regarding these things. He was in favor of simple environment inside the Church. Worship should be based on the message from the word of God and singing of hymns. Secondly according to Calvin, the whole control of the Church should be in the hands of the elected representatives of the congregation. Luther felt that since the Church is under the government control, so it is mandatory for the Church to obey the laws of the country. Calvin's liberal views got encouraging support from the colonists in America because they wanted to throw off the yoke of British rule from their necks. For this reason, the Presbyterian Church became more popular in America and it was called American Presbyterian Church. We see here the difference of views and different interpretations and understanding of the word of God, which gave birth to two factions within the protestant Church.

Luther also believed that for every believer it is mandatory to preach and witness for Christ for his salvation. Whereas Calvin believed that grace of God is given to His elected people and salvation is not earned, rather it is granted by the grace of God to the believer. Even the human faith is also gift of God.

Presbyterians Today:

In many countries of Europe like Germany, Switzerland, Holland, France and Hungry it is called reformed Church. You can see the signs of 'Reformed Christian Church' in front of many Churches in America. In Europe there are more than 60 million Presbyterians and in America their number is over 5 million. Every Church elects its own leaders, who decide about the religious matters of the Church. The elected group of leaders is called 'Session'. Many Churches combined together forms 'Presbytery'.

By combining 3or more presbyteries 'Synod' is formed. Elected members from all the Synods form General Assembly. Elected leader from the general assembly is called a 'Moderator'. At every stage an elected group of leaders consists of 50% lay leaders or Lay persons. Presbyterian Church believes in Trinity. This Church believes that God through the 'WORD' Jesus Christ controls the whole creation. God made the arrangement for salvation through the death of His son Jesus Christ. Christians believe that there is no other name than the name of Jesus Christ given under heaven by trusting whom sinners can be saved. To be saved it is essential to surrender completely to God and to accept Jesus and His sacrificial death on the cross is mandatory for salvation and in return believer receives God's grace and salvation as a free gift. In religious matters there is no book other than the Bible, which is the basis of our faith. Regarding religious matters and prayer, Presbyterians are not Narrow Minded. Modern Presbyterians use Gothic structures in their Churches or Cathedrals. They also use big Pianos, Choir, candles, flowers and plants on the altar. They also use cross without the image of Christ on it. These days you will find in American Churches two flags behind the pulpit. Out of these one is the American flag and the other one represents the Church and the Diocese. These are the symbols of their loyalty to both the country and the diocese. In every Presbyterian Church Lord's Supper is celebrated with the faith that Christ is present spiritually in the elements of bread and wine. When people were coming from Europe and Britain to America then Presbyterians came along with Puritans (4.2). Most of the Presbyterians settled in the North Eastern states and they took active part in the American Revolution.

Presbyterians from the very beginning laid stress on the education of the masses and specially the Christians, so that they may read the word of God and understand it correctly. For this purpose they appointed well educated and qualified pastors in the Churches, so that they may preach the word of God correctly and make the people understand its meaning. To achieve this aim they established colleges, Seminaries, and Universities. Presbyterian leaders have played leading role in social welfare activities. Presbyterian organizations tried to stop the child labor and implement better welfare schemes for the factory workers. With the formation of United Presbyterian Church of U.S.A. the Church played a significant role in the welfare schemes, Church Unity and World Peace. To bring unity among the Churches, "World Council of Churches" and Y.M.C.A. was formed.

Evangelism in other countries:

When the protestant movement got on firm footing, they felt that missionaries should be sent to those countries where people are away from God and they worship gods and goddesses.

William Carey was one of these missionaries, who contributed a lot towards the missionary movement. He had a dream that by preaching Jesus Christ in the whole world, people should be brought at the feet of Jesus Christ. He strongly felt that an outsider missionary would not be as successful as the local person, because he knows the local language and the culture of that area. He told that Bible should be translated into local language and local people should be appointed missionaries and local Church should bear the burden of the missionary. He felt that if Christianity has to be successful in certain area then it should be rooted deeply in the soil of the local Church and the Culture. Due to his views and the work in this regard he is known as the founding father of the modern missions. His profession was to make shoes. He worked on this profession and earned his livelihood. He spent his whole life in the service of the Lord but the woman to whom he was married being a patient of some kind of mental disease made his life more difficult and stressful and added to the problems of his life. He considered Columbus and James Cook as his heroes. William Carey accepted Jesus Christ in 1779 through the witness of one of his friends and in 1783 he was baptized. After getting Christian education in the word of God he was appointed pastor of a Church. To support his family he taught people and earned his livelihood by shoemaking.

The views of his companion Andrew Fuller had great impact on the life of William Carey. Fuller said, "If for a sinner it is essential to repent of his sins and to put faith in the message of the gospel, then it is responsibility of the God's people to preach the 'Good News' of salvation in the whole world". In 1792 William Carey wrote a book titled, "An Enquiry into the Obligation of Christians to use means for the conversion of Heathens". People raised many objections against William Carey's mission. One of the objections was the problem of reaching distant nations.

Dangers of working among the uncivilized people as it happened to St. Thomas who was one of the Disciples of Christ, who reached India in 52 A.D. and was stoned to death by the adversaries of Christianity. Then the question of financial support of the missionaries and the difficulty of understanding local language surfaced up. But Carey answered all their questions and objections. He said if the East India Company can go for its business and collecting the wealth from India, then why not people of God could work and preach the gospel without any greed and selfishness. He appealed to the Christian Churches to send missionaries throughout the world. William Carey and Andrew Fuller determined that in-spite of all the difficulties and hurdles they will carry out the commandment of the Lord and obey the words of St. Paul. "That at the name of Jesus every knee should bow, of those in heaven and of those on earth and that every tongue should confess that Jesus Christ is Lord to the glory of God the father". Philippians 2:10,11. After that William Carey, Andrew Fuller and 11 other Baptists friends made Baptist Missionary Society. Within one year after the formation of the society William Carey set for India with his family.

From 1763 East India Company had prevailed on the Indian Soil. British people were not interested at all in spreading Christianity because they knew the words of Jesus, "And you shall know the truth and truth shall make you free" John 8:32. Their interest was to rule over India and collect the wealth. British Company workers were enjoying comfortable life to the full. They because of their white skin and education treated Indians as inferior people and considered themselves superior. When senior leaders in the East India Company came to know that some missionaries are planning to come to India for evangelism, then the white British rulers conveyed to them that sending missionaries to India is not a wise step. It is not a right decision rather it will be wastage of money, a costly project and endangering lives of the missionaries. So East India Company banned the entry of William Carey in Calcutta. He being Danish moved to Seram Pur. There he started working as a Foreman in a factory making Indigo (a whitening agent for clothes). He worked there for three months. He had a lot of free time so he learned Indian languages. In 1799 two more Baptist missionaries Joshua Marshman and William Ward joined him. So they not only worked in Bengal rather did lot of work outside as well. They all studied Hindu religion in detail and they came to know the difference between Hinduism and Christianity. This helped them a lot to work among Hindus. Till 1824 Carey had translated Bible in six languages and left 24 incomplete translations. He prepared grammars and dictionaries and translated many Indian books into English.

William Carey's work encouraged many more people and so the demand for many more missionaries went up. Missionaries started coming in hundreds. Among these was a famous missionary Henry Martin and after his name Henry Martin Institute was established in Lucknow. Gradually when Christianity got deep rooted in India, Indians called Christianity a religion of the English people though British people did not do anything in spreading Christianity. Rather it was said, "When British people leave their country, they throw their Bibles in the English Channel". The credit of spreading Christianity in India goes to the missionaries who came from America, Scotland, and New Zealand. Missionary work in India is clearly reflected from the thousands of biblical messages and hundreds of hymns composed and written by the missionaries. Bishop Reginald Hebber sacrificed his life in the service of the Lord.

Missionaries of American Presbyterian mission did exemplar/y work in India in the field of evangelism and education. They established schools, Colleges, Medical Colleges, and Hospitals, which British rulers at that time did not do. Before the partition of India these Institutions were famous for their dedication and were counted among the most prominent institutions of India. In these Institutions hundreds of thousands of children from the down trodden and poor families benefited, got education and were made able to compete with the privileged people of the Indian society. Even after the partition some institutions are now playing leading role in the Indian society in general and Christian Society in particular. But certain Institutions are failing badly because of the wrong policies of the corrupt and selfish administration. Though Roman Catholic Institutions are not doing any evangelistic work, yet their education standard in schools and Colleges and medical services in Hospitals are commendable. Every parent prefers to send his children to Catholic Institutions. Even those who hate Christianity and do not want to hear the name of Christ in Christian Schools, want to spend any amount of money to send their children to Convent Schools run by the Roman Catholics.

After the partition as the time passed Indian Church realized that since our savior is one therefore all Christian denominations should come together and form one Christian Church. With this aim 'The United Church of North India' was formed. Afterwards some more like-minded denominations joined and two major Churches, Church of North India and church of South India came into being. These denominations were Episcopal, Congregational, the council of Baptist Churches in Northern India, The Church of the Brethren in India, The Church of India(formerly known as the Church of India, Pakistan, Burma and Ceylon), Methodists (British and Australasian), Anglicans, The Disciples of Christ and American Presbyterian Missions, which formed Church of North India and the Church of South India. The Mission Statement of Church of North India is "The Church of North India United and Uniting together is committed to announce the Good News of the reign of God inaugurated through the death and resurrection of Jesus Christ in proclamation and to demonstrate in actions to restore the integrity of God's creation through continuous struggle against the demonic powers by breaking down the barriers of caste, class, gender, economic inequality and exploitation of nature". American Methodists did not come into the union and they have separate Methodist Church. Efforts are being made to bring remaining churches into the union and form Church of India under one flag. It seems difficult for some Orthodox and Roman Catholic Churches, but it is hoped that Baptists and American Methodists may come into the union. These days there are many more denominations other than the groups mentioned above who are working hard to win the people for the Lord and some of these are Jehovah Witnesses, Mormons, Church of God, American Pentecostals, Syrian Orthodox Church, and Seventh Day Adventists. Out of these many are Evangelical Churches. Modern protestant Church is facing many challenges. St. Paul had stated that woman may not be permitted to serve as priests, deacons, and Bishops, but due to the shortage of pastors and lack of interest among men to become pastors has necessitated the service of women as pastors. Methodists and Presbyterian Churches have ordained many qualified women as deacons and pastors and America is on the forefront. Some of the women pastors are very successful. Many women in the Methodist and Presbyterian Churches are sharing many responsibilities in the Church as Chairpersons of the committees. I as an ordained minister feel, if a woman can be a prophet of God then why she can't be a deacon or a pastor of the Church.

It is need of the time to realize that we have one supreme savoir and all Churches who feel that way should be united. Existence of many denominations is a bad witness and is equivalent to dividing Christ into different Groups. As there is one Christ there should be one fold of His sheep. Every denomination thinks that their doctrine and faith is right which is a big hurdle in the way of union. Such denominations are Jehovah Witnesses, Mormons, Moonies, Roman Catholics, and the Cults. They have their own interpretations of the word of God.

Notes:

4.1: Presbyterian: It is a protestant denomination characterized by a graded system of Representative's ecclesiastical bodies exercising legislative and judicial powers. Presbyterian Church is traditionally Calvinistic in doctrine. Ruling body in Presbyterian churches consisting of ministers and representative elders from congregation within the district is called presbytery. The house of Roman Catholic Parish priest is also called Presbytery.

4.2: Puritans: This is a protestant group of Christians which existed in England in the 16th *I* 17th centuries. They opposed unscriptural ceremonial worship and prelacy of the Church of England. They preached more rigorous and professedly purer moral code than that which prevailed at that time. They considered themselves true Christians.

References:

1. "Protestantism and Progress" by Earnest Troeltsch
2. Historical Study of Protestantism -Beacon Press
3. "Here I stand" Life of Martin Luther by Roland Bainton
4. "The age of reformation" by Harbinson E. Harris
5. "Portrait of Calvin' By T.H.L. Parker
6. "John Calvin" the organization of reformed Protestantism by Williston walker
7. Church History in Plain Language by Bruce L. Shelly
8. "Our Religion and our Neighbors" Revised Edition by M.G.Miller and Sylvan Schwartzman

Chapter Five

Roman Catholic Church

Reformed Roman Catholic Church:

We have already studied whatever happened in the early Roman Catholic Church. For spreading Catholicism and to fight against the adversaries of Catholicism there was bloodshed. When Roman Catholic Church realized its mistakes they tried to improve upon and make Catholic faith more popular. By the end of 15th century Roman Catholic faith was most popular. Henceforth wherever I write Catholic that means Roman Catholic. After this when political hold on the Catholic Church weakened, many countries became free and with the spreading of Protestantism Catholic faith faced downfall. These circumstances compelled Catholic Church to strengthen their spiritual hold on the Church. They realized that only spiritualism would give strength to the weak Catholic Church. The spread of democracy and French Revolution affected the Roman Empire. All the states, which were under the Pope's control, became part of Italy's government. According to the agreement between Italian government and the Pope, Pope was given independent city called 'Vatican City' directly under the Pope's rule.

Pope John (XXIII) who was installed in 1958, as the Pope (1962-1965) passed in second Vatican council that all the policies of Catholic Church should be reviewed. All the drawbacks should be removed and catholic faith should be revised to meet the modern day demands, so that people should not be swayed away by the wave of Protestantism. As a result many changes were made in the Catholic Church and its faith. It was passed that worship in catholic Churches should be in local language instead of Latin. Catholic congregation should be encouraged to participate in Church worship and should be given responsibility to participate in other Church activities. There should be no bar on eating meat on Friday. To make Catholic faith universal, friendly relations should be established with other Christian denominations. Catholic faith should be molded in such a way that ditch created between Catholic faith and other denominations and Judaism be narrowed down. So the catholic Churches like in India started worshiping the statues of Mother Mary and Jesus as the local Hindus do in their temples. They offer sweets and fruits before the images of Jesus and Mary and light candles before their statues. Plans were made to talk to the Eastern Orthodox and protestant Churches. To abolish the criminal charges against the Jews regarding crucifixion of Jesus, Pope in 1965 Vatican Council freed the Jews of those charges. In 1969 a proclamation was made that efforts should be made to have cordial relations with the Jews. Catholic Christians were asked to apologize to their Jewish brothers for the excesses, which they faced at the hands of Catholics. It was declared that whatever Jews did to Christ and His disciples and believers was a history and whatever they did it is between them and God. Catholic Christians have no grudge against them. It should be kept in mind that historically Jewish nation is the chosen nation of God and love of God for Israel should never be overlooked. So due to all these things population of Roman Catholics jumped up and have crossed 1100 millions and out of these 50 million live in America.

Faith of Roman Catholic Church:

God is all Powerful and Eternal:

Catholic Church believes that God is all Powerful and never dies. Whatever wisdom and knowledge we see in the creation of this universe is above human understanding. Secrets of this creation cannot be understood or comprehended with human knowledge and wisdom, nor can we interpret and explain with human understanding. Whatever moral and spiritual characteristics we see in the human beings, these belong to God. Human wisdom, understanding, knowledge, differentiation of good and bad, free will, all these are characteristics of God and these were already present in

God before he created man and woman. God existed before the creation of this world and He is omnipresent and has no end. Man, whose wisdom is limited and imperfect can neither understand and comprehend God fully nor can know the secrets of His creation. God created man and woman out of His love so that He could enjoy their company and their love. God gave us eternal soul and our body is the supreme creation of God. God expects every man and woman to remain in the company of God and they should live a life, the example of which Christ presented before the people. Sacrificial death of Christ on the cross is the proof of God's love for the humanity. For that love God came down to earth in the body of Christ. Catholics believe in the Holy Trinity, which means that in God we have the Father, Son (Jesus Christ), and the Holy Spirit. Jesus is also called the 'Word' because He has all the characteristics of God. He was born of Virgin Mary, who was conceived by the Holy Spirit, which comes out of God. All the three are from the very beginning and none of these was created.

God's arrangement of Salvation:

God created man and woman in the state of righteousness and purity, but by disobedience to the commandment of God they sinned and separated themselves from God. By disobedience they lost the right of eternal life. A seed of Sin was sown in their lives and the same was passed on to their descendents. God created man in His own image and put all His characteristics in him but because of sin his characteristics changed and all those characteristics of sinful nature were passed on to the descendents of Adam and Eve.

The day Adam and Eve sinned, God made a plan for their salvation and their union with God. God gave spiritual laws (Ten Commandments) through His chosen nation Israel but human beings did not care for those commandments. God sent His son, THE WORD (Jesus Christ) into the world to save the sinners through His sacrificial death on the cross.

To implement that plan of salvation He chose Abraham and thereafter Isaac, Jacob, Moses, and other prophets through whom he sent His commandments for the humanity. Even then human beings kept slipping away from God and at the end He sent His son. He bore sins of humanity and was crucified to pay the price of sins of each and every human being. When we are baptized by water our sins are washed away by the blood of Jesus shed on the cross. The Holy Spirit, working in human beings tries to mold the believer in the image of God and Jesus Christ.

Catholic Church:

Christ laid the foundation of Christian Church before His crucifixion. Jesus told Peter, "And I also say to you that you are Peter, and on this rock I will build my Church, and gates of Hades shall not prevail against it. And I will give you the keys of the kingdom of heaven, and whatever you bind on earth will be bound in heaven and whatever you loose on earth shall be loosed in heaven". Matt 16:18-19, NKJV. So according to Catholics it makes clear that Christ made Peter leader and foundation of the earthly Church and gave him the authority that whatever he binds on earth will be bound in heaven. When Jesus said that gates of Hades shall not prevail that means teachings of the Church will make human beings better Christians and transform him during his life. No human being is sinless. After the resurrection Jesus has been appearing to his disciples for 40 days and prepared them for leading the Church. Before He ascended into heaven he gave leadership of the Church to His disciples. After 10 days of His ascension into heaven, on the day of Pentecost when Holy Spirit came upon His disciples in the form of tongues of fire the Christian Church was inaugurated.

After the death of Judas Iscariot, Mathias was elected to be the twelfth disciple. These Disciples established Churches in various cities, and Holy Spirit put the spiritual stamp on their works. Before the gospel was available in 65 A.D. in written form, whatever the disciples had heard from Jesus Christ, they preached to the people. After that those believers that received the word of God verbally from the disciples gave the written form. As the disciples and believers were righteous and true to their faith the same way they were honest and true to give written shape to the gospel of Jesus Christ, which made the gospel true and believable. From the book of acts it becomes evident, how the disciples honestly worked hard to preach the word of God and building His church. Acts Chapter 15 tells about first Church Council. Roman catholic Church believes that Holy Spirit had been working in founding the Church and leading the believers, leaders of the Church and the disciples. The proof of guidance by the Holy Spirit is found in Acts Chapter 10 and 15:28. Roman Catholic Church believes in 46 books of the Old Testament, this includes 39 books found in the protestant bible and 7 additional books in the Old Testament are called Apocrypha. Adding 27 books of the New Testament the Roman Catholic Bible (Jerusalem Bible) has 73 books. Seven books of Apocrypha are:

Esdras (2 books)
Baruch Judith
Esther (Part-2)
Maccabees (1&;2)
Ecclesiasticus (Part-2)

In addition to the above books there are more books, which scholars do not consider as reliable and secondly it mostly contains historical facts about Israel. These books are 1. Prayer of Azariah 2. Song of Holy Children 3. Susanna 4.Bell and dragon, 5. Prayer of Manasses.

Grace, Sin, Salvation, Paradise, Hades and Purgatory (The place of Repentance):

Holy Spirit the third personality of Godhead resides in the believer, who is blessed with the grace of God. The working of Holy Spirit in the life of believer is essential because it transforms the sinful nature and makes us acceptable to God. For this reason Jesus said, "If you love me, you will obey my commandments and I will ask my father and He will give another advocate to be with you forever. This is the spirit of truth whom the world cannot receive". John14:15-17. Second step to receive grace of God is the baptism, after which through His grace we get salvation through Jesus Christ. Through this grace we become sons and daughter of God and we receive eternal life. We cannot earn salvation through our deeds nor can we get rid of our sins. Only through the grace of God and sacrificial death of Christ we are saved. Catholics believe we can repent not only in this life; rather there is an opportunity after death, when we are in Purgatory (5.1). In Purgatory we can repent and be saved by the grace of God. Catholics believe that if a Christian dies without repenting of his sins then if his dear ones, friends and relatives pray for him and fulfill also the sacraments for his soul then his soul can be saved and can go to heaven. This faith is based upon lCor.15: 29-32.

Righteousness of our souls and becoming like Christ can only get us into the kingdom of heaven. Our first parents Adam and Eve were in that state of purity before committing sin and that is why they were enjoying fellowship of God. While talking to Nicodemus Jesus had told him same thing that unless we are born again through the baptism of Holy Spirit we cannot enter into the kingdom of heaven. Roman Catholics also believe that if a person listens to his conscience and without water baptism he accepts Jesus Christ, then Jesus works in his life through his conscience. The one who abides by the will of God, and then not only Jesus but Holy Spirit as well works in his life. Any person who did not go for water baptism but through his conscience he believes in Jesus Christ, this is called baptism of desire. When we spend eternal life with God sins like jealousy, greed and worry do not have any place in our life, rather we are like God and we enjoy the fellowship of God. The Crowns that we will get in heaven are decorated with the deeds we do in this world. At the time of death our faith, our deeds and the things we have done go with us even into the purgatory. If in this world we have lived by the commandments of God and spent life under His grace, then on the Day of Judgment we will be awarded with eternal life in heaven. Catholics believe that like the person, who was crucified with Jesus repented and believed in Jesus Christ he was promised eternal life in heaven. Likewise if we also repent at the time of death and we put our faith in Jesus we can also be saved through his grace. After the Day of Judgment there is no opportunity for a sinner to repent and be saved. Even if he wants to repent like the rich man in hell, he has no chance to repent and that soul has to spend life of torture in the eternal fire of hell. As long as the soul is resting in the world of the dead (Purgatory) he has every opportunity to repent. As long his soul is in the purgatory, our prayers, our sacrifices for him can help him to achieve the grace of God and that soul instead of going to hell can enter into the kingdom of heaven. In heaven there will be our savior Jesus Christ, the Son of God, souls of holy men and women and the angels of God. In most cases the sufferings of this life are because of his sins because God does not feel happy to see any one suffering. But if a person suffers for Christ, then his sufferings earn him salvation. The love of God for human beings compelled Him to send His son Jesus Christ in this world to suffer and pay the price of sins of the world. He took our sins on Him and underwent insulting death on the cross so that human beings may escape this torture, pain and insults. This is the expression of love of God for sinners.

Religious sacraments:

There are seven religious sacraments in the Roman Catholic Church. These are mandatory for every Catholic Church member to celebrate and receive the grace of God.

1. Baptism:

Roman Catholic Church believes that through baptism all the personal sins and the sins he inherited from his parents are forgiven and through the indwelling of Holy Spirit and we become children of God. For this Luke has written in the book of Acts 2:38-39 these are the words Peter spoke to the people, "Repent and let every one of you be baptized in the name of Jesus Christ for the remission of sins and you shall receive the gift of the holy Spirit. For the promise is to you and to your children and to all who are afar off, as many as the Lord our God will call ". In 70 C.E. it was told that get baptized in running water and if there is no running water then a person can be baptized in still water and if that too is not available then a child or an adult can be baptized in the name of the Father, son and the Holy Spirit by dipping hand in water and then putting on the head of the person to be baptized or water should be poured with a small saucer on the head of the person concerned.

2. Lord's Supper:

To celebrate this sacrament Lord commanded while eating last Passover supper with His disciples in the upper room before His crucifixion. He commanded to celebrate this sacrament till His second advent. It is written in the gospel that while eating last supper with His disciples, He took bread and gave it to the disciples saying this is my body which is broken for you on the cross. Then he took the cup with the grape juice and giving them said, "This is my blood which will be shed for you and many more on the cross for the forgiveness of sins". Even today the bread (representing body of Jesus broken on the cross) and the grape juice (blood of Jesus shed on the cross) is sufficient for the forgiveness of sins, when taken in faith. Even Jesus himself in John 6: 54-56 said, "Whoever eats my flesh and drinks my blood has eternal life, and I will raise him at the last day. For my flesh is food indeed and my blood is drink indeed. He who eats my flesh and drinks my blood abides in me and I in him" Roman Catholic Church believes that bread and grape juice used for the celebration of Lord's Supper actually changes into the flesh and blood of Jesus and St. Paul writes about this in 1 Cor 11:27-29; and l Cor 10:16.

3. Confirmation into Roman Catholic Church:

The oath of confirmation into Roman Catholic faith is taken when a child becomes an adult, and the one who takes the oath is understood to be one of the Disciples of Christ. His responsibility becomes more than what he had at the time of baptism. When we take any responsibility for the work of the Lord, then His grace abides with us. St. Paul commanded every believer to advance further in faith after the baptism as we find in Hebrews 6:1-2 "Therefore Let us go on toward perfection, leaving behind the basic teachings about Christ, not laying again the foundation: repentance from the dead works and faith towards God, instructions about baptisms, laying on of hands, resurrection of the dead and eternal Judgment."

4. Marriage:

God in the Garden of Eden established marriage between man and woman. Roman Catholics believe man and woman are united in Christ after their marriage. As the process of creation never stops, so the man and the woman through their love and marriage fulfill this God's commandment. Marriage is a sacred sacrament so it should be done in the conditions of purity of both the man and the woman. God's plan for the procreation of the world is fulfilled through the uniting of man and the woman in Holy relationship of marriage. The children born after the legal and holy relationship of marriage are God like.

5. Holy positions:

When Jesus appointed disciples for preaching the Good News, He gave them the authority to heal the sick, forgive their sins, to baptize and to spread the gospel of salvation and to preach the commandments of God. As the Christianity spread to far off places, the disciples appointed pastors, deacons, and bishops, so that God's work may be done methodically. Those who are not pastors, deacons and bishops, they too have great responsibility in the Church. Lay leader can baptize people in the name of the Father, Son and the Holy Spirit. During the Lord's Supper they can assist the pastor while celebrating the Lord's Supper, but they should be in the state of purity.

6. Forgiveness of sins:

Roman Catholic Church believes that Pope, Bishops, and catholic Priest have the authority to forgive the sins of those who confess their sin before them. They quote the words of Jesus from John 20: 22-23 to support their arguments, where it is written, "...Receive the Holy Spirit. If you retain the sins of any, they are retained". As God breathed the breath of life in the first Adam, so Jesus breathed Holy Spirit on His disciples. They became spiritual and heirs and partakers of eternal life. The eternal life which man had lost because of sin in the Garden of Eden, Jesus restored that by breathing Holy Spirit up on them.

Sins are of two types. One kind of sins is those, which result in eternal death. These sins we commit being aware and knowing the commandments of God and consequences of their disobedience and we commit these sins willfully. By this we knowingly disobey God and spurn the sacrificial death of Christ for sinners and profane the Holy Blood of Jesus shed on the cross by trampling under our feet, there is no sin bigger than this. Even the sins against Holy Spirit are serious resulting in eternal death. We have examples in the word of God. Jesus said, "And everyone who speaks a word against the son of man will be forgiven, but whoever blasphemes against the Holy Spirit will not be forgiven". In the case of Ananais and Saphira who lied to the Holy Spirit died and Peter said to them, "Why has the Satan filled your heart to lie to the Holy Spirit and keep back part of the proceeds of the land".

Second type of sins is those, which we commit under pressures of this life, human feelings, desires and ambitions or external pressures of life. The result of these is not eternal death but there is definitely punishment for these. The relationship with God is not broken, though it becomes weak and grace of God is not taken away from us, but it requires repentance on our part and forgiveness from God. God is ready to forgive our every sin provided we repent from the heart and ask for His forgiveness. Sin committed against the Holy Spirit is unpardonable. In Hebrews 10:26 it is written, "If we sin willfully after we have received the knowledge of the truth, there no longer remains a sacrifice for sins, but certain fearful expectation of judgment, and fiery indignation which will devour the adversaries. How much worse punishment, do you suppose, will he be thought worthy who has trampled the son of God underfoot, counted blood of the Covenant by which he was sanctified a common thing and insulted the Spirit of God." Hebrews 10:26-29

Such a sin is unforgivable. That is why Catholics claim that the sins, the consequences of those is not death, can be forgiven by Pope, Bishop, and Roman Catholic Priest.

7. Praying for the Sick:

Jesus gave authority to His believers to heal the sick. Even James in his epistle said, "If anyone among you is suffering, let him call for the elders (Bishop, Pastor, and Elder) of the Church and let them pray over him, anointing him with oil in the name of the Lord. And prayer of faith will save the sick and the Lord will raise him up and if he had committed sins, they will be forgiven".

James 5: 14,15. So God wants everyone in His service to obey His commandments.

Body Of Jesus:

In the gospel the Church of Christ has been named as the body of Christ. The Church of Christ is the group of Holy people who believe in God and His son Jesus Christ. Angels are also included in this and also those people who are in the purgatory. Catholics believe that those people who are in heaven can also help the believers on earth, but they do not get any reward for this. In the book of Revelation 5:8 we read, God listens to the prayers of His witnesses and the saints living in heaven. That is why Roman Catholics believe that if they pray to Mother Mary and other saints they will pass on their prayers to God with their recommendation and God will listen. They quote 2 Meccabes 15:11-14 where it is written that priest Onias and prophet Jeremiah who have gone from this world pray for the nation of Israel. Not only have that even angels prayed for us (Zechariah 1: 12-17). In certain cases even without prayer angels and prophets work for us. 2kings 13: 20-21. We find when Israel was at war then in hurry they tried to put a dead body in Elisha's grave. As soon as the dead body touched bones of Elisha the dead man became alive and sat up. Catholic Church believes in all these things.

Social Justice

There are several references and commandments in the Old Testament where stress has been laid on the social justice. Regarding poor laborer and paying his wages immediately after his day's work is over. Not to oppress the widows and orphans. Going of father and the son to the same prostitute. These three things, which come under, these headings, are: -

Human Life

Roman Catholic Church is against abortion and they give many references from the Bible to support their arguments. God knows the life before it is conceived in mother's womb. "Before I formed you in the womb, I knew you. Before you were born I sanctified you" Jeremiah 1:5. David and Job wrote similar words, "You were watching me when my bones were being formed in the womb". The omnipresent God, who is our creator and sustainer, is always watching us. To kill the child in womb means finishing his whole life for which we have no right. The people who abort the child before birth are not bad people, but abortion is the result of their wrong decisions. In America 25% women go for abortion. Roman Catholic Church helps those unmarried and married pregnant women who decide to get abortion.

Self Respect

Before God all are equal. God wants every human being whether rich or poor, black or white or from any country to live with self respect, pride and honor. He did not make anyone big or small on the basis of caste or creed. All human beings are equal in the sight of God and Roman Catholic Church supports this view.

Human Needs:

Roman Catholic Church believes that genuine needs of the weak and the poor should be met. The one whom God has given more should help those who need monetary help. In the Old Testament God commanded the rich to help the poor, orphans and widows in the society and who are under debt. Their debt should be waved off. According to the commandment of Jesus our wealth is not only ours rather we should give to the poor and meet their needs who do not have enough. Jesus quoted the parable of the rich man and the Lazarus.

According to Catholic faith Jesus is the savior of all those who trust Him and believe in the saving power of His sacrificial death on the cross. As it has been mentioned earlier Roman Catholic Church has taken out the second commandment from the ten commandments of Moses in their Bible and broke the tenth commandment into two to make it ninth and the tenth commandment. The Ten Commandments as given by God through Moses and as the Catholic Church has changed are given below.

Given to Moses	In the Catholic Bible
1. I am your Lord God. You shall have no other gods before me.	1. I am the Lord your God you shall have no other gods before me
2. You shall not make for yourself an idol, whether in the form of anything that is in heaven above or that is on the earth beneath. You shall not bow down to them or worship them.	2. You shall not make wrongful use of the name of the Lord your God.
3. You shall not make wrongful use of the name of the Lord your God, for the Lord will not acquit anyone who misuses His name.	3. Remember The Sabbath day and keep it holy.
4. Remember the Sabbath day and keep it holy. Six days you shall labor and do all your work but the seventh day is the Sabbath to your lord.	4. Honor your father and mother.
5. Honor your father and your mother so that your days may be long in the land the Lord your God is giving you.	5. You shall not murder.
6. You shall not murder.	6. You shall not commit adultery.
7. You shall not commit adultery.	7. You shall not steal.
8. You shall not steal.	8. You shall not bear false witness against your neighbor.
9. You shall not bear false witness against your neighbor.	9. You shall not covet your neighbor's wife.
10. You shall not covet your neighbors' house; you shall not covet your neighbors wife, or male or female slave, or ox or donkey, or anything that belongs to your neighbor.	10. You shall not covet anything in your neighbors' house.

Prayers read in the Catholic Church and read by the Catholics at their personal level are given at the end of this work. You may read them to find the difference between Roman Catholic and your faith and how many prayers are according to the word of God. Do you agree that Mary is the mother of God?

After reading about the early Popes and the Roman Catholic faith we find many conflicting views that led to the partition of Roman Catholic Church and creation of so many denominations. Even now when so many denominations are coming together and uniting in the name of Father, son and the Holy Spirit thinking that we have only one supreme savior Catholics are not ready for that rather in some countries they are opposing Protestant denominations.

In the recent years the Popes realized that Roman Catholic Church policies need to be revised. Pope John XXIII (1962-1965) took a bold step and passed in the second Vatican Council that all the policies of the Roman Catholic Church should be revised and the drawbacks should be removed. Catholic faith should be revised to meet the modern day demands. Later two Popes John Paul II and Pope Francis (present Pope) worked on these lines. That is why John Paul II to end the hatred for the Anglican Church toured England and met Robert Runcy, the Archbishop of Anglican Church and he welcomed the Pope by calling the Pope Brother in Christ. Pope John XXIII abolished the criminal charges against the Jews regarding crucifixion of Jesus and freed the Jews of those charges. I would in brief like the reader to know about the life and works of Pope John Paul II and the present Pope Francis.

Pope John Paul II:

Pope John Paul II (original name Karol Jozef Wojtyla) was born on May 18, 1920 in Wadowice, Poland. His early life had been tough and stressful, because he suffered the loss of his mother when he was 9 years old. Being athlete he enjoyed swimming and skiing. In 1938 he went to the Krakow Jagiellonian University where he studied theater and poetry. At that time Poland was under the Nazi rule who hated Christianity and Judaism. As he wanted to become a priest so he studied theology at a secret seminary in Krakow. After the World War II he was ordained priest in 1946. He wanted to have higher education and study theology he moved to Rome where he earned doctoral degree in theology. After that he returned to Poland and after serving several parishes he became bishop of Ombi and then after the gap of six years he was elected as the Archbishop of Krakow. As an Archbishop he played active role in the Roman Catholic Church. He being a great thinker urged the Roman Catholic Church leaders to review the Church doctrine and bring necessary changes in the Roman Catholic Church to make it more popular and appealing to the people. He was made Cardinal in 1967. In 1978 he became non-Italian Pope of Rome. He traveled over 100 countries spreading the message of peace and his faith. Because of his faith he faced assassination attempt twice on his life in 1981. By God's grace he escaped death and after recovering from his injuries he obeying the commandment of his Lord forgave the attacker.

He was an advocate of human rights and urged the people to help the suffering humanity. He was against the death sentence, abortion and the use of contraceptives. Because of his charismatic personality he influenced the political leaders of the world and as a result it brought change around the world and this was one of the factors which brought downfall of communism particularly in his country Poland. Fanatics and adversaries of Christianity criticized him for his rigid views on certain issues.

With time his health started failing and he had Parkinson disease and brain disorder. John Paul died on April 2, 2005at the age of 84. The Vatican decided to canonize him and Pope John XXIII as saints. On April 27, 2014 Pope John Paul II and Pope John XXIII were canonized as saints. He is also remembered by the two miracles done in his life. Sister Marie Simon-Pierre a French Nun who was suffering with Parkinson disease after praying to Pope John Paul II got healed. Also a 50 years old woman who prayed in front of Pope John Paul II's picture was cured of brain disease called (aneurysm). Pope John Paul II will be remembered as a beloved pope for his liberal views and strong faith in his Lord.

Pope Francis:

Pope Francis was elected as the 266th pope of Roman Catholic Church on March 13, 2013. He was born on December 17, 1936 in Buenos Aires Argentina and was named Jorge Mario Bergoglio. He is the first Pope from

South America. After graduating from high School he attended University of Buenos Aires where he received his master's degree in Chemistry. After that he attended Catholic University of Villa Devoto. Jorge Mario Bergoglio earned degree in Philosophy from the Theological facility of San Miguel. He also earned doctoral degree in Theology from Freiburg, Germany. He entered priesthood in 1969 where he was ordained priest in December. Later he returned back to San Miguel Philosophical and Theological University where he served as professor of Theology.

In June 1992 he was named as bishop of Auca. In February 1998 he was elevated to the position of Archbishop of Buenos Aires. In February 2001 he was promoted to the position of Cardinal by Pope John Paul II. After the death of Pope John Paul II in 2005 he was made president of the Bishops' Conference of Argentina where he served till 2011. In 2005's Papal election he lost to Pope Benedict XVI (Joseph Ratzinger) who won the election as Pope John Paul's successor.

{Pope Benedict XVI (Joseph Aloisius Ratzinger) was born on April 16, 1927 in marktl, Germany. He was elected Pope at the age of 78 as the oldest Pope. He resigned in February 2013 because of the reasons nobody knew. According to him he resigned on the ground of his waning physical and mental powers, yet the media suspected there were other reasons to it. His butler leaked certain sensitive documents which made the outsiders to sense something serious behind the scenes. Pope Benedict pardoned his butler for what he did and Pope had to resign. His butler Gabriele was found guilty of, "aggravated theft" and spent three months in custody and was freed as Pope Benedict pardoned him. Pope Benedict XVI was a teaching Pope, a good theologian and intellectual. He was the first Pope to resign in 600 hundred years of Roman Catholic Church history.}

In his early life of priesthood Jorge Mario Bergoglio was considered doctrinal conservative, because he opposed same sex marriages. He advocated that same sex marriages are against the God's plan. He also opposed the use of contraceptives, abortion and artificial insemination.

After visiting Brazil on July22, 2013 when he traveled back to Rome he made a surprising statement published in New York times where he told the media, "If someone is gay and he searches for the Lord and has goodwill, who am I to judge?". This statement of the Pope was received with joy by several gay and lesbian groups as a good gesture of the Catholic Church.

Pope Francis is very much concerned for the war, violence and strife going on in various parts of the world. He appealed to the people to join him to pray for peace in Syria. He appealed to Palestinians and Israelites also to find a suitable solution to the conflict between them and live peacefully and avoid the bloodshed. He held a special vigil in St. Peter's Square where he told 100,000 strong crowd of people, "When a man thinks of himself, he permits himself to be captivated by the idols of dominion and power… Then the door opens to violence, indifference and conflict." He urged the people responsible for war, violence and conflict to find a peaceful solution to the conflict. In one of his interviews he explained that a religious dialogue should take place not only on homosexuality and abortion but on other matters and find a new balance, otherwise the moral edifice of Church is likely to fall like the house of cards losing the freshness and fragrance of the Gospel." He further said, "The proposal of the Gospel must be more simple, profound and radiant. Pope Francis is not in favor of ordaining the women as priest, yet he considers women as the essential part of the Church, who can help in making important decisions regarding the betterment of the Roman Catholic Church. He has more accepting attitude towards gays and lesbians. He stated, "God in creation set us free; it is not possible to interfere spiritually in the personal life of anyone". He urged the Roman Catholic Church leaders to think of big changes in the Church. He also said, "I prefer a Church which is bruised, hurting and dirty because it has been out on the streets, rather than a Church which is unhealthy from being confined and from clinging to its own security". On the whole he is very popular Pope because of his liberal views. May God bless him, strengthen him and guide him so that he may prepare the Roman Catholic Church for the Second Advent of our Lord.

Making sign of Cross:

Cross is considered to be sacred symbol of Christianity, because Christ suffered sacrificial death on the cross to pay the price of sins of the humanity. Mostly Roman Catholics and Orthodox Christians make sign of cross with their right hand while praying or saying or listening to the various parts of liturgy. This practice actually started in the second century when Jews were being persecuted by the Romans especially in Rome and were being expelled from there during the Roman Empire. To distinguish themselves from the Jews, Christians started this practice of making sign of Cross. Catholic Christians believed in the saving power of the Cross on which their Lord died and saved His believers from the slavery and dominion of Satan. Catholic Christians start making this sign with fingers of their right hand. They start by touching their forehead with fingers of their right hand and bring down to the center of their chest and then touching the left shoulder and moving the hand across the chest to touch the right shoulder. While doing this they utter the names of three persons of Holy Trinity that is, "in the name of the Father and the Son and the Holy Spirit". Orthodox Christians also make this sign of Cross, but when they bring their hand to the middle of the chest they touch the right shoulder first and then move their hand to touch the left shoulder.

Notes:

5.1 Purgatory: a place as the intermediate state of punishment after death wherein according to the Roman Catholic doctrine the souls of those who die in God's grace may make satisfaction for the past sins and so become eligible for heaven or It is a place to purge the soul after the death of remaining sins

References:

1. Catholic reformation -Henry Daniel Rops... New York E. P. Dutton
2. History of the Church -August Franzen-revised Edited by John P. Dolan
3. The Christian world by Alan Brown -Silver Burdett Company.
4. Encyclopedia of Religion and Religions by E. Royston Pike.
5. World Religions by Benson Y. Landis
6. Church History in Plain language By Bruce L. Shelly
7. Concise history of Catholic Church by Thomas Boken Kotter N.Y. Double Day
8. A popular History of catholic Church- Philip Hughes N.Y. MacMillan 1957
9. "History of Christianity" 1650-1950 Secularization of the west by Nichols, James Hastings- Ronald press 1956.
10. "Our religions and neighbors" By M. G. Miller and Sylvan D. Schwartzman Pp 5-7; 74-111
11. Christianity for Dummies by Richard Wagner Wiley Publishing, Inc.

Chapter Six

Anglican Church

(Protestant)

According to Christian Historians, Christianity came to England in the second century. In the third century local Celtics had an organized Church. In the fifth century with the downfall of Roman rule in England, Romans left the country. Thereafter the Germans (Angles, Saxons and Jutes) (6.1) Attacked England and pushed Celtics to the west. So in the fifth century in the time of St. Aidan the people from Ireland and Wales were Christianized. In the time of St. Augustine Roman Catholic Church flourished in England. In the seventh century Roman Catholicism was declared the state religion in England. In the 8th and 9th centuries Denmark attacked England and conquered it. In the eleventh century Normans from Normandy and Scandinavia attacked England and conquered it and Danish people living there were compelled to flee. As the Normans were Roman Catholics so the Roman Catholic Church had deeper and stronger roots in England. Though nation of England seemed to be unified under the flag of Roman Catholic Church yet the trouble was brewing underneath, so the ruler and the people of England were not happy with the hurtful policies of the Pope. Pope's unreasonable interference in the religious and political matters was not less than a headache.

Actually the opposition of Roman Catholic Church had started with the appearance of John Wycliffe on the scene of Reformation Movement. Though he was a Roman Catholic Priest yet he was not happy with the undesirable policies of the Pope and the Roman Catholic Church. He opposed the Tax imposition by the Pope on the Catholic Churches and the idea that the bread and wine of the Lord's Supper actually changes into the real flesh and blood of Jesus at the time of celebration of Lord's Supper. He translated Bible into English language without the Pope's permission, so that people may read the Bible and know the truth. According to Pope's order ordinary people and general public was not allowed to read the Bible. Another person William Tyndale was not happy with the Roman Catholic Church. He opposed the misinterpretation of the Bible by the Roman Catholic Church. Because of this opposition he was got killed in 1536. He also published a wonderful translation of the Bible, which later on became the basis of King James Version (1566) of the Bible. After the death of John Wycliffe in 1384 and death of William Tyndale many more people, unhappy with the Roman Catholic Church stood up against the Pope and his Church.

Among this People Martin Luther from Germany and John Calvin from Geneva were the prominent personalities. Due to their views good part of the population of England was impressed. Most of the people and the rulers were not happy with the unreasonable interference in their religious and political matters. So the light of new views and freedom of faith was mostly loved by the people.

Beginning Of Anglicanism:

In the reign of Henry (VIll) (1509-1547) Church of England openly stood up against the Roman Catholic Church. There was no religious reason for this. Pope allowed Henry to marry his brother's widow Catherine, who was from Aragon Spain. After that Luther started opposition of Pope, because of misinterpretations of the word of God. As the writings of Martin Luther reached England, Henry started opposing seven sacraments in Luther's writings. Because of this Pope awarded Henry the title of 'defender of faith'. Henry fell in love with Anne Boleyn a beautiful woman. On the other side Catherine was very loyal and faithful to Spain. Secondly she bore six children to Henry but only one girl Mary survived. Henry wanted a male child to be heir to his throne, so Henry sought permission from Pope to divorce Catherine, but due to lack of any special reason Pope declined his request. Henry knew that if he divorces Catherine of his own, then her relatives, who are Catholics and are politically very powerful, could raise a big problem for him.

Henry continuously tried for 5 years to divorce Catherine and marry Anne Boleyn. He even tried to prove that he was never married to Catherine. Though it was easy in Catholicism, yet relatives of Catherine were very powerful and resourceful. Henry stopped paying money to the Catholic Church thinking that under this pressure Pope may permit him to divorce Catherine, but even then it was of no avail. In 1529 Henry came across Thomas Cranmer a young professor of Oxford University. He advised Henry to appeal to the learned professors of the Oxford University they included prominent priests of England as well. Thomas Cranmer promised to help Henry in this matter. Henry liked the idea and he appointed Cranmer to prepare the case and put it before the Intelligentsia of the Oxford and Cambridge Universities. When this case came before scholars of the Oxford and Cambridge Universities they gave decision in favor of Henry and it was passed in the England's Parliament.

After this Henry made Cranmer Archbishop of Canterbury. This is most superior position in the Church of England. So in 1533 Thomas Cranmer declared Henry's first marriage as illegal and got him married to Anne Boleyn whom he loved. As a result Pope excommunicated Henry from the Catholic Church and on the other hand parliament of England who was already fed up with the dictatorial policies of the Pope declared Henry as the head of the Church of England (Anglican Church). This way Church of England threw away the yoke of slavery of the Roman Catholic Church. From that day, except Mary's (who was daughter of Henry and Catherine) 6 years reign, Church of England had been free of slavery of Roman Catholic Church.

Although Pope had threatened the British Parliament to excommunicate it from the Roman Catholic Church, yet they did not bother at all about this threat. British Parliament passed many ordinances not caring for the Pope. This made it certain the breaking away of the Church of England from the Roman Catholic Church. They passed an ordinance to not to pay any taxes to the Roman Catholic Church nor any appeal will be made to the Roman Catholic Church and whole control of the Church of England will be in the hands of Archbishop of Canterbury. Under the 1534 act of succession Mary was declared illegitimate child of Henry and Catherine and Mary Boleyn's daughter Elizabeth was made legal heir to the throne of England.

At the end of that year they passed another law that anyone who will not accept the legal heir of the Emperor or will disobey the Emperor's order or will not recognize his position will be persecuted and awarded death sentence. Even though Church of England had separated from the Roman Catholic Church yet the laws, sacraments and prayers were same as that of the Roman Catholic Church. Cranmer had translated the book of prayers from Latin into English and named it Book of Common Prayer. There was lot of land property and many monasteries under the Church of England. Cranmer was asked to investigate and survey all these. Cranmer reported that the money from these properties was misused so Henry ordered that all these monasteries should be closed and all the sales money should be deposited in the royal treasury. Around 1540 Henry married several times to have a male child and finally his son Edward was born.

Cranmer's Achievements and his Death:

Cranmer not only helped Henry to get rid of Catherine rather he brought reformation in the Church of England. After Henry's death his son Edward, who used to remain sick succeeded his father to the throne. Cranmer brought many protestant changes in the Church. He allowed priests to marry. He made laws and principles for the Christian believers according to the Bible. He took out the Catholic view that bread and wine at the time of Lord's Supper actually change into the flesh and blood of Christ and he prepared new Book of Common Prayer. He permitted every Christian to take part in Lord's Supper.

Henry's son Edward died at the age of 15. After him Mary (daughter of Henry and Catherine) took over the throne. As she was strictly catholic, she once again brought Church of England into Roman Catholic fold. Those who were in favor of reformation or were leading the movement of reformation were put in jails. She got burnt many Protestants in fire and even got killed two Bishops. She removed Cranmer from the position of Archbishop and banned Cranmer's Book of Common Prayer. Cranmer was shut up behind bars. He wrote six letters of apology to Mary but it did not move her at all. When Cranmer saw that his appeals are not bearing any fruit, he wrote to Mary that he wrote these apologies out of fear. He condemned the Catholic Church, its baseless and meaningless policies regarding Christian faith. He was taken to the place where he was to be burnt in fire. At that time he was holding the list of baseless charges and all those apology letters. He first put those apology letters in fire and then he himself got burnt and thus met Martyrdom at the hands of Roman Catholic Church. Due to Queen Mary's cruel acts of suppression against the Protestants, she was called 'Bloody Mary'. Whatever Cranmer did was still remembered and his efforts were continued even after his death. Mary ruled for six years and after that Henry and Anne's daughter Elizabeth succeeded to the Throne. Mary had jailed Elizabeth before her coronation, but when she took over the throne she proved to be the beloved queen of the people. She once again broke away from the Catholic Church and brought the Church of England under the British Crown. The use of Book of Common Prayer was revived and it was being used in all the Churches. Positions of Bishops were revived and were appointed again. She took out certain things written by Cranmer from the laws of the Church. Though Church of England had snapped its relations from the Roman Catholic Church yet the system of work and sacraments were almost the same. So Church of England was neither catholic completely nor Protestant. They claimed to be Protestant yet they were rowing the boat between the Catholic and the Protestant streams.

As queen Elizabeth neither kept the Church Catholic nor the Protestant, so she had adversaries from both sides. In 1570 Pope excommunicated the queen Elizabeth from the Roman Catholic Church. Queen discovered many plots to kill her and make Mary the queen of Scots in her place. Pope helped in sending Spanish Armada fleet to war against England, but it faced a very bad defeat at the hands of English armies. This defeat was a crucial turning point in the England and European History. Pope being frustrated declared in 1596 that whatever Elizabeth did in the Anglican Church was illegal. When Elizabeth (I) took over as the queen many catholic Bishops resigned. Mathew Parker was installed as the Bishop of Canterbury. He filled up the vacant positions of Bishops and by doing so he proved that Anglican Church has nothing to do with the Roman Catholic Church. Due to this there was lot of bitterness and seeds of dissent were sown between the Roman Catholic Church and the Anglican Church.

To take away this bitterness in 1982 Pope John Paul (II) toured England and met Robert Runcy, the Archbishop of Anglican Church. Archbishop welcomed the Pope by calling pope as the brother in Christ.

Anglican Church in Present Times:

Today Anglican Church is spread all over the world. It is also called Episcopal Church. It has branches all over the world, but Church of England is the Mother church. As the English Empire lost hold over many countries and the countries got their independence, the Churches also became independent. In many countries like India Anglican Church, English Methodist churches and Presbyterian Churches have united and formed Church of North India and church of South India. According to Anglican Church of England, because of merging of Anglican Church with the Church of North of India, there is no more Anglican Church in India. Even then some rebel groups to grab properties attached to the Anglican Churches are keeping the Churches under the name of Anglican Church and running these Churches independently. Outside England the first English Church to be established was Scottish Episcopal Church and the second was American Protestant Episcopal Church, which has a membership of 3.5 million. Episcopal is a Greek word that means Bishop. In the Episcopal Church all the Churches of an area are under the Bishop and all priests are answerable to the Bishop. Episcopal Church believes that bishop is like the disciple of Christ. After the Bishop are priests and deacons. All priests and deacons can marry. In every country administration of Anglican Church can be different from other countries.

In America the administration of every Episcopal Church is in the hands of the priest-in-Charge and it is managed with the help of parish. Parish is constituted by the elected Lay Leaders called elders and the priest-in-charge is the chairman. Many parishes make a diocese. After every three years there is general conference, which takes all the decisions regarding all the Churches and makes new rules. It has two groups 1. House of deputies, which has all the pastors and Lay leaders as its members. 2. House of Bishops. Before any rule becomes a law it is essential to be passed in both the houses. After every ten years Archbishop calls a Lambeth Conference which is held in England and more than 300 bishops participate in it. The Chairman of this conference is Archbishop of Canterbury. This Lambeth

Conference does not make laws but it can advise the general conference on important issues. All Anglican congregations use the Book of Common Prayer and whole Anglican Church believes in the apostle's creed. Anglican Church and its branches all over the world are divided in two groups that are high Church and the Low Church (6.2) and they differ on certain matters and sacraments. In the Low Church the service is held in a simple way and they do not lay stress on Catholic Church matters. They do not believe in the confession of a Sinner before the priest as the Roman Catholics do. They celebrate only baptism and the Lord's Supper. Members of this Church do not pray before Mary and Christ's statues and also do not pray before the pictures of the saints and Disciples of Christ.

High church is known as the "Anglo Catholic Church" because their worship service is similar to the Catholic Church. Their Pastors listen to the confession of its members. Anglican Church keeps fellowship with other protestant Churches and they work in co-operation with them. Church of England respects bishop like Christ and his disciples. They believe in Trinity and virgin birth of Christ. In the High church they celebrate all the seven sacraments celebrated in the Roman Catholic Church but they do not celebrate as the Catholics do.

Rather they celebrate like the protestant churches. They do not recognize the authority of the Pope. They consider the Bible as the basis of Christian faith and Christian character. In America and other English speaking countries the services are held in English, but in other countries they are held in local language. Bread and wine used in Lord's Supper are taken as symbols of His flesh and blood but they do not change into real flesh and blood, as the Roman Catholics believe. All those people who believe in the crucifixion of Jesus Christ and His resurrection and accept Him as their savior can participate in Lord's Supper. They allow the married couples to divorce on genuine grounds and also permit the use of Birth Control devices. Anglican Church has played a prominent role in the American Society. Members of this church belong to all sections of the society. First Anglican Church was established in James Town in 1607 and then in different colonies it had been the state religion. When America became free and independent then its relationship with the Church of England became weak. Since very important and prominent persons were its members so it did not have any visible effect on the Anglican Church. The prominent members of the Anglican Church in America were George Washington, Alexander Hamilton, James Madison, and others. After the war with the British forces Anglican Church in America snapped its relations with the Church of England. Anglican Church has always been trying that all those who accept Jesus, as their supreme savior should unite under one flag. That is why they have been trying to bring all Christians into unity. They have brought together Protestant and Orthodox Christians. They had consultations with Roman Catholics too especially on the Biblical matters where they differ from Protestants. Leaving aside some dogmatic and Orthodox Catholics, they felt the need for unity.

After reading all about the emergence of Anglican Church we find that it was wrong policies, misinterpretations of the word of God, undue interference by the Pope in the political and religious matters of the country and his dictatorial attitude that gave birth to the Anglican Church. People like Martin Luther, John Huss, Calvin, Wycliffe, and Zwingli the pioneers of reformation acted as catalysts and movement of reformation added fuel to the fire. With the mixing of cultures, spread of education, the ways people think has given rise to independent thinking and so they chose their own ways. This was the driving force for the formation of Anglican Church and breaking away from the Catholic Church.

Notes:

6.1. Angles, Saxons and Jutes were German people that invaded England in the 5th century C.E. and merged with them to form Anglo-Saxons. Saxon- a native of Saxon

6.2. High Church. In the Anglican faith those Churches whose services resemble Roman Catholic Worship in contrast to Low Church

Low Church. These are those Anglican Churches whose services are simpler and with Jess emphasis upon Catholic like rituals.

References:

I. Encyclopedia of American Religions-Sixth Edition
2. Our Religions and Our neighbors-Revised edition By M.G. Miller and S.D. Schwartzman Pp 125-132
3. 'World Religions' Editor Geoffrey Parrinder Published by Facts on file Publications N.Y.
4. 'World Religions' by Landon Benson
5. 'Man's Religions' John B. Noss MacMillan
6. 'Religions In America' Leo Roston Ardicle, W. Norman Pittenger Pp 68-78
7. 'The story of America's Religions' Holt, Rinehart, Winston Ch. 8-Pp 130-145.

Chapter Seven

Methodists

(Protestant)

Basically there is no difference between the Methodist Church and the Presbyterian Church. Same Bible, same faith, same one God, same savior, same songs, and they have the same order and way of worship. The difference is of worldly founders and the system of administration. The worldly founder of Methodist Church was John Wesley. His father was Samuel Wesley; grand and great grand fathers were John Wesley and Bartholomew Wesley. All of them got education from the Oxford University and were priests of Anglican Church. John Wesley (1703-1791) and Charles Wesley (1707-1788) were out of the nineteen children of Susana wife of Samuel Wesley. Only 10 children survived. John Wesley's father Samuel Wesley was priest in the Anglican Church. As the children reached 5 years of age Susana used to teach them. She not only taught the books, but also taught them about the word of God and gave them spiritual lessons. John Wesley and Charles Wesley (about five years younger to John Wesley) were only close to each other.

After finishing school both brothers joined Oxford University. Charles Wesley did not like the environment there, so he organized a holy club. On Charles's request John Wesley became the leader of the club. In the beginning they discussed classic literature but later on they started paying attention to those important things of Christian faith towards which Christians paid no attention, rather neglected them in their daily life.

Members of the society run by John Wesley and Charles Wesley helped doing everything and the prayers systematically and according to the word of God. The other people who were not the members of the society made fun of them and called them 'Methodists'. This movement that started as a club in the Oxford University spread throughout the whole England and finally became the Methodist Church.

John Wesley decided to become an Anglican priest like his father. Though in his personal life he was doing God's work in a much disciplined way, yet he was not very happy. There came an occasion in his life when he met a group of Moravian Christians (7.1), who were very spiritual and disciplined Christians. They discussed and made him understand those things for which he was longing for a long time. John Wesley saw the ray of firm faith in God's love. He also felt the contentment in Christian life and enthusiasm in serving the Lord. Revelation of this firm faith and enthusiasm for doing the Lord's work was made on 24th May 1738, when he felt complete spiritual support from God at the Alders Gate Street, London. One of the society members read this statement from Martin Luther's writings according to which when God works in our life He brings transformation in our hearts and lives. All of a sudden John Wesley felt the presence of Jesus in his heart. He was assured in his heart that he has true faith in Jesus Christ and Jesus is his only savior. Thereafter both the brothers started working very hard for the Methodist Society. In these societies people not only helped each other rather they helped believers to be firm in faith. In every city and town societies will gather to establish every believer in faith and preach the word of God. Every society was composed of 12 members and their responsibility was to preach at different places. Every week members will get together and review and evaluate their work, do the Bible study, and spend time in prayer. John Wesley was very much influenced by the thoughts and work of George Whitfield and he felt that word of God should be preached to the farm workers and people on the streets which do not have opportunity to go to the Church. John Wesley also organized a group of Lay preachers who preached the word of God to the farm workers on the fields and the peoples on the streets. These Lay preachers traveled to America and sowed the seeds of Methodism on the American soil and the first Methodist society was established in New York. Barbara Heck was the founder of this society, who came to New York from Ireland in 1760. Her close relative and cousin Philip Ambry was the local preacher of Methodist society in Ireland, he too came with Barbara Heck. He was carpenter by profession. One day Barbara saw him playing cards in a gambling shop. Barbara felt bad about him; she snatched the cards from his hand and threw those in the fire. She took Philip home and told him that gambling is not good for the Christian believer; rather he should become member of the Methodist society and preach the word of God. He took her advice to his heart and organized a society at his home. After that they rented a room for society's work. One day Captain Thomas Webb an admirer of John Wesley came to the society meeting and he too started working with Barbara and Philip. After some time this society became John Street Church in New York.

After the American Revolution many priests went back to England but the American Methodist Church wanted to maintain that revival in the Church. People wanted to continue the sacraments of Baptism and the Lord's Supper but it became difficult because of the lack of Methodist priests. Only the priest could baptize and celebrate the Lord's Supper. John Wesley had to think about it. He sent Thomas Coke as the General Superintendent of the American Methodist Church, so that he may ordain the local preachers and confirm them as the priests and ordain Francis Asbury as the Superintendent. So he called conference of the Methodist workers on the Christmas Eve in the Lovely Lane Baltimore Chapel and accomplished this task. With accomplishment of this task Methodist Movement was put on firm footing in America. Francis Asbury contended that according to democratic set up of America he would accept the responsibility of Superintendent only if all the Methodist preachers gather and elect him as the Superintendent. His companions were already prepared for this, so he was elected as the General Superintendent of Methodist Church. After a couple of years he was made bishop of the Methodist Churches.

Since there were no cars or any other means of conveyance, so Bishop Asbury traveled on horse from New York to Tennessee and covered a distance of 275,000 miles. During his journey he not only did the preaching but also supervised the functioning of the Methodists Churches. Bishop is like the General Superintendent and is the Supervisor of the Churches, who come in the jurisdiction of one Conference. All Methodist Churches in his jurisdiction work under his supervision. Methodist Church is an Episcopal (7.2) Church.

Today the Methodist membership is more than 20 million and out of these 10 million 350 thousand live in America. Out of these 10 million are members of The United Methodist Church organized in 1968 and remaining are members of other denominations like the Methodist Pentecostals. Their main emphasis is to fulfill the social needs and solve the problems of the society. So Methodists emphasize on the missionary work in other countries. They also lay stress on revival and witness through spiritual life of the Church. On the other hand they work for the society's depressed people, orphans, widows, homeless, handicapped and helpless elderly people in the world. In the early years of its formation Methodist Church was divided on the subject of slavery but finally in 1939 they compromised on this issue, but even then racial discrimination continued. Before 1976 Blacks and Whites had separate Churches, but now they worship together and racial discrimination is at its lower level. Now the Blacks are pastors, Superintendents and Bishops. Rather many women are working as full time priests in many Methodist Churches. Methodist Church among the Protestants is very progressing and enthusiastic Church. This Church has done a great job regarding social welfare and for the establishment of peace both at the national and international levels. They sent missionaries to India and other countries. They opened educational, technical schools and medical colleges and Hospitals for the poor Christians where peoples from other communities also got benefited. Poor Christians who could not afford education in expensive educational institutions are now doctors, engineers, nurses and professors and working proudly with the better privileged members of the society by keeping their identity as Christians.

Jewish faith is very different from the Methodist faith. Methodist lay stress on social welfare of the society whereas Jews mainly lay stress on the Ten Commandments. In some cases there is difference between the faith and deeds of the Methodists. In many Methodist Churches worship is formal and methodical and in that way they are like the Episcopal Churches. In Pentecostal churches they shout the words of Hallelujah and Amen during the worship that depicts their spiritual enthusiasm. All the Methodists believe in Trinity, and the virgin birth of Jesus Christ from Mary. They also believe in the second advent of Jesus Christ and Judgment of sinners and their punishment at hands of Jesus Christ. All Methodists firmly believe in Christian baptism and celebration of the Lord's Supper, but they do not believe that bread and the grape juice actually changes into the flesh and blood of Jesus Christ. They believe that Christ is spiritually present there at the time of Lord's Supper. Even the little children who do not know the meaning and significance of Lord's Supper are permitted to partake in the Lord's Supper. On the other hand in Methodist Churches in India Children cannot take Holy Communion until the age of 14/15 years. They must memorize Lord's Prayer, Apostles' Creed and the Ten Commandments and then the Bishop or the District Superintendent confirms them before they are permitted to take part in the Lord's Supper. Bible is supreme and holy book for the Methodists, which is taken as the word of God and spiritual food. This word of God came through prophets, holy men of God and supreme lord and savior Jesus Christ. Through His word God directly spoke to His people. This is neither mythology nor written by the sages based upon their experiences or emotions that they received through their meditations, rather it is directly received from God through the Holy Spirit. Even though there have been changes in the Methodist Constitution but Church has been against Cigarette smoking, drinking liquor and Drug addiction. They believe that their life should be according to the commandments of their religious leaders as St. Paul wrote to Timothy in 1 Timothy 3:1-3. These words are applicable to all Churches and believers of Christ. St. Paul and Jesus Christ set an example from their lives. The District and Conference Officials control Methodist Churches. Head of Methodist district is District Superintendent and several Churches in the district are under his control. Annual Conference is under the control of Bishop that is constituted by the Lay Leaders and Pastors of the Methodist Churches. Bishop is the appointing authority of the Pastor of any Church. Every Pastor is answerable to the District Superintendent for all the activities in his church and District Superintendent is answerable to the Bishop. After every four years there is General Conference in which all the annual Conferences take part. All the decisions taken in the General Conference are applicable to all the annual conferences and Methodists Churches of the World. There are many Methodist Universities in America. The most famous of these are Boston University, South California University, Duke University, and the Vanderbilt University.

United Methodist Church:

Whenever there have been differences of opinion and interpretation of the word of God, it has given rise to the religious groups and denominations. That is what happened in the Methodist church. In 1828 there was conflict in the Methodist Church regarding the representation of Lay Leaders, which became the reason for the partition of the Church. One group became the Methodist Protestant church. In 1844 because of the slavery problem lot of discussion was going on among the various Churches. Some Churches wanted to give it a religious touch. And some wanted to keep it out of the religious circle. Their contention was that slavery is not the Church problem rather it is national government's problem and because of this Church again got divided into two groups. Group belonging to the Northern part of the country was named as Northern Methodist Episcopal Church and the group belonging to the southern part was called Southern Methodist Episcopal Church. After some discussion these three groups again became one on May 10, 1939, and named it Methodist Church. In 1946 United Brethren in Christ and Evangelical Church got united and they named the Church as Evangelical United Brethren Church. Most of the members were German immigrants. In the beginning of 1800 with the help of German speaking peoples they organized North Eastern and Mid-west United Brethren Churches. Their thinking was very close to the Methodists. Their leader Philip Otterbein and Francis Asbury a prominent Methodist leader had good relations. In those days Jacob Albright who was German and leader of the evangelical Church became pastor of the Methodist Church. He was a farmer in Pennsylvania. Since the thinking of Evangelical, united Brethren Church was the same so they got united and constituted United Methodist Church. The faith and Constitution of present United Methodist Church is the same as of these Churches listed below:

1. Methodist Episcopal church (North)
2. Methodist Episcopal church (South)
3. Methodist Protestant church
4. United Brethren in Christ
5. The Evangelical Association
6. The United Evangelical Church
7. The evangelical Church

8. The Methodist Church
9. Evangelical United Brethren Church
10. Methodist Pentecostal Church

When Methodists prepared their book of Discipline they had 24 points taken from the Anglican Church of England. All these points tell about their faith.

1. There is only one God all Powerful, Omnipresent, Omniscient and most wise. He created the whole universe. He is sustainer and controller of everything in this universe. Father, son Jesus Christ and the Holy Spirit are the personalities of Godhead.
2. Jesus Christ was born of Holy Spirit from Virgin Mary. He was crucified for the sins of the whole world. He died and was buried.
3. Jesus Christ rose from the dead on the third day and ascended into heaven, from where he will come again to judge the living and the dead.
4. Holy Spirit originates from God the father and the son Jesus Christ.
5. Old and the New Testament is the word of God and is essential for the salvation of human beings.
6. Some sacraments in the Old Testaments (like Sacrifice and Circumcision) are not essential for the Christians but the commandments that go with the teachings of Jesus Christ must be obeyed.
7. The seeds of sin committed by our ancestors Adam and Eve are inherited by their descendents so everyone is a sinner.
8. God has given the gift of free will to every human being. To use the free will wisely we need God's guidance so that we may use this gift of free will rightly and to please Him.
9. Forgiveness of our sins and being righteous does not depend on our good deeds, rather our sins are forgiven because of the grace of our Lord and savior Jesus Christ and we become sinless.
10. Our good works are the fruits of our faith and can be accepted by God.
11. We cannot do good works beyond the will of God.
12. Even after being termed righteous by God we sin, but after confession and repentance from sins God will forgive our sins.
13. Methodist Church is the group of believers of Christ where Bible is preached and according to His commandments sacraments of Baptism and Lord's Supper are celebrated.

14. No preaching is done about Purgatory nor is it mentioned in the Bible. No preaching is done about worshiping and praying to the dead saints of the Church and also there is no commandment to worship gods and goddesses.
15. Worship should be conducted in the local language of the state or country. To conduct the worship in a language that the believers cannot understand is against the will of God and also against the Christian Custom and traditions.
16. Baptism and Lord's Supper in Christian life are like the medals, which we get from God.
17. For the adults while coming into Christian faith baptism is a symbol of confession of sins and accepting Jesus Christ as savior. In the case of little children if parents desire baptism can be done on the responsibility of the parents.
18. Lord's Supper is the symbol of communion of the believer with Christ and remembrance of sacrificial death of Jesus on the cross that reminds us that Christ died to pay the price of sins of sinners. So it should be celebrated with seriousness, with utmost sanctity and taking it as a spiritual event.
19. During Lord's Supper the whole congregation of believers should participate in it.
20. Sacrificial death of Jesus is sufficient for the forgiveness of our sins. There is no value of praying for the dead, to ask them for help and praying for the repentance of their sins.
21. Priests are free to marry according to their wishes.
22. It is not mandatory that the method of celebration of sacraments in one Church and in one country should be same in other Churches and countries. Rather it can be changed according to the needs and physical environment of that country
23. All believers should abide by the laws of the country and should honor the government and freedom of that country.
24. Christians have the right to their personal property, but everyone should give in the service of the Lord and to help the poor according to the blessings that God has given him.
25. In the government courts when a Christian has to swear under oath he can do so but teachings of the Bible should never be disrespected or violated.

Faith of the United Methodist Church

United Methodist Church has the same faith as that of Methodist Church, Anglican Church and Presbyterian Church. In addition to the above noted 25 points they believe in the Apostles Creed. Apostles Creed is that writing through which we confirm our faith in Trinity. Methodists and Presbyterians believe in two creeds and during the Church service one of these two is read. Korean Methodist Church has written its own creed that is known as Korean Creed. This is not much different from the Methodist's Apostle's Creed and the Nicene Creed. Apostle's Creed, Nicene Creed and the Korean Creed can be found in the Methodist Hymnals. Nicene's Creed and the Apostle's Creed can also be found in the Hymn Books of Presbyterian churches, Churches of North and South India. For the confirmation of their faith some time they read the below given creed in unison.

A Modern Affirmation

We believe in God the father infinite in wisdom, power and love, whose mercy is over all his works, and whose will is ever directed to His children's good. We believe in Jesus Christ, the Son of God and son of man, the gift of the father's unfailing grace, the ground of our hope, and the promise of our deliverance from sin and death. We believe in the Holy Spirit as the divine presence in our lives whereby we are kept in perpetual remembrance of the death of Christ and find strength and help in time of need.

We believe that this faith should manifest itself in the service of love as set forth in the example of our blessed Lord to the end that the kingdom of God may come upon the earth. Amen.

John Wesley

Every human being has weaknesses and draw backs in his life. In the bible we find so many examples where even the people after God's heart and chosen by Him had weaknesses one or the other. Such examples are Abraham, Moses, Aaron, Solomon, Saul, David, Samson, Peter and sons of Zebedee James and John, yet they were God's favorite and served their Lord God. John Wesley though did remarkable work as founder of Methodist Church, yet he stumbled in the initial stages until he met Moravian Christians and he was enlightened by the Lord for His work

Till eighteenth century people were struggling to get away from Roman Catholic Church. Though many denominations had been formed yet even within the denominations people were not happy, because of the methods of worship and there was confusion in the breakaway groups and denominations. Most of the Christians especially the Deists who believed in the system of worshiping nature and affirming the existing of God while denying the validity of revelation and also denied mysticism, prophecy and miracles. They believed only in the Christianity that appealed to the mind rather than heart. John Wesley and like minded people felt the need for revival movement in the Christian faith. Moravian Christians were already working in that direction. Their faith was based on the Bible, prayers, and good deeds to lead a life of holiness and righteousness.

John Wesley and his brother Charles Wesley were trying to establish a Methodist faith which too felt the need for purely Bible based Christianity. After achieving success in England, John Wesley decided to go to Georgia United States where colonists were trying to attract migrated believers to join their Churches. With the aim of preaching Methodist ideology he and his brother Charles Wesley with two more evangelists went to Georgia as Missionaries. While being in Georgia he became Chaplain in Savannah where there were Choctaw and Creek tribes. He hoped to evangelize these tribal people who were ignorant of Christian faith. To achieve his goal he met chief of the Lower Creeks. But these tribal people did not show much interest, so John Wesley and his companions made a little impact on their lives.

He was really upset and disappointed because of this unexpected failure. There he came in contact with the local Magistrate and his family with the hope that he may prove to be a big help. As he was mixing with his family he fell in love with his daughter Sofia Hopkey. He made many proposals to Sofia and her family for marriage with the girl, but her father declined this proposal. John Wesley felt that his pride and sentiments have been wounded, so he again renewed his determination to evangelize and convert local tribal people. So neither the Magistrate nor his daughter agreed for marriage nor he got success in converting the tribal people. Sofia Hopkey was given to another man in marriage. He really got frustrated. On the day of Holy Communion John Wesley being the Chaplain retaliated by refusing Holy Communion to Sofia and her family. Due to this revengeful attitude her parents and parents-in-law filed number of charges against him and they spread the rumor that he had tried to make Sofia his mistress.

In the court of law he struggled to defend himself, but he failed and he was suspended from his pastoral duties. Sensing persecution he decided to run away. He was ordered by the court not to leave the colony, but he walked through swamp and forest on December 2, 1737 and boarded the ship from Charles Town and went back to England. After that he wrote in his journal, "What I have learned, why, what I least suspected, that I who went to America to convert others, was never myself converted to God". As he was pondering over his future he came in contact with the Moravian Christians and that was turning point in his life. When he got enlightenment and felt the presence of God and His son Jesus Christ in his life he stated six themes which not only were Methodism but became the basis for early Adventism too.

1. The need for simplicity.
2. The need for gospel order.
3. The need for holiness.
4. Identification with the poor and the oppressed.
5. A prophetic relationship with the religious establishment.
6. Religious enthusiasm and openness to God's spirit.

Ellen white the co-founder of Seventh Day Adventism was greatly influenced by the teachings of John Wesley. Methodists' commitment to holiness and Godly living made great impact on seventh Day Adventism.

Thus after the enlightenment John Wesley had charismatic personality which put Methodism on firm footing.

After reading about the history and faith of the Methodist Church we find there have been splinter denominations on the basis of difference of worldly opinions but it is a good that these splinter groups realized that this is not a good witness to the gentiles and they decided to come together and formed United Methodist Church. Hope they will one day realize that Methodists and Presbyterians have same Supreme savior and they will come together before the second advent of Christ and work together to bring the lost sheep into Christ's fold.

Notes:

7.1. Moravians- A protestant denomination arising from a 15th century religious reform movement in Bohemia and Moravia. This group believed in purity of character and leading a life according to the word of God. Some of them were proud of their faith and considered themselves righteous and living a life acceptable to Christ. They were evangelical and most of them were doing the missionary work.

7.2. Episcopal. Church organization governed by the Bishops. Many Protestant Churches including Anglican Church are Episcopal.

References;

1. United Methodist Primer 'by Chester E. Custer-Discipleship Resources
2. Meet the Methodists by Charles L.Allen -Abingdon Press Nashville.
3. United Methodist Way By Brabson L. Thurston Discipleship Resources.
4. Methodism's World Parish by William K. Anderson -Methodist Publishing House.
5. Church History by Bruce L. Shelly
6. A brief History of synopsis of the public History of the Church published by G.H.S.P. Christian Truth Book Room Bombay
7. The United Methodist Members Hand book by George E. Koehler- Discipleship Resources
8. John Wesley and the eighteenth century by Maldwyn Edwards 1955 Epworth London
9. John Wesley and his world by John Pudney Scribner N.Y. 1978

Chapter Eight

Quakers

(Protestant)

After the drawbacks in the Roman Catholic Church and human factor of the pope, new sects and denominations started surfacing in the Christian faith and Quakers are one of them. In the middle of seventeenth century when the first English translation of the Bible appeared Christians started reading the bible and came to know what biblical Christianity is. Certain groups of people did not agree with the Christianity of that time. They felt that Churches have forgotten the real Christ and Christians have drifted away from the apostolic faith and teachings of Jesus Christ which His disciples and early Christians had practiced. That Christianity was based on the words and examples that Christ had stated in the New Testament.

George Fox a shoe maker and leather worker of England was one of those people who were called 'Seekers', because he was struggling to find answers to the questions regarding true Christian faith which he had in his mind. Ultimately according to him he had a vision and revelation. He stated to his fellow seekers that a voice came to him and revealed that, "There is one, even Christ Jesus that can speak to your condition. Gorge Fox who was very active and influential, attracted many followers by his message and speeches. His other leading disciples were James Naylor, Richard Hubber Thorne and Margaret Fell and many more. That was a time of English Civil War(1642-1651) and time of confusion. George Fox along with his leading followers targeted desperate seekers. That being the time of upheaval, social and political unrest, they attracted disgruntled and scattered Baptists, disillusioned soldiers and common people unhappy with the Christian faith they had and formed a sect known as 'Quakers'. The other names given to the society were 'Children of Light'; 'Light Bearers' ; 'Friends of Truth'; and finally this society was called 'Religious Society of Friends' or "Quakers".

English word 'Quake' means to shiver or shivering. Because in the middle of seventeenth century this group of believers during the worship or prayer while listening to the message or praying were overwhelmed by emotions and would start to shiver or quake, so this group of shivering people was called "Quakers".

There was lot of opposition from the mainline established Churches and its leaders in power. Quaker leaders assured their followers that God could speak to common people through His son Jesus Christ provided they believe in Him, without paying heed to opposing Churchmen, pay tithes, or engage in deceitful practices. Since in Northern England there was majority of unsatisfied and restless people, so that became fertile ground for Quakers to sow the seeds of "Quakerism". They made northern England as the base. There was lot of opposition from the government, English Church and the Puritans(8.1) and they were termed as heretics because of their faith and laws. Though Lord Oliver Cromwell (1653-6158) himself was a Quaker, yet many leaders were arrested and jailed, but the enthusiasm and the work of missionaries failed to slow the movement. Even the Cromwellian authority was at stake. Margaret Fell who was very close to George Fox and a great help in organizing meetings later married him and tried to organize the seekers into one community, because she felt that without an organized group Quakers will fall apart.

James Naylor's Campaign:

James Naylor was very popular Quaker minister. He differed with the standard beliefs of the Quakers. In 1656 he rode into Bristol in the heavy rain accompanied by some of his fellow men and woman chanting, 'Holy, Holy, Holy'. Followers threw their garments on the ground where Naylor was riding, thus copying the royal entry of Jesus into Jerusalem. By doing so they were trying to say that 'Light of Christ' is present in every person.

So most of the people believed the James Naylor is Jesus Christ. These people were arrested by the authorities and handed over to the parliament. They were tried for their conflicting views and sent to Bristol jail. But these efforts by the authorities did not deter the work of the Quakers. Even George Fox when he started preaching Quaker faith was jailed and Quakers were persecuted for their conflicting views.

With time many controversies arose particularly in the period 1660-1670 when John Perrot a respected minister raised the issue that whether men should uncover their heads during prayer. Later this issue was resolved. George Fox and some other leaders advocated equal rights for women, but William Rogers, John Story and John Wilkinson disagreed with the heightening influence of women among Quakers. In 1666 a group of leading Quakers ruled that those who had different views and do not follow Quaker rules should be excluded. So women were given equal rights in the Quaker faith. Quakers who were called 'Friends' believed in the spiritual equality for women and the women were allowed to take more active role in the affairs of Quakers. Women meetings were organized to involve women in more modest, feminine events.

Persecution of Quakers:

According to their faith they claim that they always spoke truth, so Quakers did not take oath in the court of law. They refused to join the army. They claimed that in every human being spirit of God resides and God does not want to kill people. To get attention of people in other churches Quaker men and women interrupted their services. They paid no tithe to the Churches. They do not take off their hats before elders or rulers or those in high position. So they have controversial views for which they were opposed and criticized by the government. In 1650 George Fox was arrested and imprisoned. From 1650 to 1670 he was arrested and put in prison several times. Even his followers were arrested and jailed, so they had hard time in England. English Parliament passed two acts and made their life more miserable and difficult. First was Quaker Act of 1662 which made illegal to refuse to take oath of allegiance to the king and the country. Those who refused to take oath were not allowed to hold meetings openly or secretly. They believed that their religion was superior to their country.

Second was Conventicle Act of 1664 which reaffirmed that holding of secret meetings by Quakers who do not take pledge of allegiance to the country or the king is a crime. Because of their persecution and opposition by the government some Quakers arrived in Netherlands in 1655 along with William Ames and Margaret Fell's nephew William Caton and they started residing in Amsterdam. In Amsterdam they met Mennonites. Even in Netherlands they had hard time because even here they encountered persecution.

William Penn that had Dutch mother visited Netherlands in 1671 and saw the persecution of Quakers. Due to the persecution in England and Netherlands many Quakers moved to New England colony of America with the hope that they will not face persecution in the New World. Even here the English and Dutch Quakers who had moved to the Colony of New England (U.S.) faced tough opposition. Among the first comers were Mary Fisher and N. Aston who were imprisoned and sent back. In 1666 William Penn came to America and met members of Friends Society (Quakers). After visiting Netherlands and meeting English and Dutch Quakers he came back to America in 1674. In 1681 he took permission from Charles II ruler (1660-1685) of England to establish a colony in America and for that he paid 16,000 pounds. In 1682 he established the colony of Pennsylvania to help and settle the members of the Friends Society. According to him that was 'Holy Experiment'. As William Penn provided liberal atmosphere to the Quakers first, later they were followed by Dutch Calvinists. German Lutherans, German Reformed Christians, Amish, Mennonites, Wesleyan Methodists. All these Churches found a cordial environment to settle and grow.

Quakers Beliefs:

As the Society of Friends (Quakers) has split into various groups, so they have different beliefs. Yet at the very center of Quaker faith lies the concept of "Inner Light". They believe that in every human soul there is present certain element of God's own spirit and divine energy. This element was known to early friends as, "that of God in everyone" seeds of Christ or the seeds of light. This is according to John 1:9 "The true light which enlightens every human being that cometh into the World.

Baptism:

They are not particular about baptism, because it is a formal observance, so baptism is not necessary.

Fellowship or Communion:

They believe spiritual communion with God is experienced through silent meditation.

Bible:

They believe that bible has good and true things, but everything is not true. According to them Bible is not complete and perfect guide.

Creed:

Quakers do not have written creed, rather they believe in personal testimonies, professing peace and humility.

Equality:

Religious Society of Friends believes in equality both for men and women, yet some conservative Friends are divided on this issue of equality for women.

Heaven and Hell:

They believe God's kingdom is now. The concept of hell and heaven is a personal matter of every person. Some believe it is a matter of speculation.

Trinity:

To believe in Father, the son and the Hoy Spirit and the virgin birth of Jesus is a personal matter. Most Quakers believe God revealed himself through Jesus Christ. Large numbers of Quakers are more concerned in emulating Jesus and obeying His commandments than the theology of salvation.

Sin:

Most Quakers believe that humans are born sinless, so are inherently good. They believe that even the sinners are children of God and God tries to kindle His light within them.

Sacraments:

They do not have traditional ritual of baptism, yet they believe that if a person lives in the example of Jesus that is a sacrament.

No oaths in courts:

Quakers passed the law that no member of their society will or take oath in the court of law by keeping hand on the Bible, they argued that it is against the word of God and they always speak the truth.

Most of the Quakers opposed the theory of evolution as told by Charles Darwin. One of the Quaker Scientist stated that this theory was not compatible with the creation of the creator, yet some young Quakers who believed in the doctrine of progressive revelation with evolution ideas supported this theory.

Worship Services:

Quakers do not worship like other protestant or Catholic Christians; rather they spend most of their worship time by being quiet and waiting for the message from God through any Quaker member. If during the worship any person feels he has message from God, he can come forward before the congregation and preach the message. Sometimes no one speaks and they spend whole time quietly. This type of service is called un-programmed worship. These days modern Quakers have started copying evangelical protestant groups. They have programmed worship service. They worship with hymn singing, music, Bible reading and message by the preacher. They have trained and qualified pastor. Those having un-programmed service sit in a circle. They do not call worship place a Church rather they call it a meeting house or a steeple house.

They do not call days of the week or months by their common names, but They call first day, second day and the first month second month and so on. Their reasoning for this was that the days and months have been named by the pagans after the names of their gods and goddesses.

Slavery Abolition:

When Quakers migrated to America slavery was very common and very much acceptable. Most of the Americans had slaves to work in their homes and on the farm and it wasn't considered bad. So Quakers too owned slaves. The slave owners catered to the physical and spiritual needs of the slaves. With the passage of time around 1688 Quakers felt that having human slaves is not good. Two prominent Quakers John Wolman and Anthony Benezet spoke against slavery system. They asked their fellow Quakers, "What thing in the world can be done worse towards us, than if men should rob or steal us away and sell us as slaves to strange countries". So a group of Quakers with some Mennonites convened a meeting in German Town, Pennsylvania to discuss the matter of abolition of slavery. Francis Daniel Pastorius prepared a document stating that, "To bring hither, or to rob and sell them (slaves) against their will, we stand against". So from 1775 to 1776 American Quakers worked on freeing slaves. Efforts made by Quakers had a great impact on President Ben Franklin and Thomas Jefferson who in Continental congress were able to convince the members to ban slavery. Quakers not only worked for the freedom of slaves rather worked for improving the conditions of African race. George Washington encouraged the freed slaves to join the fight for American freedom from British rule. So 5,000 African Americans served in George Washington's army. Consequently most of the states like Virginia, New England, Mid Atlantic states, and North Western territories passed antislavery laws to abolish slavery.

There was still slavery in Southern states, so to free the slaves in these states an underground rail road was formed and Quakers played major role in this effort. Quakers not only helped the slaves to get freedom, but also worked for prison reforms. As prisoners were ill treated so Elizabeth Fry and her brother Joseph John Gurney campaigned for human treatment to prisoners and they fought for abolition of death penalty.

Quakers by their own law were prohibited from being involved in the field of law and politics, but with time they started taking part in politics. Joseph Peas a business man was elected to the U.S. parliament in1832 and Noah Haynes Swayne served on the United States Supreme Court.

Splinter Groups:

No religion or denomination is without subgroups. Elias Hicks around 1827-1828 took stand against the strong discipline regarding doctrinal questions. Those who supported Hicks were called Hicksites (Hickmites). And those who opposed were known as 'Orthodox'.

Gurneyites and Wilburites:

Hicksites Separations encouraged the two Quakers Joseph John Gurney and John Wilbur of Rhode Island. Gurney emphasized the scriptural authority and favored working with other protestant Christian groups. Gurneyite Quakers favored planned worship with paid pastors, singing hymns, music, bible reading and message, so they left silent type of un-programmed worship.

John Wilbur advocated the authority of Holy Spirit and worked to prevent the dilution of the Quaker tradition of Holy Spirit filled ministry. As he criticized and opposed Gurney, so Wilbur was expelled from the yearly meeting in 1842 and he formed his own 'Wilburite' group.

Beaconites:

Initially Friends in Britain were strongly evangelical following the orthodox doctrine, so they were least influenced by the Hicksite breakup. Actually Beaconite controversy surfaced in England on the publication of book, "A Beacon to society of Friends" published in 1835 by Isaac Crewdson. He was minister in Manchester Meeting. The breakup group included Isaac Crewdson and 48 fellow members of the Manchester meeting. A number of them joined the Plymouth Brethren and they brought the issue of simplicity of worship in the society. Evangelical International was another group. This group was staunch conservative evangelical which broke away from Gurneyites. They permitted their member Churches to practice the outward sacraments of Baptism and the Lord's Supper. They strongly opposed Homosexuality and abortion. In addition to these there were more splinter groups.

So we find it is the doctrinal, social, and political issues which prompt the people to have different views and hence there are splinter groups in the same denomination.

Notes:

8.1: Puritans was a group of 16th and 17th century Christians in England and New England (U.S.A) opposing unscriptural and un-ceremonial worship and the prelacy of the Church of England. They practice and preach more rigorous or professedly pure moral code than that which prevails. They lay stress on strictures and austerity in the matters of religion and conduct.

References:

1. "Religious History of American people" by Sydney E. Ahlstrom – Yale University press 1972.
2. "Great traditions of American Churches" by Winthrop Hudson.
3. "World Christian encyclopedia" 1982 by D.B. Barret.
4. "Religions in America" 1945 W.L. Sperry.
5. "The American Churches" 1947 W.W. Sweet.
6. "World Religions" from ancient History to present Ed. Geoffrey Parinder N.Y. Facts on file Publications.
7. 'World Religions' Benson Y. Landis.
8. "What is Quaker" by Richmon P. Miller Pp 163-175.
9. Wikipedia free Encyclopedia.
10. Quakers Hand Book of Religious society of Friends.
11. The Quakers in the Puritan England … Barbour, Hugh 1964
12. The beginning of Quakerism… by Braithwaite, William C…1912
13. Quakers in America …. H. Thomas 2003
14. William Penn's Holy Experiment…1962 Edwin B. Bronner
15. A short History of Quakers ……John Punshon 1984

Chapter Nine

Baptists

(Protestant)

When and Why the Baptists?

In 1525 an ordinance was promulgated by the Protestants in Zurich (Switzerland), that all Christian children should be baptized. Some parents objected to this order and said they cannot get the little ones baptized who do not know even the meaning of baptism. They argued that baptism means confession of sins with the mouth and repentance from those sins and confessing Jesus Christ as the personal savior before the public. Little children do not understand any of these things. They contested that every child should be baptized when he is able to understand the meaning of baptism or he is an adult. They also contested the Roman Catholic claim that with baptism all past sins are forgiven. No one becomes a true Christian by being born in a Christian family. To become a true Christian one has to confess his sins and confess Jesus Christ as personal savior before the public. He has to make confession wholeheartedly and with responsibility. A little child cannot confess his sins with his mouth nor he can confess Jesus Christ as his personal savior. A little child does not understand the meaning of Baptism. Such people formed a separate group called Ana-Baptists. They may have been baptized in Catholic Church as a child but on being an adult and member of the Baptist Church they will have to take second Baptism. Ana-Baptist meant baptized second time. Those who declined child baptism and became Ana-Baptists were either imprisoned on the orders of the protestant government of Zurich or killed by drowning them in water. Out of these people was Hubmeier Balthasar, who was a priest from Switzerland and many people started following him. He was tortured in Jail. After his release he went to Germany. There he organized a considerable large group of Ana-Baptists. As a result Catholics and Lutherans opposed him because Ana-Baptists opposed child baptism. Many Ana Baptists met martyrdom. Many Ana-Baptists were asked to leave Germany. In 1528 Hubmeier was burnt to death and his wife was killed by drowning in water, but Baptists movement did not stop. In Netherlands their leader was Menno Simmons. His followers in Netherlands were called 'Mennonites' (9.1). After that some Englishmen came from England and after meeting some Ana Baptists, they too became Ana- Baptists. Out of these Englishmen some went back to England and started Baptist movement. So around 1615 Baptist congregation came into being. In the early days this movement was slow but when John Bunyan became Pastor of the Bedford Church in 1672 this movement started spreading rapidly. This is the same John Bunyan who wrote the famous book 'Pilgrim's Progress'. The whole life he lived in poverty and faced shortage of the necessities of life. He spent 15 years in Jail because he did not have preaching license as a priest. That was a time in England when no one could preach without license. In 1939 Roger Williams brought many people into Christian faith in Rhode Island Colony in America. The population of Baptists in America is around 30 million and about 3 million live outside America. They take active part in American politics. Baptists feel that every person in the world should have complete religious freedom, because religion is the personal matter of every person, so no government anywhere in the world should interfere in the religious matters of every religion as long as they are law abiding citizens of the country. When Mexico government imposed restrictions on the religion in Texas (Texas was one time part of Mexico), it was Baptists who fought for the freedom of Texas. In Baptists every Church is independent, yet they have some associations to work together and keep in touch with the working of other Churches like Presbyterians and Methodists. There is no fixed or special creed in Baptist faith. There is slight difference in faith and working of different Baptist Churches, but in certain Churches there is lot of difference in faith and working. Mostly Churches are above narrow thinking nor are they too rigid except baptism.

All Baptists believe in Trinity that is God the father, Christ the son and the Holy Spirit. They all believe in the Virgin birth of Jesus Christ from Mary. Some of them believe in Hell and Heaven. Like Methodists and Presbyterians they celebrate Lord's Supper every first Sunday of the month. Inside the sanctuary normally, at the back they have water tank where they baptize the believer in running water by immersion. They believe in evangelism and missionary work. The world famous evangelist Dr. Billigrahm belongs to this Church. Missionary work is part of their faith. In America the Baptists missionaries have done lot of work among American Indians, people with African background, and Spanish speaking people in South Eastern countries. So every Baptist started working in his own way, because they believe in religious freedom. In America there are 27 denominations of the Baptist Church. Out of these some Churches are purely white and some others have black congregations and they are called 'Black Churches'. The biggest organization is constituted by the Southern Black Churches. This organization is politically very active. Southern Baptists do not like to work with other protestant churches.

In North Eastern states of India there is majority of Baptist Churches. The credit for this goes to the dedicated missionaries. In Korea also Baptists exist in large number and Korean Church is very strong. After reading about the Baptists we find though they are very rigid but there exists difference of opinion on certain matters and as a result they have 27 denominations. In this case I will say the cause of 27 denominations in Baptists is the difference of opinion regarding the word of God, different interpretations and understanding of the same word of God that they believe. Baptist Church has views different from the Methodists and Presbyterians. They believe in the Baptism by immersion whereas most of the protestant Churches like Anglicans, Methodists and Presbyterians baptize by sprinkling of water on the head. In the early years racial discrimination was also one of the causes of split in the Baptist Church. Baptist Churches do not have any creed like the Presbyterians and Methodists.

Notes:

9.1: Mennonites. This is a protestant sect deriving its name from Menno Simmons leader of the Ana-Baptists in Holland (Netherlands). The faith originated in Switzerland about 1525 and from there spread to other European countries and America. Each congregation decides its own form of worship but all agree upon baptism only of those old enough to accept Christ, the necessity for man's regeneration, refusal to bear arms or take oath, and rejection of worldly concerns. The Group is marked by simplicity of dress and habits. One of the most conservative branches is the Amish.

(Our religions and Neighbors. By M.G. Miller and S.D.Schwartz-P-277)

References:

1. 'Our religions and our Neighbors' by Milton G. Miller & Sylvan D. Schwartz Revised Edition Published by The Union of American Hebrew congregations New York N.Y.
2. 'World Religions' By Dutton
3. 'Religions in America' by Simon and Schuster. What is a Baptist Pp 14-21 an Article by William B. Lipphard.
4. 'The story of American Religions' Holt, Rinehart, Winston. The Baptists Pp23-38 Chapter 2.
5. 'World religions' Edited by Geoffrey Parrinder
6. 'Church History in Plain Language' by Bruce L. Shelly World Publishing London.

Chapter Ten

Mennonites

(The Anabaptists)

It is a breakaway group from the Baptists. They had differences with the Baptists regarding doctrinal, political and social issues. Though Baptists supported baptism by immersion after confession and repentance from the sins, yet they were very much politically involved in government and social affairs. When Zurich government issued orders to baptize all children the Baptists opposed this. Among the Baptists was Hubmeier Belthasar a priest from Switzerland who took the lead that Christians coming from Roman Catholic, Lutheran and other protestant Churches who have child baptism must be baptized again. With his views he organized a large group and they were called Anabaptists. Roman Catholics and Lutherans opposed this group.

Also when Ulrich Zwingli was working to get away from the Roman Catholic Church, there was a group called Swiss Brethren who also wanted to breakaway with the Roman Catholic Church, so they formed a group of Swiss Brethren. Zwingli wanted these brethren to join him, but they refused to join his struggle.

Swiss Brethren and Mennonites:

The Church in Zurich, Switzerland was state sponsored Reformed Church, which advocated child baptism. When this Church ordered that all children should be baptized, there were Baptist groups of people who opposed this move. They argued that sin entered human beings through our ancestral parents Adam and Eve with the knowledge of good and evil, when Adam and Eve disobeyed by eating the forbidden fruit. Since little children do not have knowledge of good and evil, so they cannot sin. And hence there is no need for child baptism. They should be baptized only when they grow up and can differentiate between good and evil and are able to confess their sins. Those who denied infant baptism started studying the Bible. Conard Grebel started preaching against child baptism without preaching license from the government of the state, so for this offence he was put in prison several times. George Blaurock another priest having the same views preached along with Conard Grebel and said that name Christian should be applied to those people only who truly believed in Jesus Christ and practiced His teachings. He further stated that the people who observed state sponsored church rituals like infant baptism and Eucharist are not true Christians. But these ideas were rejected by Ulrich Zwingli who was prominent leader of reformed protestant church. So these people formed a small group called 'Swiss Brethren'. When Zwingli approached members of this group and asked them not to disturb the unity of the church they refused to co-operate with him. The group of Swiss Brethren continued their meetings secretly and baptizing those adults who had infant baptism, so they were called Ana-Baptists (meaning baptized again), so this group separated rejecting the hierarchy and coercive policies of the old church. Their main emphasis was on obedience to the teachings of Jesus Christ of love and non-resistance and to imitate the life and character of the Lord and savior Jesus Christ.

As Roman Catholics believed that at the time of Holy Sacrament of Eucharist bread and wine actually change into flesh and blood of our Lord, they contradicted and said Christ is present in the body of the believer who truly believe in the redemptive power of Jesus and practice His teachings. This faced criticism and opposition from the state and the Church. The authorities termed them as the enemies of the European religion and the social institutions. Ana-Baptist beliefs were declared as devil inspired and antisocial. So the prominent leaders of this group were arrested, imprisoned and expelled. Felix Manz was killed by drowning in water on the charges of rebaptism. Conard died of plague at the age of twenty seven while he was exiled. George Blaurock was burned alive for his Ana-Baptist beliefs.

Michael Sattler left Catholic Monastery and became Ana-Baptist evangelist. He called a conference of all Brethren groups and issued a declaration of "Brotherly Union". This declaration has seven articles and was called 'Schleitheim Declaration'. The seven articles are mentioned below in brief:

No infant baptism: Only those adults should be baptized who confess their sins, repent from their sinful life and believe that their sins are forgiven through the sacrificial death of Jesus Christ and they believe in the resurrection of Jesus Christ.

Excommunication Ban: If any member after adult baptism and commitment to the fellowship of Ana-Baptists slips away and commits sin he will be excommunicated from the congregation. He will not be permitted to take part in Lord's Supper, so that all other members may celebrate Lord's Supper in one spirit and love.

Breaking the Bread: Those who join in the Lord's Supper should be one in body of Christ and baptism. Those who wish to drink from the cup in remembrance of the shedding holy blood of Christ cannot be partakers of the table of devil and of the Lord. All those who take part in the dead works of darkness cannot take part in this Holy Sacrament.

After separation from the evil and wickedness of devil which he planted in the world we are united in Christ. We do not have fellowship with the people who run in the confusion of their abominations. We keep away from the weapons of war and violence and we believe in the words of Jesus, "You shall not resist evil".

According to the words of St. Paul, "The Shepherd of the Church shall be of good report, who can warn, read, teach, exhort admonish and rightfully lead the people in prayer and breaking of the bread. If he needs help another member can support him. If he leaves, dies or is martyred another member of good report shall take his place immediately.

Sword (Government): The sword is another order of God outside the perfection of Christ. He punishes and kills the wicked and guards and protects the good people. The ban or excommunication is for a member who has sinned and is simply to warn him not to sin anymore. The government punishment is according to the flesh whereas that of the Christian is according to the spirit.

Oaths: (The people who fight and take oaths). In the Old Testament it was permitted in the name of God, yet Jesus has forbidden all swearing. He said, "Your speech should be yea or nay, anything other than this is evil.

So because of their beliefs most of the leaders of Swiss Brethren were martyred or died, but these articles became the basis of Mennonite and Amish people's tenets.

Menno Simmons (1496-1561) of Netherland liked these beliefs of Swiss Brethren, so he too joined the struggle and he decided to choose between state sponsored traditional Church and authority of scriptures. When he saw the Anabaptists suffering, dying, and undergoing Martyrdom he too decided to follow this path. When his brother along with other Anabaptists was attacked and killed he left the position of Catholic priest of low counties and started working for the Anabaptist movement. He became very prominent leader of this Movement in Netherland. The people who followed Menno Simmons were called 'Mennonites'. This movement spread very rapidly in other countries as well. The Mennonites who lived in countries dominated by Roman Catholic or Reformed Churches suffered persecution and oppression. Especially the Swiss Mennonites because of the suffering, torture and suppression fled to neighboring countries where they could be tolerated. They settled in Hinterlands and valleys of Jura and Vosges mountains and adopted agriculture as their way of life.

In the contemporary society Mennonites are taken as religious Christians Denomination with member of different ethnic origins. Some consider them both as ethnic and religious sects. Still there is difference of opinion, some considering them as a religious group and others as a distinct ethnic group. Some historians say it is an ethnic religious group. They are considered as plain people who are indistinguishable in dress and appearance from the common people.

Mennonite Beliefs:

Though Mennonites believe and favor seven articles of Schleitheim declaration yet their beliefs in short are:

1. Sacrament of Baptism - They believe that a member be baptized with water by immersion, sprinkling, or pouring water from the pitcher. This sacrament should be done publically and the person to be baptized should pledge to follow Jesus Christ through the power of Holy Spirit. They believe baptism is signing an agreement of commitment to follow Jesus Christ and also to the membership and service to the Mennonite denomination.

2. Bible - Mennonites believe the Holy Scripture of the Bible as the word of God given through the Holy Spirit for instruction in salvation and to lead life of righteousness. It is fully reliable and trustworthy to lead true Christian life with faith in Jesus Christ.

3. The Holy Communion - To take part in Lord's Supper is symbol of remembrance of His sacrificial death and of the New Covenant which Jesus established by shedding His holy blood on the cross.

4. Eternal Security - They do not believe in eternal security, because everyone has free will either to choose sinful life or the means of salvation. You have assurance of eternal security only if after baptism you continue in faith and close relationship with Jesus Christ.

5. Government - Since there are different views of different groups of Mennonites, so to vote is the decision of group of Mennonite. Conservative Mennonites do not vote, but liberal Mennonites normally vote. The same rule applies for the Jury duty. Since Jesus warned against swearing an oath or judging others, so the conservative Mennonites abide by the words of Christ. As they try to avoid the law suits, so they prefer negotiation and reconciliation. Some Mennonites take public office jobs and government employment as long as it does not interfere in their work for Christ, which is their priority.

6. Faith in Heaven and Hell - They believe that who has Christ as the centripetal force of their life, they will certainly live with Christ in Heaven

and for others who do not believe in Jesus it will be eternal separation from God, so they do not speak about Hell.

7. The Holy Spirit - They believe that Holy Spirit is the eternal Spirit of God, who also dwelt in Jesus and after His resurrection it empowers the Church and is the guiding force in the life of Christian believer.

8. Jesus Christ the son of God - They believe Jesus Christ is the son of God born to Virgin Mary through Holy Spirit. He is the savior of human beings to trust and believe in Him. He is perfect human being and fully God. By His sacrificial death He reconciled the humanity to God.

9. Ordinances - They do not refer to holy rituals of baptism and Holy Communion as sacraments rather call Ordinances. They believe in seven biblical ordinances that is confession of faith, Holy Communion, Washing of saint's feet, marriage, ordination of bishops, ministers, preachers, deacons, elders, anointing with oil for healing and holy kiss. Holy kiss is allowed only for the same sex but the modern Mennonites shake hands instead of kiss.

10. Pacifism - Able bodied Mennonites do not serve in the army on the ground that Jesus taught to love one another and also there is commandment that says that do not kill, even killing in war is against their belief.

11. Sabbath - They observe Sunday as the Sabbath, because Jesus arose from the dead on the first day of the week.

12. Salvation - They believe that salvation is the gift of God's grace. If a believer accepts the gift of God's grace, he repents and trusts in God alone and lives a life of obedience to God and His son Jesus Christ, then Holy Spirit works as the agent of salvation and the believer is saved.

13. Trinity - They are 'Trinitarians' because they believe in Trinity, the Father, the Son and the Holy Spirit who make one God head.

Worship Services:

Mennonites have Churches like the evangelical denominations. Worship service is conducted by a minister who leads the worship service. He delivers the message, leads in prayer and members give testimonies. Many of the Mennonites who have become modern use organs, pianos, and other musical instrument during hymn singing unlike the Amish who do not use any musical instrument. Each Mennonite district has different rules regarding telephone use. Some conservative Mennonites do not allow use of telephone like the old order Amish. They dress simply and women are required to wear modest dress and head covering (Bonnet). Three groups Mennonites, Brethren and Amish Mennonites make use of worldly conveniences such as cars, telephones, electricity and mechanized tools for farming.

Splits:

With the passage of time there arose disagreements within the Mennonite faith which resulted in the fragmentation of the group. The reasons were doctrinal, sometimes social and sometimes geographical. Some members wanted to have Sunday school like other evangelical Churches and participate in protestant style Church evangelism, but the others wanted to remain more conservative, so that progressive group has separated and became Amish Mennonite. Many divisions took place along the family lines.

Since Mennonites were not willing to serve in the army, they were given option. They can stay in the country if they serve in the army, but with the change of government they were again persecuted and forced to flee the country. In Netherland they were allowed to live in areas of poor soil. They were required to do farming and if they make the land arable they will be exempted from the military service. But when the land became arable and fertile they were compelled to flee and face suppression. Exemption from military service was withdrawn and heavy taxes were imposed upon them. So because of the persecution in Switzerland they fled to different countries.

In 1768 Catherine the great of Russia acquired lot of land north of Black Sea which is now (Ukraine) after the war with Ottomans. Russian authorities invited Mennonite farmers living in Prussia to farm this semi arid and grass covered land. As they were successful farmers they made the land arable and had large agriculture estates. With time they became industrialists in cities as well. After the Russian revolution of 1917 and civil war (1917-1921) all their farms and industries were taken over by the government. Not only that they suffered great persecution at the hands of tyrant communist government which was against Christianity. Hundreds of Mennonites including women and children were killed by the Russian Bolsheviks. People who practiced Christianity were imprisoned and killed by the Russian government. So many Mennonites fled to United States of America and Canada.

In the Second World War in 1941 when Germany attacked Russia many Mennonites fled with the German army and they were accepted by the German government. Soviets thought the Mennonites collaborated with the German army so they expelled Mennonites to Siberia as part of internal deportation. As they were living in labor camps the Russian government gave them an option to migrate wherever they liked. So most of them migrated to Germany. When William Penn visited Germany he met Quakers and Mennonites. He heard the stories of their suppression and torture in various states. When he came back to United States he acquired the colony of Pennsylvania and invited Quakers and Mennonites to this colony under the 'Holy Experiment'. In early eighteenth century 100,000 German Mennonites immigrated to Pennsylvania and they were known as 'Pennsylvania Dutch'. Most of them settled in Lancaster County area and acquired large tracts of agriculture lands because they were offered to them at cheaper rates. When they came here they promulgated the idea of separation of state and the Church and abolition of slavery. More and more Mennonites followed and immigrated to U.S. and settled in Ohio, Indiana, Illinois and Missouri. Along with them migrated Amish the breakaway group from the Mennonites. They also settled in Canada. In the First World War Canadian Mennonites were exempted from military service. In world War II they were given option of non-combatant military service to serve in medical and dental corps, making roads and parks. Even in the United States they were given the same option during the Second World War, but to serve in Civilian Public Service (CPS) instead of military. So Mennonites, Amish and Brethren in Christ performed the works of soil conservation, forestry, fire fighting, agriculture, social services, making roads and health services. For this they were not paid any wages and got minimum support from the government.

Education.

They did not want to send their children to government owned Public Schools rather they wanted to have their own Schools and their own curriculum for giving them faith based education with the stress on agriculture, but the state authorities opposed this. In Quebec (Canada) when they wanted to have their own schools and independent curriculum the Quebec government imposed a ban on this. Government ordered that either you send your children to government public schools or you have to follow the same curriculum in your schools as is followed in other public schools. If you do home schooling even then you have to follow the government approved material. They presented their concerns to the Quebec government but their pleas went unheard and the government imposed restrictions which threatened their faith and religious traditions. So most of Mennonite families left Quebec and migrated to different states in U.S.

Families Values:

They believe in the purity of social and family life. They recognize the legitimacy of purity of unmarried life of singles and sanctity of married life of couples. Single men and women are expected to be chaste and marriage should be taken as life long, monogamous, and faithful covenant between man and woman. They discourage divorce and it is allowed only in extreme cases when living together becomes impossible due to some genuine reasons. There was a time when divorce was very rare but in recent times it is becoming more common. Same sex marriages are not permitted in Mennonite and Amish society. Female pastors were not ordained but liberal Mennonite Dutch Churches have started having female pastors.

Mennonite women normally make dresses at home for all the family members. They take care of the Children and do all the household chores.

Main branches of Mennonites are conservative and liberal the reformed Mennonites. Reformed Mennonites consider themselves as the first keepers of the old way and true followers of Menno Simmons. They consider bible as their guide. Another denomination is Holdeman Mennonite or the Church of God in Christ Mennonites. They emphasize evangelical conversions and strict Church discipline. They use modern technology, but discourage intensive use of internet and avoid television, cameras and radio. Most of the Mennonites use horse driven buggies for local use. Modern Mennonites use tractor for farming, but some oppose it and use horses and mules to pull the agriculture implements.

Main Mennonite branches are;
Mennonite Church of U.S.A.
Brethren in Christ
Mennonite Brethren
Mennonite Church in Canada
Conservative Mennonites
Church of God In Christ Mennonite

There are Mennonite Churches in Mexico, Belize, Argentina, Bolivia, Ethiopia, Congo and Tanzania.

Chapter Eleven

AMISH

(The Simple People)

Origin of Amish dates back to the protestant reformation in Europe when Christian groups were breaking away from the Roman Catholic Church because of the repressive policies of the Pope and the church. Lutherans, Reformed and Anglican Churches were the first to distance away from the Roman Catholic Church. Ulrich Zwingli while trying to form a reformed Church was trying to unify the other Christian groups. Due the differences on ideology and doctrinal issues a group of Swiss Brethren was formed. Though Menno Simmons liked the ideology of Swiss Brethren, yet there were certain doctrinal, social, and political issues which compelled Menno Simmons to form his own group called Mennonites. With the passage of time even the Mennonites changed and they broke up into several splinter groups and Amish are one of them. In 1693 Jacob Amman in Alsace became the leader of the religious group who were against War and swearing in courts and did not want to join the army and they wanted exemption from the military service. He and his group in Alsace had difference of opinion with the Swiss Brethren and Mennonites in Switzerland.

In the beginning there was difference of opinion on the celebration of Lord's Supper. He advocated that Holy Communion should be observed twice in each year instead of once as was the custom with the Swiss Brethren and the Mennonites. The Swiss leaders like Benedict Schneider and Hans Reist pleaded that in the Old Testament times high priest entered the Holy of Holies once in a year. So they advocated that yearly Communion should be sufficient, but Amman did not agree. Then he raised the issue of social avoidance (Meidung). He advocated that excommunicated members should come under the rule of social avoidance. Swiss Mennonites (Anabaptists) were practicing excommunication according to the Schleitheim articles of faith, but Amman followers accepted the Dutch or Dordrecht confession of 1632 which had upheld social avoidance part of Meidung and foot washing. Jacob Amman who advocated social avoidance and foot washing were not being observed in Mennonite and Swiss Brethren assemblies. Swiss Mennonites rejected Jacob Amman's Meidung resolution.

Alsace group of Mennonites supported Jacob Amman and Amman refused to yield and compromise on his demands thus Mennonites of Switzerland, Southern Germany and Alsace (Amman's followers) got divided into two factions. Those who followed Jacob Amman were called 'The Amish'. Not only that Jacob Amman attached great importance to the wearing of simple clothing and to avoid worldly style of dressing. He also condemned trimming the beard and wearing fashionable clothing. Anyone in his group disobeying will be punished. Amish used hooks and eyes on their clothing for that they were called 'Haftlers. Whereas Mennonites used buttons so they were called 'Knopfters' (The button people). These were some of the causes of breaking of Amish from rest of the Mennonites. The basic beliefs of Amish and Mennonites are same. Amish are stricter about their faith and observance of the tenets of their faith. Jacob Amman was 37 years old when he formed his separate Amish group. Basically he was Anabaptist farmer tradesman. He was son of Michael and a tailor like his father.

They believe in the biblical story of creation and the Garden of Eden where Adam and Eve lived in the company of God among plants, birds, and animals. That is why majority of them are farmers and using animals for farming. Human salvation is possible only through the obedience to God and responding to His love. They believe that all the godly gifts they receive from God is His blessing which they do not deserve and for that they must try to prove worthy and faithful and should be thankful to God. For that they try to walk in righteousness, obedience, submission and humility and lead life of non-resistance.

Humility and love towards fellow Amish is their main priority. They believe they live in this world but are not of the world (1Peter 2:11). They believe they must live separated from the perverted world and should not partake in the acts and deeds of darkness. They consider that they and their Church is the bride of Jesus, so that when they meet their Lord the groom they should be unblemished. That is why they try to maintain purity of the community and personal life. So the disobedient and unruly must be expelled. Strife, jealousy and violence have no place in the Amish community and personal life. Holding public office, government job or political participation is not allowed.

Amish normally do not evangelize or proselyte the outsider, but they try to keep their baptized members from leaving the Church and go to other religious denominations. Amish members cannot have worldly facilities like automobiles, T.V. radio, and other comforts of modern living. If they do they can be excommunicated and shunned. As they believe in the purity of Amish life so drunkards and adulterers will be excommunicated. Excommunication from the Amish Church membership is exercised only after the offender has been properly warned and if he remains unrepentant and unwilling to refrain from his transgression and rebellious behavior.

Professions:

When Amish along with Quakers and Mennonites moved to America most of them settled in Lancaster County of Pennsylvania, where under 'Holy Experiment' William Penn offered them liberty and freedom of religion and also offered agriculture land at cheap rates. Since the land was flat and arable so they were happy to settle there. After that some Amish started moving to other states because they needed more land for agriculture. So they moved to Ohio, and Idaho. Their main profession is farming where they grow Corn, Soya, Tobacco, Wheat, Barley, Rye, Oats, and vegetables along with Dairy farming. For the farming they do not use tractor and other motorized devices, rather they use agriculture implements pulled by horses and mules. Their reason for not using tractor is that it does not make manure and also it ruins the land by making the fertile land compact and on sowing the plants do not take deep roots thus it reduces the yield.

Christian Denominations

The whole family including the boys and girls are encouraged to work on the farm. They do not send their boys and girls for higher education, so they have their own schools where they are taught by a teacher in one room school. After 8th grade schooling when the boys are able to work on the farm they are encouraged to take farming as their profession. After they get married either they work on the family farm or a separate farm land is acquired for him. Since with time availability of agriculture land is becoming more and more difficult they move to other states and places where land is cheaper and is available. Because of the shortage and non-availability of agriculture land Amish are taking to other professions. The other professions are dairy farming. Amish in Lancaster County have been permitted to use milking machines and milk tanks operated by diesel engines.

To make additional income the women and children sell their products on the roadside stalls. These products are vegetables, honey, fruits, dry goods, lawn chairs, brooms, home baked bread, and plants. Women also make beautiful quilts, rugs, hand painted dishes and plates.

Due to increasing cost of farming, non-availability and shortage of agriculture lands and the less profits the young farmers are thinking of other professions. Ohio has the largest number of non-farming Amish. They work in shops and are taking other trades within the Amish community. These trades are Carriage Makers, Cabinet making, Carpentry, Black Smiths, Butchers, Shoe making, Bee keeping, Carpet makers, and Orchard growers. They are also having appliance stores, Bakery shops, furniture and farm equipment, Printing presses, Silos, making wood storages and mobile homes. They are also taking up heavy industry like steel fabricating plants and Machine shops.

Since they have their own Amish Schools, so some Amish are taking to teaching as well. You will rarely find an Amish doctor, because they do not send their children to college because college training is forbidden.

Amish are not allowed to have electricity, telephone connection, central heating and air conditioning. Beards for all married men but no moustaches are mandatory because army men have moustaches, long hair for men as to cover part of their ear, uncut hair for women, hooks and eyes on their coats, without collars and lapels are essential. No education beyond elementary grades both for boys and girls, so that they can just read and write and know basic mathematics. There is exception to this rule for business men and those who are in high positions and in government civil jobs or having their own industry.

Family Life:

Amish family life is very simple and more attached to the nature and based upon the tenets of the Bible. Father is the head of the house that normally looks after the farm and attends to the outside matters. Whereas the wife looks after the home and attends to the family matters. Amish family may have six to seven children. Homes are big with spacious rooms. House may be double or triple storied and may have more than one dwelling units, where the whole family lives with grandparents, newly married couple, father and mother with rest of the children. It is duty of the children to take care of parents and grandparents when they retire. Retired Amish do not seek financial aid or social security from the government, yet they pay their taxes honestly as commanded by Jesus, "pay to the Caesar what is Caesar's and to God what is God's."

Household appliances like refrigerators, washing machines, and driers are run by propane gas, compressed air, or kerosene or they make use of solar energy. For hot water they make use of propane gas. Car batteries are used to operate computers, cash registers, and other electric devices. They make use of solar energy for drying their clothes using clothe line which you find outside every Amish home.

Amish are a monogamous family. House wife and children take care of the garden around their house where they grow vegetables and flowers. Typical Amish women preserve fruits, vegetables and meat for the family use. They preserve fruits, make pickles and also preserve carrots, tomatoes, beans. If the family has more fruits and vegetables and the preserved stuff they sell to the passerby on the roadside stall or they go to the farmers market to sell their produce. Women and children that are able help the adults in the farm work.

Homes are painted with sober colors. You will not find pictures, photographs, or ornamental articles on the walls. Yet they use curtains with sober colors, calendars, homemade quilts, blankets, kitchen articles, and decorative plants. Duty of mother is to train and discipline the children after the Amish tradition and teach them humility and obedience both to parents, elders, and to God's ten commandments. Children and parents visit relatives and friends every other Sunday to keep the family relationship alive and also for the purpose of knowing each other and also children can play together. Children play with dolls and homemade toys, wagons, and scooters, but not battery operated toys. Musical instruments are not permitted in the family. Young boys and girls do singing during worship service on Sundays. After the worship service boys and girls sixteen and older stay together and play games. If a boy likes the girl he can take her home, but they have to keep the sanctity and purity of their life until they get married. If some children when they become adults cross Amish boundaries and start using alcohol, tobacco, watch movies and T.V. listen to radio and other entertainment sources, parents thinking them adults ignore them, yet the parents expect them voluntarily reject the worldly ways and return to the Church. Statistics shows majority of them return to the family and the mother Church to join. Unique characteristic of the Amish community is they help each other in house and the barn building if they are damaged by storm and hurricane.

Amish Dress:

As the Amish dress themselves plainly, that is symbol of Amish community unity, so they are called 'Plain People'. Their dress and clothing is governed by Ordnung (Amish life Code), yet it may slightly vary from one district to another. Men wear black and dark suits with hooks and eyes and no outside pockets. Men trousers have no fly and use suspenders to hold the pant. The coats have no collars or lapels. For the worship service they wear black suit, with coat and vest and white shirt underneath and a black bow. All men and boys wear straw hat with a black ribbon around it.

All Amish women wear the same type of dress which they sew at home. They make dresses for each family member. Amish woman is expected to wear black Cape (or Bonnet) and an apron while going for Church service. Young girls and women while working in the farm wear grey aprons. Men, Women and children normally wear black shoes outside but at home women normally walk bare foot. Children while going to school wear sneakers. The dress code for all Amish is a binding according to Ordnung code. Any disobedience to these rules is an offence and may lead to excommunication.

Worship Services:

There are two categories of Amish, 'House Amish' and 'Church Amish'. House Amish conduct their services in the house of a member or in the barn. Every Sunday the services are held on rotating basis from house to house. There is a committee that moves the furniture from one house to another. The benches are backless. They pray on their knees. There is hymn singing and sermon by the preacher. Every organization has preachers, a deacon, and a bishop. House Amish think having Church building is worldliness and copying other Christian denominations. Whereas the Church Amish worship in a Church building. Communion services are held twice a year and are followed by feet washing. Baptism is done by pouring water on the head of the member to be baptized. Liturgy and doctrine is the same for the house and the Church Amish communities.

They feel Church must be pure, unspotted and without any blemish both in the community and personal life, Church as a whole is the bride of Christ and must be presented to Him unblemished at His second advent. They tell the members either to obey or perish. They consider themselves to be strangers and pilgrims in this world according to Peter who said this world is not our real home. Real home is living with Christ. They strive every way and everyday to prepare for the heavenly kingdom and work of their salvation will be complete, when they hear the welcome words of Christ their Lord at the last judgment, "You blessed of my father come and inherit the kingdom that has been prepared for you from the foundation of the world" Matt. 25:34.

Amish Wedding:

Amish boys and girls have liberty to choose their life partners. After they decide to marry they inform their parents and the deacon. Deacon then visits the parents of both the boy and the girl and seeks their consent.

After this he announces the wedding which is normally solemnized on Tuesday or Thursday in the month of October after the fall harvest. House Amish solemnize the wedding at the bride's house where friends and relatives gather from both sides. Meals are prepared by the family friends. Minister gives due instructions to the bride and the groom telling them the duties and ethics of the married life. Both dress in Church going dress. In addition bride wears white cape and apron. After the wedding bride packs her white dress and it is never used again until the woman dies. Then this white dress is used for her shroud at the time of her burial. After that they start living in separate unit of the house and start visiting relatives. Groom's father gives him separate farm, furniture, machinery, animals, cooking utensils, and house furnishings to start separate life or if he decides to live with his father he will help the father at the farm.

Note: Cape and Bonnet are head coverings for the women. Cape is a triangular piece of cloth with long cords to tie at the back. Bonnet is a special kind of cap made by the women with cords to tie below the chin.

References:

1, Amish the Old Order by Lucy Hanley American souvenirs and Gifts.
2. The old Order Amish of Lancaster county Pennsylvania by Calvin G. Bachman
3. Brothers in Christ, The history of Anabaptist congregation Scottdale Pa. by Blanke Fritz Herald Press.
4. Anabaptism neither Catholic nor Protestant Water loo, Ontario by Walter Klaassen Press.
5. Amish Culture and Economy by Gerald S. Lestz Science Press.
6. Amish People New York Atheneum By Carolyn Meyer.
7. The Mennonite Immigration to Pennsylvania vol. 28 Norris town by Henry Smith.
8. Amish Society by John A. Hostetler Fourth edition published by John Hopkinn University press Baltimore and London.

Chapter Twelve

Seventh Day Adventist

(Protestant)

Though there were many denominations before Seventh Day Adventists, yet this denomination came into existence, which claimed to be true followers of Jesus Christ, because William Miller found drawbacks in those denominations and started thinking on different lines. He was born on February 15, 1782 in Pittsfield, Massachusetts. He was one of the sixteen children born to his parents. Since his father was very religious and God fearing, he used to take his family to the church in the family's Horse driven Buggy.

On being adult he joined the army. Since he was hard worker and a loyal person, so he was promoted to the rank of captain during the war in 1812. Because of the Christian environment in the family he was interested in reading the word of God and so took interest in religious matters. He was not happy and satisfied with the Christian environment around him. He being disappointed chose the path of spiritualism. According to this thought God does not interfere in any of the man's work. After the creation, God has left the world to run by itself and He wants that Man and Woman should solve their problems by themselves. After some time he became disappointed and disheartened.

After retirement from the army he came back to Lo Hampton, New York and started working on his farm. Even the ideology of Spiritualism did not help him and for some time he started going to the Baptist Church to seek answers to his questions. Many questions were troubling him inside his troubled heart. In 1816 finally he decided to study the Bible to find answers to too many questions in his heart. He read many more books related to the Bible. Without the guidance of any teacher he studied the Bible thoroughly. He felt that whatever things about the religion have been passed on to him and whatever things leaders talk about are different from the truths given in the word of God. After studying the Bible continuously for two years he realized that after 25 years around 1843 Christ is to come again and then he gave a second thought to his theory and predicted that Christ's Second Advent date is October 22, 1844. Some believers had thought that before the Second Advent there would be a period of 1,000 years in which there will be peace and prosperity and after that Christ will come. To be sure about his predictions and to be more informed he studied the Bible in more detail and thus became more convinced about the word of God. He wanted to share his view with the people, but people thought him to be illiterate farmer and no one paid heed to his views. They reasoned that he did not get any religious education from any well-known University or religious institution. He started spending more and more time in prayer. To seek answers to his questions he started praying alone in thick grove of trees. He promised God that if anyone calls him for prayer he would definitely go with him. When he came home then exactly after one hour his nephew Gilford came to invite him to preach in the Dresden Baptist Church coming Sunday so that he can share his views with the people. Miller accepted this invitation. By this God opened door for His service. In the coming 13 years he preached in 500 cities and delivered 4,000 messages. More than 200 priests and 100,000 people heard and supported his views about the second advent of the Lord. All those people who supported miller were called Millerites. This movement was known as the Millerite Movement. Miller's views about the second advent of Jesus Christ were based upon the prophecy of prophet Daniel mentioned in his book in 8:14. According to the rules of interpretation of prophecy 1 day is taken equal to one year. So by considering 2300 days as 2300 years he made his calculations. Sir, Isaac Newton also tried to discover many things from the biblical prophecies and wrote about it. Since Daniel's prophecy was made in 457 B.C. So counting 2300 years from then, he prophesized October 22, 1844 as the day of Second Advent of Jesus. When that day arrived not only Miller got disappointed rather all those got disappointed who were ready to meet their loved ones who had already died, because neither Jesus came back nor the dead were raised. Because of unfulfilled Predictions of Miller many of his supporters left him and went back to join their old Churches and some of them started their own Churches. Miller felt a big shock because of this failure, which he had never expected. Even then he had considerable number of supporters. Frustrated people were not ready to listen to the excuses from Miller. He had to face sarcastic criticism of the people, who made fun of him. He had to face people who published sarcastic remarks and his caricatures in News Papers. Even then a small group was left with him that was searching the truth. Miller though disappointed and frustrated started once again to look into the word of God and find out where he made the mistake in calculating the date of Second Advent of Jesus Christ. Calculation about the number of years was correct but to say that these years are for the second advent of Jesus Christ is not correct. From his second time study of the Bible he found out before the second advent of Jesus 1,000 years are not the years of peace and prosperity, rather before his Second Advent troubles, wars and evils will increase. After that to curb the troubles, wars and evils Jesus will come and His rule of peace and prosperity will start. With this interpretation followers of Miller got satisfied and got more confirmed in their faith. They accepted the calculation regarding the number of years and miller admitted that he was mistaken about the happenings in those years. While studying Bible they also discovered that the Sabbath day, since the people honored the creation and now this seventh day is also related to the Second Advent of Jesus Christ. Joseph Bates who was captain of the Sea Ship, and had been observing seventh day as the Sabbath, also came and joined them. He started working for this organization, which by now was called as the 'Seventh Day Adventist Church'. Hiram Edison who was also supporter of this faith tried to investigate that where Miller made the mistake. He supported Miller as for as the calculation of the number of years was concerned, but what is going to happen in those years was not correct. Actually October 22, 1844 was not the date of Second Advent of Jesus Christ, rather it is the beginning of second part of His priesthood in heaven and in that way this prophecy was fulfilled. Many people tried to research about the prophecy. A 17 years old girl Allan Herman had a vision while she was praying with her friends in Portland Maine; she got new power and guidance from God. She saw in the vision that whatever Miller and Hiram Edison are saying is correct and they are on the right path. If they continue like that Jesus will continue guiding them. A young priest James White was very much influenced by the vision of Allan Herman. After that both got married. They both worked for the Seventh Day Adventist Church. Because Seventh Day Adventists consider seventh day as the holy and they strongly believe that the second advent of Jesus Christ will be on the seventh day. For all these reasons this Church was called 'Seventh Day Adventist'. James and Allan White emphasized on the importance of seventh day to be celebrated as the Sabbath. Both of them along with Hiram and James Bates emphasized on the importance of Bible study. They provided proper guidance to the people who wanted to understand the word of God correctly. In a short time thousands of people started the study of the word of God. They called the first Sabbath Conference in 1848 on Rocky Hill Connecticut. There they mainly laid emphasis on the study of Bible and the Prayer. Their difference from other denominations was that instead of Sunday they recognized Saturday as the Sabbath and the Seventh day, which was consecrated by God as the Sabbath day. Secondly they emphasized that the second advent of Jesus Christ will also be on the Sabbath day. Keeping all these things in mind and after thorough thinking they named their group as the Seventh Day Adventists. Like the Seventh Day Adventists many Protestant Churches believe in the second advent of Jesus Christ, but they claim nobody knows the time and day of His coming except God the father. When this Church was founded there were 3,500 members only but today their number in the whole world is about 10 million.

What do they believe?

Every Church is a congregation of believers. Every person may have different way of life, different food habits and likings and, the different way of dressing, but where rules of religion and faith in God are concerned is same in every Church. All the Adventists are tied together with one thread of faith and are members of one Church. In all the countries like India, Pakistan, Peru, Cambodia, Canada, America and other countries of the world, all Adventists are tied together with one thread of Faith. Their faith is based upon the word of God. Their interpretation is one. The main points of their faith are given below.

God and His Word:-

Seventh Day Adventists believe that word of God reveals the will of God for human beings. This word is the foundation of their faith. Seventh Day Adventists believe that God is omnipresent and is omnipotent. He has no beginning and no end because He is eternal. God has three personalities that are God the father, God the son and the Holy Spirit.

Salvation of Human beings:-

Seventh Day Adventists believe that God created man and woman in the state of purity or holiness, yet God's plan failed because of the sin they committed through disobedience. Now the descendents of Adam and Eve are born with the seed of sin. According to St. Paul every human being is a sinner and he needs a savior. Adventists believe that Jesus came in this world, and He lived a Holy life. He gave His life on the cross to pay the price of sins of the world and rose again on the third day from the dead. Grace of Jesus Christ is free for everyone who accepts him as his savior wholeheartedly.

Seventh Adventists believe that we cannot earn our salvation by doing good deeds; rather our good deeds are fruits of our faith, which a believer bears because of His grace. It is only through His grace our good deeds are accepted by Him. As long as we do not believe in Jesus Christ, our good deeds are like dirty rags.

Satan:

Seventh Day Adventists believe that Lucifer was one of the important angels of God. Who rebelled against God in Heaven, and God expelled him out of the heaven and threw him on earth along with all those angels who supported Him. The same Lucifer is today's Satan who opposes God's plans and creates obstacles in God's work. He misleads human beings and compels them to follow other paths and faiths. He works through his followers and through them tortures and kills Christian believers and stops them from preaching the word of God and is enemy of Christ, Christianity and Christian believers in different countries of the world, so that he may torpedo the God's plan of salvation for the humanity. It is the same Satan or devil that entangles human beings in bad habits of revelry, drunkenness, lewdness, lust, adultery, and strife to take the believers away from God. The word of God tells about the fall of man and to rise again in Christ. At the end this earth will belong to the believers who confess Jesus Christ as their savior and walk according to His will in their daily life.

Christ and His Believers:

Seventh day Adventists believe that Christ is seated at the right hand of God, the father in heaven. He is the representative of the whole humanity. He, through His servants is trying that more and more people may believe in Him and enter the kingdom of heaven. They believe in the second advent of Jesus Christ, which is very near and this reality every human eye will witness.

Seventh Day Adventists believe that at the second coming of Jesus Christ all the believers who died in Christ will be raised and Christ will give them eternal life. So the dead are not alive in heaven rather they are resting in their graves on earth and they will be there till the second coming of Jesus Christ. At the second advent of Christ His 1,000 years reign will start. After His 1,000 years rule he will judge all the people and He will wipe out the sin and punish the sinners and after that there will be no more sin. Jesus will again create the world of believers that will be perfect. His believers will be able to live according to His Godly will on this earth. There will be no more pain, suffering, sin, thieves or dacoits, adulterers or liars, drunkards or Idol worshipers.

Life of Christian Church:

Seventh Day Adventists believe in the organization of the Christian Church and Christian fellowship. Those who believe in the Seventh Day Adventists faith, for them baptism is mandatory. After confessing Jesus Christ as the personal savior, baptism by immersion is essential, because Jesus set example for this by getting baptized from John the Baptist in the Jordan River. They do not believe in the Baptism by sprinkling of water nor do they accept the baptism of children. All Adventists have one aim to prepare the people to meet Jesus Christ at His second coming. To achieve this goal they want every believer to keep the company of other believers, personal Bible study, and share the word of God with the other people. By sharing His love with others and fulfill the needs of the needy. At work and the other people we meet every day to witness before them about Christ and our faith. God blesses those who believe in Him with spiritual gifts so that they may serve Him. Holy Spirit will be our guide and helper until Jesus comes back at His Second Advent. Seventh Day Adventist believes that Jesus blesses his believers with spiritual gifts who are obedient to Him. Lord's Supper is celebrated after every three months. To meet the needs of the Church they give tithes, so that God's work may continue and the worldly needs may be met. For this they contribute to the best of their ability.

Christian Life:

Seventh Day Adventists claim that they are representatives of Jesus Christ, so their way of life, their talk, and every deed and action of their life should be witness for their savior. In their everyday life they keep in mind that everything they do, their way of dressing, their sources of entertainment should be based upon their faith. They pay special attention to their family relations, married life and acknowledge that these are sacred relations whose foundation was laid by God in the Garden of Eden. They believe that our body is a blessing from God and we should take care of this. So by obeying the commandments of God they pay special attention to their health, so that they remain physically healthy and holy.

Sabbath:

Adventists do not recognize Sunday as the Sabbath rather they take Saturday as the Sabbath and the seventh day of the week. They claim that God did the creation work in six days and rested on the seventh day, which He called the Holy Sabbath. They not only obey and follow the commandment regarding Sabbath rather they obey all the Ten Commandments in the true sense and spirit. There is no such commandment or indication in the Bible according to which day of Sabbath can be changed to another day. To take Saturday (seventh day) as the Sabbath is totally different from those who take Sunday as the Sabbath. Because of this thinking all those who were away from God came into Christ. Peoples from different backgrounds joined Seventh Day Adventist Church. This way they have understood the God's love and honored God's commandment and recognized Him as the Creator of this world. This is the faith of all the Adventists and this faith has kept all the Adventists tied together in one thread of faith.

Who Are Seventh Day Adventists?

Seventh Day Adventists never think they are sinless. Every Adventist confesses that he or she is a sinner and they can only be saved by the saving grace of their savior Jesus Christ. They believe that every human being is precious in the sight of God. The effort of every Adventist is to share the living word of God with other people, wherever and whenever they get opportunity for that. There are certain things, which only the Adventists teach and these are not taught by the other Churches.

They are very careful about what they speak, what they do, and how they entertain themselves. Will their God and savior be happy with all these things and they will be acceptable to Him? They pay special attention to their food habits. They always keep in mind that their body is the temple of God and is the place for the Holy spirit to live in. Many of the Adventists are vegetarians. They believe that God commanded their first parents to eat only the fruits and vegetables. (Genesis 1:30,31). Those who are Non-vegetarians do not eat lot of meat and avoid eating pork according to God's commandment. Many Adventists do lot of exercise to keep their body hale and hearty, because it is house of God. They keep away from intoxicating foods and beverages, Liquor, beer, and smoking. According to one survey a Seventh Day Adventist lives 7- 10 years longer than the other people. They do not watch obscene movies and T.V. shows. They like to dress in simple clothes. They have done laudable wok in the education field.

Normally the worship service in Adventist church is held on Saturday mornings and is divided into two parts. The first part is the Sabbath School. For Sabbath School the congregation is divided into different groups, right from the children to adults. In the Bible school they play games and learn hymns. All Churches have the same syllabus, so that systematic religious education is imparted to every Adventist.

Second part is the worship. During the worship they sing Christian Hymns of praise and intercessory prayers are done for the needy and those requested for special prayers. If anyone inspired by the Holy Spirit wants to give testimony for the spiritual uplift and strengthening them in faith, he or she is given chance to share his words with the congregation. There is pastor's message from the Bible. In the absence of the pastor any other prominent member can conduct the service and deliver the message from the Bible. Seventh Day Adventists come to the Church to worship their Lord God, to share their experiences and matters of faith with the other fellow members, so that they may encourage each other and become spiritually strong in faith and refresh themselves spiritually and be filled with the power for the work to be done during the coming week.

The Area Conference pays pastor, so that he may not feel that he is dependent on the congregation and he should deliver Sabbath message to please the congregation. Congregation of the Church may be small or large every pastor is paid the same salary. They have not made any changes in their faith. Whatever it was in 1863, it is still the same today. Local conference supervises the work of local Churches. Many local conferences form one union conference. There are 9 union conferences in America. Union Conferences brought together form Divisional Conference and then is the General Conference. Formation of these conferences is based upon Bible teachings in the Mosaic period. Moses' father-in-law Jethro had advised Moses to divide the whole work into groups of 10,50,100 and 1,000 and appoint supervisors on them. So the whole Seventh Day Adventist Church is divided into different groups who are responsible for the work of their groups but all have one central faith based upon the father, son and the Holy Spirit. Regarding The Seventh Day Adventists I have to repeat my statement that reason for the formation of this denomination was the difference of opinion with the other existing Churches. They had different interpretations about the Sabbath and the second advent of Jesus to which they did not agree, and hence it gave rise to this denomination as the Seventh Day Adventist. Even this Church has many splinter denominations, which came into existence because of difference of opinion and views. Some of these are:

Davidian Seventh Day Adventist Association.
General Association of Davidian Seventh Day Adventists.
Seventh Day Adventist reformed Church. (Rowenite)
Seventh Day Adventist reform Movement.
Seventh day Christian Conference.

References:

1. 'Adventism for the New generation" By Steve Daily -Better living publishers Portland.
2. "World Religions" latest edition by Dutton
3. "Religions in America" by Leo Rosten. "What is a Seventh day Adventist" an article by Arthur S. Maxwell Pp 176-184.
4. "The story of America's Religions" by Hartzell Spence Chap.10. "The Seventh Day Adventists" Pp 165-182.
5. "Our religions and our Neighbors" revised edition by Milton G. Miller and Sylan D. Schwartzman
6. "Church History in Plain Language" by B.L.Shelly- World Publishing.
7. "Adventism in America" A History by Garyland Grand Rapids W.B.Eerdmans publishing Co. 1986.

Chapter Thirteen

The Church of Christ, the Scientist

(Christian Science)

Church History

In every human brain whenever a fire of difference of opinion and different interpretation of the word of God is ignited his mind and soul get upset and he feels troubled because of the storm of different ideas and thoughts. He starts questioning the faith and the actions of the mainstream religion, and as a result new sect, group or denomination is formed. If we study the mainstream religions in India like Hinduism, Islam, Sikhism and Christianity we find so many breakaway groups or sects with their own religious philosophy and their own religious mentors. Some of these groups throw mud on other religious groups and try to justify themselves by finding faults and drawbacks in the group from which they broke off. Some of the supporters of these sects do not know what they really are because they will kneel down and bow down their heads anywhere. They are supporters of Rajneesh wearing Rudraksh Necklace (13.1), also go to, Radha Swami Commune (13.2) also they bow down in the temples of Hanuman (13.3), Shiva (13.4), Ram(13.5), goddess Kali (13.6). Radha Swamis have two groups Beas and Sikandar Pur groups(Sucha Sauda). Likewise in Islam there are more than 1 00 splinter groups. In Hinduism and Sikhism there are innumerable splinter groups with different ideologies and every group thinks that their faith and doctrine is right. Not only that rather due to the caste system some of them think that they are superior to the other groups. Why Christianity should be left behind the other groups? It has more than 400 denominational groups and sects. So any breakaway group from the mainstream religion who has their own philosophy and own living religious leader are called Cults by the main stream denominations. The Church of Jesus Christ, the Scientist is though termed as Cult by the main stream denominations yet these people do not like to be called a Cult, because they consider themselves as one of the main denominations of the mainstream Christian faith. The founder of Church of Jesus Christ, the Scientist is considered Mary Baker Eddy (1821-1910). She founded the Christian Science. She was brought up in a good Christian environment. She had a great interest in Christianity and Bible study. From the childhood to adulthood she had been sick. As she was not getting healed she started looking for other means of healing. She wanted to think about those means that were other than the medicinal methods. The English methods of treatment and medicine had failed on her. After the death of her first husband she started studying about other methods for healing. She married again in 1853 so that she could keep her son from her first husband with her, whom she had left with another family because of her failing health. At the age of 41 she started getting treatment from a watch repairer Phineas P. Quimby. He was not highly educated but he treated people with Hypnotism and magnetic devices. He was of the opinion that if a person is mentally healthy then he will have good physical health. Quimby believed that the recovery of a sick person mainly depends upon his determination and his faith and his trust on the healer. Eddy (Mary Morris Baker Eddy) was student of Quimby till his death (1866). In his companionship her health improved but after Quimby's death her health deteriorated again. During snow season she slipped and got seriously injured. People thought she wouldn't survive. When she was lying in bed she read about the healing power of Jesus. She felt that healing is not acquired by the internal physical actions; rather it is achieved through mental power and from the spiritual source of God. She prayed and trusted God with all her mental strength and she got recovered very fast. For a long time she continuously kept herself aloof from the mainstream of life, during which she studied the Bible and tried to investigate that how she got cured so fast. She wanted to share her knowledge, experiences, methods and resources by which people can keep them away from sins and achieve good health. She authored her first book,

"Science and Health" and afterwards she changed its name to "Science and Health with Key to Scriptures" Till now this book has been published in 17 languages. This book is also available in Braille script for blinds, Cassettes, C.D's.and computer soft ware. People feel she stole the matter from the teacher Quimby's writings and got printed under her name.

Some people feel there is dualism between mind, spirit and matter. Quimby emphasized the supremacy of the mind matter, and was highly antagonistic towards Christianity, yet Eddy was firm believer and she opposed Quimby's philosophy. But at one point she supported Quimby's idea that for healing one should be mentally strong and determined. Finally she concluded that for healing God's involvement through human mind is very essential. Without God mental strength cannot bring healing, only God grants healing. Some people feel that she has plagiarized the writings of German American philosopher Francis Leber, but there is no proof for this. Her explanation was that her ideas are based upon the new interpretation of the biblical scriptures but not on the human ideas. She also stated that her ideas and writings are not an addition to the biblical writings. She studied the Bible from the scientific perspective. Her claim was that she had investigated those biblical facts, which Christians have believed from the very beginning and had been practicing in their everyday life.

Her book was published when there was lot of upheaval in the society. The reason for this was Darwin's Theory of evolution. Marxism, Feudalism, Industrial revolution and also because of the financial crisis the people were in a fix. Many Americans supported Mary Baker's views, but the main stream Christians opposed her ideas. People objected to the attachment of the word science with Christian faith.

Her book was published in1875. In 1877 her second husband divorced her and she married Gilbert Eddy and after her husband's name she was known as Mary Baker Eddy. Though her book published in 1875 was quite controversial, yet many Christians admired the book.

In 1879 she laid the foundation of the 'Church of Christ the Scientist'. Her supporters chose her all over in charge and leader of that Church. After that she changed the name of the Church to "First Church of Christ The

Scientist". Till the end of her life (1910) she looked after the affairs of that Church.

According to one survey the number of members of this Church in the world is about 400,000 out of which more than 100,000 live in America and others live in about 60 countries including Germany and Britain. They have 1600 congregations in America and 60 in Canada. They have opened reading rooms for the public where people can go for the Bible study and to read the books regarding the Bible literature. In 1908 she started a news paper called 'Christian Science Monitor'. The workers of this paper have bagged 6 Pulitzer awards.

Their Faith:

The Christian Scientists believe that Christian Scientists Church is one of the mainstreams Christian sects, which is based upon the works and teachings of Jesus Christ. The main aim of the Church founded by Mary Baker Eddy is to give practical shape to the teachings and works of Jesus Christ so that basic Christianity may be revived and lost element of Christian healing may also be restored. They do not have written creed like the Methodists and Presbyterians. The main points of their faith are: -

1. Christian Scientists believe that Bible is a Holy word of God. It is true and is inspired by the Holy Spirit. They believe it is a complete guide to get eternal life.

2. They believe God is omnipotent, omnipresent, omniscient and eternal. They believe Jesus Christ the only beloved Son of God and the Holy Spirit as the guide and helper of the believers and Jesus Christ is the image of God and is like Him.

3. Christian Scientists believe in the forgiveness of sins by God. They believe that God will bring an end to the sin and the evil. As long as one keeps sinning God continues to punish him. 4. Christian Scientists believe in the sacrificial death of Jesus Christ. The salvation of a man is only through Jesus Christ. 5. They believe sacrificial death of Jesus on the cross is the result of God's love for the humanity. They also believe in the love of Christ, His righteousness, His life and His power to heal the sick.

6. They believe that Jesus achieved victory over sin and death. Christian scientists believe that crucifixion of Jesus and His resurrection served to uplift faith to understand eternal life, even all-ness of soul, spirit, and the nothingness of matter.

Christian Scientists affirm by saying, "We also solemnly promise to watch, and pray for our mind to be in us which was also in Jesus Christ; to do unto others as we would have them to do unto us; and to be merciful, just and to follow God, act upon the Holy word of God is the main aim of Christian Science. God is loving, all powerful, and omnipotent father and Jesus Christ is His beloved son. Earthly life of Jesus is the proof that we who believe in Him are also His children. Life of Jesus Christ is an example and the way shower.

Healing and Medication:

If you talk to Christian Science people they will tell you that they neither take medicine on being sick nor they go to a doctor. This is true for the Christian Science people but they are not against doctors. They respect the doctors and their profession but instead of medicine or going to the doctors they spend more time in prayer, because they believe that they can get healing through prayer. They felt the effect of prayer more powerfully in their lives. The regeneration of heart and mind that brings about physical healing is a most significant element of healing. Teachings of Jesus Christ are central in the Christian Science faith. His omnipotent love is even today effective for healing in our lives. If we read the history of Christian Science, which is not very old, even then we find thousands of examples where people have been healed through faith and prayer. These healings are not based upon the blind faith but it is a proof of being one with God. How to be one with God we come to know after reading Christian Science literature. It is the result of drawing closer to God through coming to know the loving kindness of His divine laws and the perfection of His spiritual creation. Christian Scientists normally pray for themselves and find healing. If a sick person needs someone else's prayer they call another Christian Science person to pray. The one who prays for healing can be a man or woman. Such people spend more time in prayer to get the healing power through prayer. They claim that healing power is not their own rather this is blessing from God and He heals. The prayer healer who is

Christian Denominations

called a practitioner prays with patience and humility under the guidance of God's voice and directions and he does whatever God asks him to do.

What They Do:

Christian Science people read Bible every day and study about science and health. Essential part of this study is the weekly message, which is based upon Bible, science and health. For daily reading is the message, which is delivered on Sunday at the international, level. There is no ordained minister in the Church. The people who deliver message are those who study the Bible, investigate through it, and read about science and health. They study those messages that they receive from the mother Church. Where the Church services are held in English they use King James Version of the Bible. They use the other translation versions for private study of the Bible. Science and health are considered two different topics and for these, they have two different pastors.. Lay Christian Science practitioners are trained on the basis of prayer and Church rules, so that instead of medicines they may serve the public through Science and Health. Mother Church prepares all the rules so that Christian Science movement may run on in the right direction and with proper guidelines. For the proper functioning of the mother Church there is a board constituted by the 5 members. There are some basic sacraments celebrated in the Church but they have different interpretation for that. According to their interpretation baptism means the purification of thoughts and deeds. Lord's Supper is the spiritual union with God and this is celebrated with utmost respect and silently through prayer.

Controversial Things of the Church:

Like other groups and sects who break away from the mainstream religious denominations, this Church also faced considerable criticism and opposition. Some of them were those who termed this sect a 'Cult' and hence opposed this group. Some criticism came from fundamental and rigid religious denominations. Main cause of their opposition was the weird interpretation of the word of God. For this reason mainstream groups called them a 'Cult', but Christian Scientists reject this term. They claim that like other denominations, Christian Science church is also a denomination. Their church and reading rooms are open for everyone and their church service is like the other denominations.

Faith and Treatment:

For a very long time there has been a tension between Christian Science practitioners and medical doctors. Medical doctors do not believe and recognize the means and methods adopted by Christian Science for healing, yet this controversy does not go to the judicial courts like the Jehovah Witnesses. In Jehovah Witness families and churches the discussion and controversy between parents and their children takes them to the law courts. If there is some controversy between the Christian Science and the medical health department, then there is a directive from the mother Church to avoid going to the law courts and support the medical and the health department. Church always tells its members that if they have serious health problem or a complication or any disease, which can spread to others, he or she should tell the Church. They should get the shots or injections for the prevention of diseases. At the time of birth of a child they should either go the hospital or call trained and certified midwives or nurses. Church strongly feels that spiritual methods of healing are mostly effective. Some- members- feel if a church member needs the help of a medical doctor he should be free to do that and Christian Science treatment should not be binding on the member. They claim that they use the same healing methods on the patients that Jesus Christ used in His time.

After reading all about the controversial life of the founder of this denomination, faith and doctrine of this group no one will be willing to include this denomination in the main stream denominations of Christian religion. Mary Baker Eddy was actually upset and dissatisfied from the other Churches because of her failing health and she started looking for the alternative which gave rise to this denomination. As for as I can say there are healers in the mainstream denomination as well, who believe in the Father, Son and the Holy Spirit. People get healed in other denominations if someone prays with faith in the name of Jesus The Supreme Physician. Apostle James has written about it citing the example of Elijah. James 5: 13-18

Rev. Dr. Salatiel Sidhu

Notes:

13.1 Rudraksh is a special kind of necklace worn by followers of Rajneesh and Shiva. It is made of round fruits of a tree.

13.2. Radha Swami is a sect and they have a living guru, who preaches to the Radha Swami congregation. The sect has followers both from the Sikhs and the Hindu Communities. For all Radha Swamis Meat and Liquor are forbidden. Their teachings are mainly based upon Sikh and Hindu scriptures. They also quote from the Bible without any reference to the Bible.

13.3 Hanuman is the monkey god and a central figure in the great Epic 'Ramayana'. He helped Rama to rescue his wife Sita from the demon Ravana king of Lanka (now called Ceylon) and for this Rama decreed that Hanuman should also be worshiped when his followers worship him(Rama). Some people who believe in celibacy worship him for his male power and the strength. According to one myth Hanuman and his army of monkeys built the bridge of rocks connecting Kanya kumari southern tip of India to Lanka for the Rama's army to go to Lanka and fight Ravana.

13.4 Shiva is the destroyer god. In association with other gods and goddesses, he brings about floods, earthquakes, famines, and other disasters, yet the Hindus believe that as the destroyer Shiva is really a force for good, he helps bring about the end of things. He is also worshipped for his male power. Image of his male organ (Shivlinga) is worshipped in Shiva temples.

13.5 Rama a Hindu god is incarnation of Vishnu. Vishnu is believed to represent a union with Brahman and is the creator god, who took physical form to overcome evil. Vishnu passed so far through 9 incarnations and tenth is yet to come at the end of the of the world. and two of these are Rama and Krishna. The religious work Ramayana depicts the life and works of Rama. The 10 incarnations of Vishnu are:

1. Matsya (Fish/ Half man and half fish)
2. Kurma the Turtle.
3. Varaha (gigantic boar).
4. Narasimha (Half man and half lion).

5. Vamana also called dwarf Avatar the tiny Brahman.
6. Parashurama.
7. Rama.
8. Krishna
9. Buddha (some say it was Mohini avatar).
10. Kalki, yet to come. He will appear at the end of Kal Yuga (going on now) to herald the end of the world.

13.6. Kali (black) also called Durga is the favorite of Robber's caste. She is considered cruel goddess who is pictured as devouring human flesh and blood dripping from its protruding tongue. In India and Nepal (a Hindu majority state) animal sacrifices are offered to this goddess.

References:

1. "Science and Health with key to scriptures" by Mary Baker eddy Reprint 1991.
2. "Mary Baker Eddy' by Gillian Gill -Perseus Press
3. "Mary Baker Eddy- The years of Trial" by Robert Peel published by Rinehart Holt and Winston, N.Y. 1971.
4. "Christian Science" a source book of contemporary Materials. The Christian science publishing society Boston MA (1990)
5. "Dictionary of Cults, Sects, Religions and Occults by G.A. Mather & L.A. Nicholas published by Zondervan Grand Rapids 1993 Pp73-75.
6. "Our Religions and our Neighbors" Revised Edition by Milton G. Miller and Sylvan D. Schwartzman Ppl48-151.
7. Manual of Mother Church 'First church of Christ' in Boston Massachusetts by Mary Baker Eddy 1908.
8. "World Religions" Edited by Geoffrey Parrinder -Facts on file publication N.Y.

Chapter Fourteen

JEHOVAH WITNESSES

Jehovah witness is a sect not accepted and recognized by the mainstream Christian denominations. They have controversial views and beliefs, and some of these views being against the word of God. This sect came into being because of weird interpretations of the word of God and especially unacceptable beliefs about Jesus Christ. That is why it has been called a cult by the main stream denominations, but Jehovah Witnesses are not ready to accept this terminology. Jehovah Witness is the people who do not celebrate birthdays. They do not celebrate Christmas or Easter. One of their arguments is that exact dates of these important days are not known. These dates, which are fixed to celebrate these days, are not correct, especially the Easter date changes every year. These people even do not take blood whenever it is needed to save the life of a patient. The interpretation for this is that giving blood to anyone is equivalent to drinking blood, which is forbidden in the Bible. These people keep fixing dates of the end of the world. They believe paradise promised by God is a reality and one day this very earth will change into paradise. They are also called 'Millennialists'. They believe that Christ at the time of His Second Advent will return to the earth for final apocalyptic battle of Armageddon and after that His reign of one thousand years will start and then the final judgment

History of Jehovah Witnesses:

Founder of this sect was Charles Taze Russell (1852-1916). His father was a cloth merchant living in Pittsburgh Pennsylvania. In his early years, he was impressed by the ideas of William Miller the founder of Seventh Day Adventists so he joined the Seventh Day Adventist movement. William Miller predicted that Jesus would come again in1843. He reconsidered his prediction and changed the year of His Second Advent to1844. When his second prediction proved wrong he confessed his mistake and declared that this date is for Jesus' ministry in the heavenly temple. This mistake by Miller made many Adventists to leave this movement and join other denominations. Many Adventists started studying and researching through their Bibles. Among them was N.H. Barbour of Rochester New York. Both of them in 1877 published two books "Three Worlds" and "Harvest of this World". It was N.H. Barbour who wrote in this book that Christ has already come into this world in 1874. He will come again in 1914 in His glory with His angels and till his death he did not change his views. One certain Biblical issue they did not agree was this, so Charles Russell and Barbour parted their ways. Charles Russell founded Zion Watch Tower. Barbour predicted that 1,000 years reign of Christ will start in 1914. For all his work he was earning money through his Cloth merchant business. In 1884 he changed the name of his sect to "Watch Tower Bible and Tract Society" Russell wrote 7 books "The studies in the scripture". His view was that we couldn't understand the Bible just by reading it. To understand the Bible completely one has to read his books. Though Russell was not highly educated yet he wrote the books, which are base and foundation of Jehovah Witness faith. Russell was president of this sect till his death in 1914. After his death Joseph F. Rutherford took as the president. His views were quite different from the views of Russell. He made many changes in the doctrine of Jehovah Witness and interpretation of the Bible. He changed the teachings of Russell and implemented his own teachings but many members of the Watch Tower Society did not like this and these people broke away from the Watch Tower society and made their own groups. The main groups were Dawn Bible Students, and the Layman's Home Missionary Movement. In 1931 this movement's name was changed to Jehovah Witness. To bring revival in this movement Rutherford prepared young people who went door to door for preaching about this movement.

With the death of Rutherford in 1942 Nathan H. Knorr took over the reins of this movement. For spreading this movement he thought of many methods like the businessmen. He opened training schools for preachers. This movement progressed a lot, money wise and number wise because of the business tacts. Till the death of Knorr in 1977 the number of its members reached 2 millions. After this the vice president Fredrick Franz took over as the president. He was highly educated but because of misrepresentation under oath in the court trial in1954 in Scotland he was discredited on account of failing to cast a simple Bible verse (Genesis 2:4) back into Hebrew. He had prophesied that in 1975 this world would come to an end. People sold their homes and their properties and put themselves into the service of Jehovah Witness movement. When this prophecy did not come true then people got upset and there came chaos in the society. Franz had to struggle hard to keep his position in place. Many high-ups in the society had many differences with Franz. He even terminated the services of his nephew Raymond from the Board of Directors.

What do the Jehovah Witness Publish?

They do lot of work through the books, magazines, and tracts they publish. In the early years they published every month only 6,000 copies of Watch Tower Magazines in English, but now they publish more than 20 million copies in 110 languages. Their Magazine 'Awake' is published in more than 40 languages with 1060 million copies every month. The other worth reading interesting books are: -

I. Revelation. It's grand climax at hand. 2. You can live forever in paradise on earth.

3. Bible God's word or Man's. 4. Knowledge that leads to everlasting life.

They have their own Bible Translation known as, "New World Translation" The purpose of this translation is not to bring out the best translation rather it has been done according to their views and doctrines and through this they teach their members about Jehovah witness views. Through their books and the Bible their effort has been to prove that Christ is not God and His position is not equal to God. They have tried to contradict the statement in John 1:1 that 'WORD' (Jesus Christ) was God. In these translations they have cleverly used the word 'god' for 'WORD'. (Word was god).- The same they did for Philippians 2:9 and Colossians 1:16-17. In these verses they have tried to tell that Jesus was one of those who were created by God. This meant that Jesus was not from the beginning rather

He was created by God. This is something, which the Christian World is not ready to accept because He is begotten son of God.

What do they believe?

Jehovah Witness people believe that they are witnesses of God who is called only 'Jehovah'. They think that people loyal to Jehovah are His true witnesses. They quote the long list of witnesses given in Hebrews 11:1-12:1; Revelation 3:14. They say Abel, Noah, Abraham and Jesus are witnesses of God. In 1931 when they changed the name of this sect to Jehovah Witnesses, their decision was based on the verse Isaiah 43:10 where it is written that, "you are my witnesses and my servant whom I have chosen says Jehovah".

Jehovah witnesses claim to believe the Bible, but instead of believing the Bible they deny the main doctrinal points of the Bible and misinterpret the Bible according to their own views. That is why Edmond C. Gross an ex-member of the Watchtower society said, "Jehovah witness are the apostles of denial" They deny the Trinity, the oneness of God the father, Jesus Christ the Son and Holy Spirit. They even deny the heavenly dwelling and the place Hell, as declared by Jesus in John 14. They do not believe in the resurrection of Jesus on the third day. They also deny the Christ's promise that at the time of his second advent every eye will see him. They believe that salvation is not gift of God through the sacrificial death of Jesus on the cross rather salvation is through listening to the leaders of Jehovah witness and their loyalty to them and Jehovah witness faith. Jehovah witness leaders claim to be the brothers of Jesus. So your behavior and loyalty to them will determine whether you will be eligible for eternal life or just like the weeds and wild plants you will be thrown in the eternal fire.

They not only deny the trinity rather take this thing as a joke. They say that those who want to worship through God, they can't think of three headed God. They said the idea of trinity is the idea of devil. They often declare that believing in trinity means worshipping three Gods. All these ideas and views are against the views of the Bible. It is clearly written in the Bible that every person in the trinity is eternal (Psalms 93:2, Micah 5:2, Hebrews 9:14) and each one took part in the creation and inspired the prophets in writing the word of God and every person in the trinity is called God. (Psalms 100:3, John 1:3, Genesis 1:2, John 6:27, 20:28, Acts of the Apostles 5:3-4) Actually Jehovah witnesses are polytheists, they believe in two Gods who are separated from each other. One is God called Jehovah and the other Jesus Christ the god created by Jehovah, through whom whole world has been created. In Matthew 28: 19 Jesus commanded to baptize the people under the names of three persons that is father, son and the Holy Spirit. These three personalities though being three persons are one.

They deny the God Head of Jesus:

Jehovah witnesses say that Jesus was not Jehovah rather; He came into the world as an ambassador of Jehovah and revealed all the characteristics of Jehovah. Bible tells that Jesus is the incarnation of God, which is evident from the works, and personality of Christ. (Romans 10:9-10, John 8:58, 20-28, Hebrews 1:8, Matthew 1:23, Colossians 2:9)

Holy scriptures tell that, whole creation came into being through Jesus Christ (John 1:3, Colossians 1: 16-17) Isaiah declares the whole creation came into being through Jehovah (Isaiah 44; 24). This clearly shows that Jesus and Jehovah are one.

They deny the resurrection of Jesus:

St. Paul writes, "if there is no resurrection of the dead then Christ has not been raised and if the Christ has not been raised then our proclamation has been in vain and your faith has been in vain"

(1 Cor 15:13-14). Jehovah witnesses claim that Jesus did not rise from the dead physically, rather he rose from the dead spiritually. Their uncertain view is that either his body changed into gases or Jehovah carried his body miraculously to heaven. Christ who will reign this world was physically hanged on the cross, but he was raised spiritually which cannot be seen with these human eyes. The Christ that was seen by the disciples could both change into spirit and physical body. This kind of views is held even by the non-Christian faiths that claim that their religious leaders are alive spiritually. They did not rise from the graves yet; their souls were alive even after the cremation. Then according to St. Paul, "If Christ has not

been raised, your faith is futile and you are still in your sins" Jesus himself declared before his death that he would rise again physically after his sacrificial death (John 2:19-21). The same thing he said to the Jews that he will rise again on the third day. In support of this he showed to Thomas nail marks of his hands and his side, which was pierced with the spear and Thomas, touched those nail marks and put his hand on the pierced side and believed. Jesus said to Thomas "Spirit does not have bone and flesh" and he ate before them.

Jehovah witnesses deny the visible return of Jesus:

Jehovah witnesses claim that at the time of Second Advent of Jesus, human eyes will not see him physically because he will not return to his earth bodily. Keeping this in view they have already declared that Christ has already returned to this earth in 1874 and then they changed this date to 1914 and his reign has already begun. This change of dates is only feasible on his spiritual return. Christ clearly told that people would claim and say that I am Christ or Christ is at that place. Christ told that every eye would see Him on His return, and His return will not be in secret (Matthew 24:23-27).

Jehovah witnesses deny the immortality of soul:

Jehovah witnesses believe that soul only lives in the physical body. When physical body is finished soul also dies. For this reason human death is not different from the other animal's death. This view of Jehovah witness does not agree with the Biblical teachings because St. Paul says "that a believer will live with His savior Jesus Christ after his death" and same thing Jesus told his disciples in John 14 (Philippians 1:21-24, 2 Car 5:6-10) Jehovah witness also believe that Christ was created as Archangel Michael and the same angel appeared as Christ in the physical body. When Christ rose again spiritually the physical existence of Christ was finished and that of Archangel Michael too. Jehovah called back the spirit of Christ into Heaven, so Christ and Archangel Michael are the same.

There is no Hell:

According to Jehovah witnesses' faith there is no hell or place of torture where sinners are punished. Jesus said, "Hell or Gehena is a place prepared for the Satan, his angels and his people" (Matthew 25:41). So it is clear that Hell is a place where Satan and his followers will be punished (Matthew 13:42, 25:46, 26:24)

Number of People going to Heaven:

Jehovah witnesses believe that only one hundred forty four thousand will go to heaven. This claim is based on Revelation 7:4. They claim that number of people going to heaven is more than this but out of Jehovah witnesses one hundred forty four thousand people will stay with the Jehovah and for the remaining number this earth will be changed into paradise. So these people will live away from Jehovah on the earth but these views are against what is written in the Bible. Jesus has promised every believer to keep him in His fathers' house (John 14:2-3, 1 Thess. 4:13-18, Luke 23:39-43, 2 Cor 5:8). As already has been stated that during major surgery or whenever any patient needs any blood they do not take blood. They say that Jehovah has told not to take other peoples blood (Genesis 9:4). Jews were commanded not to eat the blood with the flesh because every living being life is in the blood. Because of this rigid faith, many Jehovah witnesses have lost their lives.

They do not celebrate Christmas on the plea that no one knows the correct date of the birth of Jesus. They do not celebrate Easter because according to their belief Jesus did not die on the cross where there is painful death. They do not celebrate holidays and birthdays. According to them celebrating ones birthday is like worshipping him. They do not recognize the human government and saluting the national flag is like idol worship.

Misinterpretation of the word of God:

Whenever they misinterpret the word of God they support it by saying that this interpretation is from Jehovah. In Matthew 24:44-47 it is written, "Therefore you also must be ready, for the son of man is coming at an hour you do not expect. Who then is faithful and wise servant, whose master made him ruler over his household, to give them food in due season? Blessed is the servant whom his master, when he comes will find him at work. Assuredly I say to you that he will make him ruler over all his goods" Jehovah witnesses claim that the faithful servant is Watchtower Society, which gives spiritual food to the believers on time. Charles Russell claimed that all workers of the Watchtower Society including Rutherford are the right servants of Jehovah, but wife of Charles Russell objected to this statement and said Christ talked about one servant so that servant is only Charles Russell. For ten years after his death Charles Russell, was only considered the servant but after this the statement was changed and Watchtower Society was considered the servant as a whole. They also declared that if anyone praises Charles Russell as Jehovah's servant then this is equal to human worship, which Jehovah hates. In doing all this they sin because if leaving aside Charles they consider the whole society as the servant of Jehovah then they disrespect Charles Russell, who is considered as the prophet and the servant of Jehovah. If they consider Charles as the prophet and the servant of Jehovah even then they sin because in that way they do human worship. In spite of all these irrelevant beliefs and misinterpretations of the word of God they do not like to be called a Cult and point fingers to the other denominations. If you see their budgets and their flourishing works then it seems that financially they are sound and so the publishing of magazines and books is in full swing. Not only in English but also in most of the other languages this literature is published.

Jehovah witnesses do not participate in the political matters of the country; rather they pay more attention towards the activities of the society. They give top priority to Bible study and whole family is supposed to participate in it. The main aim of this Bible study is to know the commandments of the society to spend life with honesty and integrity in character and dealing with other people and as a family and individually spend righteous life. As far as possible they do not marry outside the Jehovah witness's community. In the world wherever there is epidemic, earthquake and Tsunami or floods. They reach there and help the victims. In 1994 when there was civil war in Rwanda, they did lot of good Samaritans works among the refugees. They established field hospitals, sent clothes, blankets, food, and Bible related literature and helped more than seven thousand people. Though they do not recognize human governments yet they respect government officials. In the whole world they have about eighty five thousand congregations. The place where they worship is called kingdom hall. Their elders both men and women go from house to house and distribute Bible Tracts and share their views and doctrine with the people. They give their literature free of cost. The expense for printing books and magazines is met through the donations of the people. They do not take offerings or tithes.

According to the recent survey their number is more than six million and their work is in 232 countries and has about eighty six thousand groups. In America their number is about 1.55M and has 11,000 congregations.

After going through the faith and doctrine of Jehovah witnesses we conclude, how the misinterpretation of the word of God has given rise to the split in the Seventh Day Adventist movement and creation of new denomination which mainstream Christians call a Cult the Jehovah Witness. In spite of all the criticism and opposition from the mainstream Christians they have held to their faith and trying to enhance their faith and people are coming into their fold.

References:

1. Guide to Religions and Cults by Ronald En roth
2. "Who are Jehovah Witnesses" by Milton G Henschel PP95-102
3. "Religion s in America" by Leo Rosten
4. Encyclopedia of Religion and Religions by E Royston Pike
5. The oriental cults in Roman Britain 1965 by E Harris and J.R.
6. Our Religions and our neighbors 1971 by Milton G Miller an d Sylvan D Schwartzman
7. "The Bible God's word or of Man's" Watchtower Bi ble and Tract Society.

Chapter Fifteen

Unification Church

(Moonies)

History

Today Unification Church is the Church of followers of Sun-Ming Moon. The followers were initially called Moonies. Sun-Ming Moon was born in a small village in North Korea on January 6, 1920. He was sent to Seoul for his high school education. There he started attending a Pentecostal Church, which had great impact on his life. According to him on Easter of 1936 he was sitting on top of a hill when Jesus Christ appeared before him and he was told, "You have been chosen to complete the work which I had started"

In Pyong Yang a Secret Church was operating. One of the members of that Church had Prophesied that soon a Korean Christ will appear. So for Sun-Ming Moon there could not have been a better opportunity to declare himself as a prophesied Korean Messiah and prove him just that. During the Second World War Sun-Ming Moon was studying Electrical Engineering in Tokyo's Waseda University. It is not clear whether he completed this degree or not. In 1944 he went back to North Korea and gathered some people who would follow him. In 1946 he came back to South Korea where he met Paik Moon Kim. Before Sun-Ming Moon could do anything Paik Moon Kim declared himself the promised Korean Messiah. He established a monastery under the name of Israel. Moon lived in this monastery for 6 months and then went back to Pyong Yang and founded "Broad Sea Church" where he started preaching his own principles which he had formulated while being in the monastery. He also then changed his birth name Yong Myung Moon to Sun-Ming Moon (15.1)

Anti Christian:

Because-of communist government in1946-50 he was sent to jail twice where he was tortured. In his book, "The heart of our father" his sufferings under the communist government have been compared to the sufferings of Christ. According to one story when conflict was going on between North and South Korea where he was preaching he got arrested. He was beaten and tortured at the police station. Because of internal and external injuries he had lost a lot of blood and fainted. He being taken as dead was thrown out of the police station. His followers who were waiting for him outside also took him as dead and took him for burial. As they were taking him for burial they realized there was still life in him. They took him to the secret place and provided the necessary medical aid. He got cured after a couple of days and started preaching again.

Some people say his arrest was not because of his preaching but because of adultery and bigamy. About his life people have conflicting views. According to one view in June of 1950 when United Nations bombed North Korea many prisoners escaped communist jails and Moon escaped with them. According to another view United Nations officials freed them. After being freed he sped to South Korea with his followers and started working as a laborer at Pusan Harbor. During 1950- 54 he with his companion Hye Won Yoo, started teaching and preaching his new principles of his religion. Yoo invented an air gun that brought prosperity to Moon and he got lot of money for his sect.

In 1954 Moon established a Church in Seoul under the name "The Holy Spirit Association for the Unification of World Christianity" Later on, it was called the Unification Church. In 1954 his wife left him because Moon criticized her by saying that "she does not understand my mission" On July 4, 1955 he was arrested again and put in jail along with some of his followers. Initial charges against him were cheating but later on he was charged for adultery and promiscuity. His followers were mainly men that had deserted their wives. After being released from jail in 1960, he got married again. His wife's name was Hak Ja Han. Both of them named their marriage as "Marriage of the lamb". They called Moon the father and his wife the mother of the world. Moon declared that November 21 is a complete and lucky day. He also declared that from 1960 onward during the coming 21 years his wife will give birth to 12 children. These 12 children will be like the 12 Disciples of Christ and 12 gates of heaven. This way his prediction was fulfilled. He also went on to declare that every child of his is sinless and righteous. So these 12 children and their parents are the symbols of Unity in the Church.

For bringing Unity in the Church Moon visited United States in December 1971. In January of 1972 while delivering his first message in New York he asked all Americans to leave all their denominations and get unified. Set your relations right with Christ and get yourself and your community ready for His Heavenly Kingdom. Moon had also declared that in 1981 Christ heavenly reign will begin on this earth and Moon will reign as the Prince of Second Advent in place of Christ. So neither the heavenly kingdom began in 1981 nor world recognized him as the Christ of heavenly kingdom. Then he changed his statement and declared that this will happen in 2001. This delay is because world is not ready for the heavenly kingdom. Even in 2001 has come and gone and evil is still on the rise. Violence and wars are still rising yet kingdom of heaven has not come. He was fully hopeful that Kingdom of Heaven will begin in 1981 and he will celebrate the marriages of 10,000 couples on this day. He was also expecting that whole America would get unified in faith till 1981. While in America many people followed him and his mission amassed lot of wealth. With this money he established a seminary in New York, established diplomatic National bank, erected New York Hotel, started Washington Times daily Newspaper and also many other businesses and industries. In July of 1982 he was imprisoned for 18 months and was fined 25,000 US Dollars for cheating and stealing income tax.

Faith of Unification Church:

More than the Bible the faith of Unification Church is based upon the book "Divine Principles" authored by Moon. The followers of Unification Church believe that principles written in the "Divine Principles" is the divine manifestations, which were revealed to Moon on the fulfillment of time. God sent His servant Moon at the right time so that he may answer the basic questions to his disciples regarding this life. This book serves two purposes. One, to keep the Moonies tied together in one thought and gives right guidelines regarding their faith. Secondly, to contradict and prove wrong the faith and thoughts held by the people from other denominations regarding the New Testament. In this book it is written that the Bible is not a complete book for the believers therefore it is essential that there should be new revelations and new interpretations to understand the Bible. Bible itself is not the truth but it tells about the truth.

This book is divided into three parts i) First Adam ii) Second Adam Christ iii) Third Adam who will appear at the time of the Second Advent. First Adam and Eve were creation of God that fell into sin. Second Adam was Christ who was crucified and killed by Jews. Messiah of the Second Advent is the one who will establish his kingdom on this earth. These three Adam's will fulfill the purpose of God, which He had for this universe.

First Adam:

According to the book "Divine Principles" God was present as a male personality before the creation of the world, yet at the time of creation he acquired double personality that is both male and female that is the father and mother. Due to this double personality He created Adam and Eve as innocent creatures that is as brother and sister. He filled His love in their hearts for each. They lacked the level of maturity at that time. God wanted them to grow spiritually and become mature before they live as husband and wife. But because of their sin, God's plan for them was disrupted. No one till today was able to understand this story rather they thought Adam and Eve really ate the forbidden fruit and broke God's commandment. According to their book, the tree of fruit of eternal life is the Adam and tree of knowledge is Eve. According to this book when Lucifer saw God's love for Adam he felt jealous. When Lucifer saw Eve he felt she was a beautiful woman and felt desire for her, so he established illicit relations with her. When Lucifer had intercourse with Eve, her eyes opened and she realized that she had done something wrong. She realized that her real husband was Adam. When Adam came to know, she enticed him to have sex with her.

Adam did not know that having sex is sin and that Eve already had intercourse with Lucifer. So this was the fruit, which God had forbidden them not to eat. So this sexual misconduct was the cause of their downfall. By committing this sin they lost the spiritual and physical companionship of God. Before this sin they were naked and were not ashamed of one another but after committing this sin they realized they were naked and started feeling embarrassed and ashamed. So they covered the same body parts with which they had committed sin. This book goes further and says that out of the sexual relationship between the Satan and Eve, Cain was born who is a symbol of Satan and human relations. Out of this relationship between Satan and human beings communism came into being. Out of the relationship between Adam and Eve, Abel was born who is a relationship between God and human beings. Democracy is the outcome of relations between God and humans. This way Communism is from Satan and Democracy is a gift of God. After the downfall of Adam and Eve in the Garden of Eden, God has been trying to restore the same position of Adam and Eve, which they had with Him. Noah, Abraham, Solomon, David and other persons being imperfect, God could not succeed in His plan. Then He sent His Prophets and at the end he sent Jesus Christ who was faithful to God.

Second Adam:

According to The book "Divine Principles" many Prophets came before Jesus Christ to prepare the way for Him. For other nations Gautam Buddha and Confucius came to prepare the Asians to receive Jesus Christ. Socrates came to prepare the Europeans for the same purpose. The mission and purpose of all these runners was to prepare this world to receive Christ and bring them together under the name of Christ. But due to Crucifixion of Jesus this plan also failed. Moon also said that John the Baptist was responsible for Crucifixion of Jesus. John the Baptist created doubts in the hearts of Jews about Jesus and because of this Jews did not accept Jesus as the Messiah and their Savior and King. Moonies do not say that Christ committed anything wrong or that He was not faithful to God, but that Christ made a mistake in understanding Jews. Christ did not have any other way out or the option, so He decided to lay down His life for His followers and His believers so that the sinners may be saved from their sins.

If Christ had not been crucified he could have found a suitable companion for Him and married. Then through His family he could have established that Kingdom of Heaven in this world and also could have accomplished Physical and Spiritual salvation of human beings. Satan attacked His physical body and killed Him. According to Moonies a man may have close relationship with God but he cannot accomplish the task of physical and spiritual salvation of humanity. According to that book Christ's resurrection on the third day was spiritual. Whenever He appeared in front of the disciples that spirit could take a physical form as well. This way time and death did not have any effect on him. So when he appeared to His disciples and appeared before 500 people it was his spiritual appearance. This baseless and concocted story of this sect certainly hurts the beliefs of Biblical Christians and those who consider Christ as their savior and Son of God but the Bible opposes such remarks and writings and imaginary stories. Likewise when God speaks in the Bible, he does not mean the three personalities but He speaks alone and he speaks as above the angels and the whole creation. In John 1:1-3 whatever is mentioned that means He took part in the creation of this world and He is like one of them who being perfect human being helps in the growth of humanity. Moonies believe the word of God and His principles are the principles of creation of man and woman. Where he is faithful and loving father there he is loving mother too, so that he may give new birth to humankind fallen in sin. So that He makes His children the children of righteousness and goodness, and that mother is The Holy Spirit. So divine personality of Christ is limited to His perfection. So He can be called a god but not God While on this earth he was an ordinary sinless person. Christ delivered human beings spiritually but he could not redeem them physically because Jews killed Him. So therefore coming of the Lord and Messiah of the Second Advent is essential, so that He may accomplish the unfinished work of Christ, which is God's plan.

Lord and Messiah of the Second Advent:

This sect believes that to make any human being spiritually perfect, the person should be Utmost Perfect on this earth. There is no difference between a Christian and an Old Testament saint, however strong believer he may be, because none of these could get rid of old sin and the Satan. Therefore it was essential that the Lord and Messiah of the Second Advent may be born on this earth and may accomplish the unfinished work of Physical Salvation of human beings. According to their calculations Abraham was born 2000 years before Christ, and therefore second Adam will come 2000 years after Christ. For this reason they changed the year of Second Advent of Christ from 1981 to 2001, even that statement did not come true. They also predicted that the Messiah of Second Advent of Christ would be born in Korea, Japan or China. They clarified that because Japanese worshipped another deity called Ama Somi Kami, so Christ cannot take birth in that country. China being communist country is following Satan, so Christ cannot take birth in that country either. So it is evident that Christ will be born in Korea and that Messiah could be Sun Ming Moon. Declaration regarding Lord and Messiah of the Second Advent will neither be made by Sun-Ming Moon not by his followers rather people will understand by themselves and acknowledge Moon as their Messiah. Those who do not accept and acknowledge and will not follow his teachings, God will punish them and people by themselves decide that who is the Lord and Messiah of the Second Advent. Because of Christ's death people could not accept Him as the Messiah, but under the name of Lord and Messiah of Second Advent all religions will be unified and Moon will be their Messiah and the Lord. Moon also warned that Christian Priests and Jew Rabbis who will be present in the day of the Second Advent of the Lord and Messiah would torture him. Those Christians who think they are on the road to heaven are actually running on the road that ends in hell.

More Emphasis on family life and Worldly Matters:

Though Jesus and St. Paul did not lay more emphasis on married life yet they emphasized that as far as possible that those who want to serve the Lord should keep away from the woman. Because the people leading family life get more involved in their family responsibilities and cannot serve their Lord whole heartedly. Married person remains entangled in responsibilities and tries to make happy his wife and family, but unmarried person who is in the service of the Lord tries to please his Lord only. I personally feel Moon the leader of Moonies sect has not only insulted Jesus by calling Him an imperfect man rather he has challenged God and contradicted the Holy Word of God. When Jesus got baptized in river Jordan and he came up from the water The Holy Spirit descended upon Him and voice of God came from heaven, "You are my beloved Son, in you I am well pleased" The same voice was heard when He was on the mountain with his three disciples. If He was not a perfect man and He was imperfect ordinary person then this Voice of God from heaven cannot be for Him, because every human being born of man and woman is not perfect. Secondly purpose of First Advent of Jesus was not producing children and increasing population of this world as Sun-Ming Moon has produced 14 children and out of them 2 died.

Begetting children is not difficult task; those who have no contribution in the salvation of human beings and sinners are producing children. This world needed a savior who could salvage the sinners drowning in the ocean of sin, who could pay the price of their sins and redeem them to get them back to heaven to live with their God. So Christ happily chose to face the insulting death of torture, disgrace and accomplished the work of salvation that nobody could do. By involving in Voluptuousness with women and keeping many wives for enjoyment, one cannot accomplish the work of salvation. Those who run after wealth and have billions of dollars in cash and kind cannot be the redeemers of this world Jesus said, "The Son of man (Jesus) does not have place to lay His head" The people who live in royal palaces and are pleasure seekers, from their mouth words of salvation do not sound good. Jesus along with His twelve disciples walked on the dusty roads of Palestine for three and a half years with a shoulder bag and dirty slippers and preached the word of God and message of salvation. He told the people to walk on the path that leads to kingdom of heaven. Guru Nanak Dev, founder of Sikhism left the comforts of his home to preach about One God. He traveled all over India and also carried message of one God to Sri Lanka, Burma, Mecca, Medina, Turkey, Saudi Arabia, Baghdad, Kabul, Kandhar and Siame. Some scholars feel that Guru Nanak Dev also visited Israel along with his companions Bala and Mardana. Did they have millions or billions of dollars and enjoyed the pleasures of this world and had royal palaces to live in and enjoy? Moonies are married in groups of thousands as in India Naamdhari Sikhs do. On these weddings Moon and his wife bless the married couples and then all drink the sacred wine, which they compare with the Lord's Supper. This way old sins of married couples are washed away. On November 29, 1997 about 39.6 million married couples all over the world and 28000 couples in Washington DC celebrated the anniversary of their marriage. This celebration was heard on radio and watched on television all over the world. This sect has started many welfare social and religious programs.

Before coming to America their number was very small. In 1976 their number in America was about 6000. People did not like the preaching and principles of this Church so they started leaving this sect and their numbers started dwindling. To appease the people they started many social welfare programs because of which people got impressed and their number started rising again. In 1998 their number in America rose to 50,000 and 3 million worldwide. According to one survey 70 million married couples have received blessings of Moon and his wife and they all drank the sacred wine. Because of the anti biblical doctrine and principles of Moonies mainstream Christian Denominations called them a cult. Misinterpretations of the Bible verses and Christ's teaching, and criticism of Christ's personality and Moon calling himself Lord and Messiah of the second Advent is being opposed by the biblical Christians. These things are contradictory to the Bible teachings. For all those who claim to be Christ or Messiah's of the Second Advent Christ had already warned 2000 years before, "then if someone says to you look, here is the Christ or there do not believe it. For false Christs and false prophets will rise and show great signs and wonders to deceive, if possible even elect. See, I have told you before hand... For as the lightening comes from East and flashes to the West so also will the coming of The Son of Man be" (Matt 24:23-28), "Many will come in my name saying, I am the Christ and will deceive many.... but you do not go after them"(Matt 24:4-11)

Mainline denominations that have fundamental beliefs in the biblical truths have concluded that Unification Church is satanically inspired sect in an effort to mislead the faithful Christians who are trying to unite under the banner of Christianity. 'The writers of 'The Great American Cult Scare' David G. Bromeley and Anson D. Shupe have quoted Jerry I. Yamamoto from his book "The Puppet Masters":

"Moon may have a strong hold on his followers, but the strings do not begin with him. Moon himself is more deceived than those whom he deceives. Moon is not the puppet master. Moon is the master puppet. Satan is the puppet master" After reading all about the principles, doctrines and life of founder we conclude that this sect's foundation is mainly laid on the imaginary concocted and baseless explanations of the word of God which contradicts the biblical faith and the truth. This is one sect but there are many more like this so called Christian and Non-Christian sects who have misinterpreted the Bible for their own personal interests and gains and are misleading the people away from the path that leads to God and His Heavenly Kingdom. Such misunderstanding and misinterpretations of the word of God has given rise to denominations that do not deserve to be called Christians but a cult.

Notes:

15.1. Yong Myung Moon.
Yong means "dragon"
Myung means "shining"

Moon is a common surname in Korea, which means, "letter" So Yong Myung Moon means a Shining Proper Letter.

References:

1. "What is a Unitarian" by Karl M. Chworowsky PP. 185-194
2. Our religions and our neighbors by Milton G. Miller and Sylvan D. Schwartzman PP. 132-136
3. "A guide to Cults and New Religions" by Ronald Enroth PP. 151-172 essay by J. Isamu Yamamoto
4. "The Early Years "Refuge books UK 1997 by M. Breen
5. "The Making of Moonies" Basil Blackwell Oxford Press 1984 - by Eileen Barker
6. "Moonies in America-Sage Publications 1979 by David G. Bromley and AD Shupe
7. Encyclopedia Handbook of Cults in America - Garland Publication in NY 1986 by Gordon Melton.
8. Strange Gods by David G. Bromeley and Anson D. Shupe Jr. Beacon Press Boston

Chapter Sixteen

Church of Jesus Christ of Latter Day Saints

(Mormons)

Church History

According to the definition of 'Cult' and by the main stream Christian denominations this sect has been termed as a Cult. No sect like this one is ready to accept the name 'Cult' for his or her group, because they claim to be one of the main denominations. These sects blame and criticize other religious groups and claim that they are right. The founder of this sect was Joseph Smith Jr. When people were migrating to America from England, Scotland Germany, France and Spain, ancestors of Joseph Smith also came with English and Scottish migrants. At that time colonies were being established in North Eastern parts of America. Country was wide open and Native Americans were simple and backward, so it was golden opportunity for the migrants to settle. Here they could live freely and happily. His father Joseph Smith Sr. and mother Lucy Mack Smith came to a place in 1816 with their 8 children and settled at Pal Myra near New York. In 1776, his ancestors took part in the freedom struggle under the leadership of George Washington. This family was very religious God fearing and lived life according to the Bible, but they were not members of any church. That was the time when most of the Christians were not members of any Church, because Churches were not organized yet. On the other side different groups were trying to lure Christians to join their denominations and were trying to convert people into Christianity from other religions. The whole priest community was busy and zealous in this work. People were free to join any church of their choice during those times. This movement was in full swing from Kentucky to New England. In 1820 this movement reached New York and there was news in Rochester paper that in Palmyra, Massadon, Manchester, Lyons and Ontario 200 people accepted Christianity. Under this movement Lucy Mack and her three children became members of the Presbyterian Church. Joseph Smith Jr. was 14 years old at that time. Joseph Smith thought about all those priests who were one in converting people but had different views on membership of the church. Every priest wanted that the converts would join his church. Seeing this he got confused that where should he go and which church should he join. He could not decide which church was wrong and which one was following the right path. He concluded that all churches couldn't be right. To decide this he turned to the Bible and in James 1:5 he read "If any of you lacks wisdom, let him ask of God, who gives all liberally and without reproach, and it will be given to him" Joseph Smith believed these words, so he decided not to join any church but he will seek guidance of God. He said he will ask God for wisdom and understanding and he will definitely give me wisdom to decide that what should he do. They had a family farm close to New York, a part of which was thick forest, so to seek guidance from God he went to the forest. It was a clear and beautiful day of spring in 1820. According to Smith it was his first day in life when he prayed alone to God in loud words. On his knees he put his question before God. While praying thick darkness surrounded him and he felt as if his death is very near. Then all of a sudden he saw a Pillar of light, which came and rested on his head. It was brighter than the sun. When that pillar of light rested on his head he saw two people. Their glory was beyond apprehension and explanation. They were in the air and one of them pointing to the other said, "He is my beloved son, listen to him." Controlling myself, I asked the person with bright dress which church should I join?" He answered me and said, "You shall not join any church". He further said, "these are the people who claim with their lips to be my people and teach my commandments to them but they do not obey my commandments and accept their power"

When he told this whole story to the priest, the priest responded that it was all devils work. After Christ and his disciples there are no more visions and also at such a tender age this vision is not possible. So, he was left alone, rather people laughed at him. Nobody paid any attention to his vision and he became disappointed and sad. Joseph Smith claimed that his vision was like the one Saul saw when he was going to Damascus. Rather Agrippa did not believe him after listening to the whole vision story. Some people laughed at him and some called him mad even though that was a real story. The same thing happened in my case even though I saw two heavenly persons and even talked to them. While narrating my vision story people made fun of me. How could I deny what I saw in the vision? Joseph Smith was happy that God showed him the way and that he talked to Him and was told the truth.

Angel and the Book of Mormons:

After this vision Joseph Smith was at peace and was happy that God talked to him and showed him the right path. Even then people were making fun of him and called him a daydreamer, son of a farmer, yet he continued working at his father's farm. According to Joseph Smith he was a weak young man. He made a lot of mistakes in his youth and he lived in fear that God may reject him. He was always aware of his mistakes. According to Smith, "As I was preparing to sleep on September 21, 1823 at night, I knelt down before God and confessed all my sins and mistakes and asked God for His forgiveness. I beseeched God "Lord forgive sins of my youth. Grant me your knowledge and guide me to the right path" As I was praying brightness in my room started increasing and my room was lit up like a bright noon day and in that bright light a person with glorified face was standing in the air near my head. His feet were not touching the ground and he was wearing a bright shining robe. His clothes were so clean and white that no one can wash and make it that white. His head, hands and feet were bare. His face was full of glory and his eyes were shining. When I saw him I at once got perplexed, but soon my fear went away. He addressed me by my name and said "My name is Moroni, and I have come with the message from the presence of God" He said to me "God has entrusted me with a job and that His name will be preached throughout all the nations" He told me that a book written on gold plates is buried at one place. There is a mention of all those people who lived in America and from where they came with those plates are Urim and Thumim, the precious stones. After that he narrated certain things from the Old

Testament and told me certain prophecies. He warned me that after the recovery of those gold plates, the breastplate, Urim and Thumim do not show to anyone otherwise you are sure to die. In the vision he showed me the place where the Plates were buried. After that the heavenly body disappeared into heaven and all the light went away with him and my room once again was totally dark. As I was still pondering over these things the same person appeared again and the angel left for heaven. I was still in a fix and thinking about these visions, the same person appeared again the third time and warned me about my family circumstances. He warned me that if my family came to know about these gold plates, they might like to take those plates and sell them for money, so I had to be very careful. Third time again he disappeared into heaven. After the daybreak I went with my father to work in the farm and told him about these happenings. He told me all this is from God. After that I went to the site where the plates were buried as told in my vision.

Getting the Plates:

Joseph Smith and his family were living in Palmyra New York and the hillside where the plates were buried was about 4 miles from their place. Angel Moroni had shown everything to Joseph Smith so he straightaway proceeded to that place. As he tried to remove the rock to get the gold plates he felt a sever shock like an electrical shock. Second time again he felt the same shock and so it happened three times. As he lifted up his head he saw the same Angel Moroni. He told Joseph that by telling his father he had broken God's commandment, so now you cannot get these plates, you will have to wait for 4 more years. You come every year this day and I will keep telling you directions. So Joseph Smith did likewise. He kept visiting the Comorah Hills every year and Angel Moronie kept meeting him there. Finally on Sept 22, 1827 the day came when Joseph Smith was to get those plates and he did, but the Angel warned him that no one else should see these plates and he will not hand over the plates to anyone. After receiving those plates Joseph Smith kept hiding those plates from people from place to place. Before receiving the plates he married Emma Hale from Harmony, Pennsylvania. When his father-in-law came to know about the vexation of Joseph Smith, he called him to Harmony, Pennsylvania. After reaching there he copied the writings from the plate on to a paper and then started translation work. He used Urim and Thumim for translation work. He did not know certain words so he approached Martin Harris and Prof. Charles Anthon. They supported the translation done by Joseph and for translation to be correct they certified in writing. When Joseph Smith was about to leave with his certificate, Prof. Anthon called him back and asked him to return the certificate.

Prof. Anthon asked him to tell about the translation and the gold plates. Prof. Anthon asked him to show the plates. Joseph Smith expressed his inability to show the plates. Hearing negative answer Prof. Anthon tore the certificate into pieces and said that this is concocted and impossible story. Later on Martin Harris helped Joseph Smith translating those parts, which were beyond Joseph Smith's understanding.

Martin Harris's wife asked her husband to bring those translated papers, because she wants to see these papers. When he approached Joseph Smith requesting for those papers, Smith declined his request, but on Martin's insistence smith gave him the papers. After a couple of days it was found that the whole translation work was stolen. Joseph Smith realized his mistake and repented but nothing could be done at that time.

On April 6, 1829, his friend Oliver Cowdrey came to meet him and he asked Joseph Smith about the story of gold plates. Joseph Smith related to him the whole story. The left over part of the translation that he had read to Oliver Cowdrey, Oliver Cowdrey said this story is all about the people who left Jerusalem 600 years before Jesus and came here to settle. God has inspired Lehi, telling him that devastation of Jerusalem is very near, so those people fled Israel and came to America by ships and boats. When they reached here people got divided into two groups Nephites and Lamanites. Nephites were God fearing people but Lamanites were wicked and quarrelsome community. They had preserved that background history, which had mention of all their Prophets, priests and Mosaic Law.

Because of Nephites Israelites background and their hope in the coming of Christ, Jesus did not forget them. After his resurrection, on the third day Jesus came to America and met these people and preached to them the good news. Jesus fulfilled his words which He had spoken in the gospel of John 10:16, "and other sheep I have which are not of this fold; them also I must bring and they will hear my voice and there will be one flock and one shepherd" Christ told them that "I will establish for you a Church in America" and told them all the principles of that church.

After this these people followed these principles for a long time but as the time passed they forgot these things and they got away from God. Among them was one person by the name of Mormon. He kept a record of all these things with him. He inscribed these things on the gold plates and handed over to his son Moroni. When he saw the devastation of Nephites at the hands of Lamanites he buried those plates by the side of Comorah Hills. After his death he as an angel kept coming back to tell the secret of these gold plates. These plates were given to Joseph Smith after 14 centuries. Descendants of lamanites can be seen today among American Indians.

Baptism of Joseph Smith and Oliver Cowdrey:

Joseph Smith and Oliver Cowdrey took a pledge to advance the Mormon movement. In this movement Joseph Smith was known as the prophet and Oliver Cowdrey as the assistant. They read about baptism in the old records. Joseph Smith was not baptized so far, because he was not a member of any church, likewise Oliver Cowdrey did not know whether he was baptized or not.

So both of them went to Susquehanna River in solitude. This happened on May 15, 1829. As they were praying in the thick grove of trees by the riverside, to them appeared a person with shining and glorified face and he told them his name as John, the Baptist.

That heavenly person told them that "I have come under the authority which has been given to Christ's disciples Peter, James and John" They hold the keys of priesthood. It is the same priesthood, which was given to Aaron's family by Jehovah. He laid his both hands on their heads and said "I hand over the same responsibility to you, so that you may preach the good news of repentance and baptize people by immersion for the forgiveness of sins." He asked them to baptize one another by immersion. After the heavenly person left the place Joseph Smith baptized Oliver Cowdrey and then Oliver baptized Joseph Smith. After that Peter, James and John appeared to them and gave the responsibility of priesthood to them.

Translation and Witness:

Translation work was finished in June of 1829. Then he read that in the original script it is mentioned that this translation will be deemed correct if three persons appointed by Jehovah God read this translation and certify by signatures with the certificate that this is really the word of God and this translation has been under his commandment, wisdom and guidance. Those who directly or indirectly contributed to this translation were Martin Harris, Oliver Cowdrey and David Whitmar. Joseph Smith requested them to be a witness to this translation.

So all four of them in the summer of 1829 went to a forest near the home of David Whitmar. To know the will of God they prayed to God one after the other, but they did not get any answers. They prayed over and over and still got no answer. Martin Harris told them that his presence is an obstacle in getting the answer to their prayers, so leaving them he went to a spot away from them. Then the other three started praying again and they saw even at noon there was a bright light around them. In that dazzling light there stood a heavenly body in the air holding the plates. He is turning those plates like leaves of any book. He told that these plates are from God. The translation that you have done is correct. I allow you to certify this translation to be correct by putting your signatures. After this Joseph Smith went to find Martin Harris and to his surprise he found Martin Harris on his knees and praying. Joseph brought him back to join them. Then four of them prayed again and saw that heavenly being again with gold plates in his hands and he repeated his words. After this vision three of them wrote a statement of 300 words and certified the translation with their signatures. After about 3 days eight more people saw those plates and certified this translation to be correct. In 1830 the owner of a printing press printed 5000 copies of this book for $3000. At that time and even now, this book is called the book of Mormons. So far 3913 changes have been made in this book.

On April 6, 1830 there were six young people gathered in David Whitmer's house and foundation of the Church was laid on that day. The same day Joseph smith saw a vision when he was appointed the Mormon prophet and apostle of Christ. Since that day Joseph Smith is known as the first prophet of Mormons. At that time Church was known as "Church of Jesus Christ" and later on the words "Latter Day Saints "were added.

Book of Mormons and the Bible scholars:

Before his death Joseph had said, "Hey brothers the book of Mormons on this earth is the right and true book and this is the foundation of our religion. Anyone who reads and acts upon the laws of this book will be closer to God". After printing this book in 1830 about 3913 changes have been made in this book, which includes the spellings, and grammar mistakes and other changes which have been made without the aid of Urim and Thumim.

Book of Mormons tells the story of people who came to America from Jerusalem 600 years before Christ. Among those people was God fearing Nephi and Laman. Lamanites were away from God; they had a fight with Nephites and routed them. Mormons say that God cursed Lamanites and their skin turned dark and they are Native Americans.

Last prophet of Nephites was Moroni, who wrote everything on the gold plates and he hid breast plate, Urim and Thumim by the side of Comorah Hill and he appeared to Joseph Smith as an angel. These gold plates were returned to Moroni after the translation work was completed and after that these plates existed no more on the earth.

When officials of Archaeology section of the Smithsonian Museum were approached they denied any proof about the gold plates and the book of Mormons and they do not have anything related to this story. People have different views about these plates, Urim, Thumim, and the book of Mormons. In the Fahn Baroodi's book "No man knows my History" it is written that this book is the creation of Joseph Smith's mind. Some scholars feel that, Solomon Spalding based the book of Mormons on the unpublished novel, because he died before this novel could be published. Also there is a rumor that Sidney Rigdon, a companion of Joseph Smith stole the unpublished novel of Solomon Spalding and helped Joseph Smith to translate this work into book of Mormons. After some years he had differences with Joseph Smith and his membership was terminated from the Mormon Church. Then he claimed that he had nothing to do in the translation and publication of the book of Mormons. The third view is that Joseph Smith stole certain views from the book "View of the Hebrews" written by Anthon Smith and published in 1825. There is a solid proof that Joseph Smith took certain things from K.J.V. Bible and West Minister's Confession and Josiah priest's books, "The wonders of nature" and" Providence Displayed" which were published in Albany New York in 1825. Fourth view is that he saw these visions and Satan incited him to write this book. According to St. Paul's words this is also possible, "But even if we or an Angel from heaven, preach any other gospel to you, let him be accursed".(Gal. 1:8) This is also possible that the book of Mormons may be based on all the above mentioned controversial Charges.

Religious Doctrine of the Book of Mormons and Covenants:

Joseph Smith had claimed that the Book of Mormons is the foundation of their religion and whosoever follows the principals of this book will be closer to God, but many of the things about Mormons faith are not included in this book. Harry Ropp while commenting on this book wrote 13 things what Mormons do but they are not written in this book.

Structure of the Church:-

2. The Melchizedikian priesthood.
3. The Aaronic Priesthood
4. Many gods
5. God is exalted and superior man.
6. Human beings ability to become god.
7. The three levels of heaven
8. Polygamy
9. The word of wisdom
10. The pre-existence of human spirit.
11. Eternal Progression
12. Baptism for the dead.
13. Celestial Marriages.

Joseph justified himself by saying that most of the things he received from God in vision. The book named "Doctrines and Covenants" was published in 1833, which is called the book of commandments. After making many changes this book was again published in 1835. 71 sections were added to this book. Many parts of the book were either taken out or changed. Out of these, section 7 is said to be hand written by Apostle John. In the first book of commandments, the translation had 111words less. Did God tell Joseph Smith that his first translation is wrong? If Joseph Smith did it knowingly; even then Joseph Smith had claimed that this translation had been done with the help of Urim and Thumim. Mormons and Joseph Smith claim that these things were revealed to him through the visions but they do not clarify or assert that Jehovah God has certified these revelations and translations.

From 1835 - 1921 the messages of faith, which Joseph Smith delivered, were being published in the book "Doctrine and Covenants". Some of the messages were taken out all of a sudden such as in the third message where it is written 'God is eternal and does not change nor there is any variableness with Him, but He is same from everlasting to everlasting, being the same yesterday, today and forever without variation'. But today they are teaching that God is an exalted man who progressed and one day he became God. Joseph had prophesied that New Jerusalem will be built in Zion. Though he prophesied in 1833 yet no Jerusalem was built in Zion or the Jewish temple was built where there is Aksa Mosque. According to Bible if the prophecies made by a so-called prophet are not fulfilled, then he is not a prophet from God.

Mormons history also tells that black people will go to heaven as servants of the white people but afterwards on June 9, 1978 Spence W. Kimball president and prophet of the Mormon Church declared that even the blacks could become priests. He said that this order he received from God. He also declared that gold plates, hand written parchments of John and Abraham are the basis of Mormon faith. But no one has seen these documents and neither plates were shown to anyone rather excuses were made that these documents have been lost or stolen and gold plates returned to Moroni.

Views about Jehovah God:

Whatever views Mormons have about God they are neither supported by the 'Book of Mormons' nor by the Holy Bible.

God has a physical body:

Mormons believe that God has a physical body. Human beings today on earth and God are from the very beginning. Their existence is spiritual and eternal. Today's God was born out of the union of another God and His heavenly wife and he became human being. Because he successfully lived a righteous life on this earth so from human he became God. That is why God is glorious and perfect human being. He has bones and flesh but he has eternal spirit in him. To support the human form of God they cite the reference from Exodus 31: 18 where it is mentioned about the finger of God and writing of Ten Commandments on the two stone tablets which were given to Moses and the magicians said to Pharaoh, "this is the finger of God, (Exodus 8:19, Luke 11:20 and Psalm 8:3). But Harry Ropp contests to say that these things do not prove that God has a physical body. In Psalms 91:4 Psalmists writes that, "He will cover you with His pinions and under His wings you will find refuge..." Does this verse prove that God is big hen? In the book of Mormons God has been portrayed as a big spirit but he has nowhere been mentioned as a glorious human being. When Moses insisted to see God, then God told him, "See there is a place by me where you shall stand on the rock and while my glory passes by I will put you in a cleft of the rock, and I will cover you with my hand until I have passed by and then I will take away my hand and you shall see my back; but my face shall not been seen" Ex 33:21-23. This incident in the Bible they explain by saying that the hand was not Gods rather it was Christ's hand. How ridiculous is this interpretation that even before Jesus' birth he had a physical body and he was physically present with God.

Mormons believe God is from man and he is the righteous and spiritual form of man, so man can also become God. According to them God's plan is that we also should become God one day.

When we become God then our off springs will be descendants of spirits, as all spirits are off springs of God. These views about God prove that there are many Gods.

Book of Mormons and Holy Bible tells that God is eternal and He never changes. (Psalms 90:2) "From everlasting to everlasting you are God and you never change" Isaiah quotes God in 43:10,11 "I am he. Before me no

God was formed, nor there any after me. I am the Lord and besides me there is no savior" So this proves that God does not have any father.

Mormon denial about the conception of Jesus by the Holy Spirit:

According to Mormons we all are off springs of God and his wife in heaven. They claim that God came to Mary as a man and because of their physical relationship Christ was born that is why he is called Son of God. God has several wives in heaven. According to Brigham Young the President and Prophet of Mormons, Christ was conceived like our children and was born the same way, yet according to their book Alma 7:10 it is written that Christ was conceived by the Holy Spirit and Born of Virgin Mary.

Mormons do not believe in the Unity of God Head:

They take Father, son and the Holy Spirit as three different personalities. These three make a Council and run the Universal System. These three are separate Gods. Bible claims the Unity of God head, yet Mormons preach that there are several gods. On the other hand in the book of Mormons where there is mention of three witnesses it is written, "all glory and praise be to the Father, Son and the Holy Spirit who is one God". Many statements in the book, "Doctrine and Covenants "are' contradictory to the statements recorded in the Book of Mormons. Book of Mormons confirms of Unity of God head that includes Father, Son and the Holy Spirit but their faith is contrary to this.

In spite of all the controversies and drawbacks even now people are joining Mormon Church, which is also called the Church of Latter-Day Saints or LDS, The forceful factor behind all this is not their faith rather hard work of their elders and preachers. Their members are rich and give heavy donations and because of this they have highly impressive and expensive Church buildings.

Opposition of Mormon Church

Due to the rules and principles of the Mormon Church, which are contradictory to the scriptures of the Holy Bible, this sect had to face severe opposition wherever they started to settle and preach. They were not welcomed at all in any community and were not allowed to stay there. In 1844 Joseph Smith was murdered and they were compelled to flee from Nauvoo Illinois in the severe winter. After their exodus from Illinois they fled to Iowa, even there their enemies tortured them and they were not allowed to set foot on that soil. So President Brigham Young and the council of 12 disciples moved from Iowa in 1847 and reached Salt Lake City, Utah where they finally settled. Before that they largely suffered at the hands of their adversaries and kept moving and fleeing in severe summers, chilly and freezing winters, traveling in rain and snow yet they remained true to their faith. When they finally got settled in Salt Lake City they started missionary work in 1849 doing a lot of preaching work in Western Europe, England, Scandinavian countries. Even though they were mobbed and jailed, but their spirit of tolerance strengthened more and more and they made thousands of converts. Preachers traveled to Italy, France, Malta, India, and Chile and to the Islands of the Pacific. In America they made known their faith to the people in Phoenix, Arizona, Boise Idaho and now they are scattered all over the United States. In the early days of the movement they were prejudice of the black people and so blacks were not accepted into the membership of this Church. Because of this racial discrimination this movement suffered a setback but in 1978 because of the declaration of their president and prophet Spenser Kimble blacks were also accepted into the membership of this Church. They can serve and work in this LDS movement. This decision made the Mormon movement again popular and the number of this sect started growing.

They call their worship place a temple. On special occasions only the people with Mormon faith can go inside, others can see the temple only from outside, they are not allowed to go inside at all. For weekly worship meetings and religious studies they use other building in the complex and that room is called Kingdom Hall. Anyone can go there and join them. In the main temple they celebrate 4 sacraments mainly Baptism, Repentance, Baptism for the Dead who did not accept Jesus while they were alive, Special worship meetings, religious offerings and Sacraments for the family occasions.

After the Second World War this Church made a lot of progress. This sect has branches all over the world. In 1999 the membership of this sect was around 5M and in America they had 10,000 congregations. In Canada they had 420 congregations and about 150 thousand members. Recently their number in 160 countries has been estimated to be 9.5 Million. Because of certain objectionable matters, controversial principles and interpretations of the Biblical scriptures their members started breaking away and formed other denominations like the reformed Mormon Church.

Re-Organized Church of Latter Day Saints:

Those people who were left behind after the exodus of Mormons from the eastern and Mid-west part of America established this Church. Briggs was the most loyal elder of L.D.S. Church in Nauvoo Illinois. In 1848 he came in the company of James Jessy Strang but after some time due to some conflict with Strang, he left him and joined the Church run by William Smith. In 1851 he left William too and in 1851 he claimed to see the vision and said God has told him that He will not leave His people. God will soon raise a strong and powerful prophet from the seed of Joseph Smith (2 Nephi 2:46-47). Zenos Gurley was the senior vice president of Nauvoo Church. He remained faithful friend of Brigham Young till his exodus to Utah. After that he too joined the company of Strang. But he left company of Strang because of Briggs as he too had claimed to see a vision.

William Marks was the president of Nauvoo State. He was excommunicated from the Church when he helped Sidney Rigdon. In 1852 Gurley and Briggs came together and established a new Church. They decided to install Joseph Smith (Ill) as the prophet and president of the Church. In 1853 Briggs became the president. Since Joseph Smith (III) was quite young, so he was elected president after six years. Many rules and principles of this Church were the same as that of the original Church. On April 6, 1860 this Church was named Reorganized Church of Latter Day Saints. At that time it had membership of 300 members only.

This re-organized Church opposed polygamy. They were against the marriages for the dead. This Church opposed the statement of the original Church that God was man before and man can also become God. In this re-organized church everybody could go into the Temple and no special dress is needed for that as required by the original L.D.S. Church. Yet they are very particular about the presidency and the prophet hood, which will go to the family of Joseph Smith (III) only. So from 1860 till today presidency and prophet hood is with Joseph Smith's family, but it is not so in the Utah L.D.S. Church. In 1990 no member of the Smith (II) family was prepared for this position, so in 1996 they decided to install Grant Muckri as the president and the prophet of this Church.

This reorganized Church is kind of democratic Church under God. Its membership is open to everyone. This Church's work is spread over Nigeria, Japan, South Korea, South India, Brazil, Mexico, Hattie, New Zealand, Philippines, Australia, French Polynesia, England and Germany. In 1996 membership of this Church was about 2.5 Million.

Restoration Branch Movement:

In 1980 the drawbacks in the early branches of the Church were realized, so many changes were made in the rules and syllabus of the Church School. In the early L.D.S. Churches women were not permitted to speak and serve as pastors, but in 1984 the president at that time declared that even the women can be given the responsibility to serve in the Church. After the proper education and training they can be ordained as pastors. It was emphasized that book of Mormons and the Bible translated by Joseph Smith should be followed strictly. Omitting article 156 Doctrines and Commandments should also be acted upon. All independent L.D.S. Churches can become members of this Church. The other denominations of Church of Jesus Christ of Latter Day Saints are:

1. Restoration Church of Jesus Christ of Latter Day Saints
2. Church of Jesus Christ (Bickeronite)
3. Church of Jesus Christ (Cult rites)
4. Church of Jesus Christ (Drew)
5. Church of Jesus Christ of Latter Day Saints (Strangites); and so on.

Though the presidents and prophets of these Churches are different yet there is no much difference in their religious matters, principles and sacraments. Out of these different groups of the same sect, who is right and who is wrong only God can decide. Whose principles, rules and doctrines are in contradiction to the Bible that person and religious group is against God. The one who opposes Christ opposes God. At the end I will quote St. Peters words from Acts 4: 12,

"Nor is there salvation in any other, for there is no other name under heaven given among men by which we must be saved".

After going through the history, doctrines, principles and faith of the Mormons it is clear that this sect and breakaway groups are surrounded by controversies and misinterpretations of the word of God. Due to the unbelievable interpretations of the word of God, man-made stories about God, birth of Christ and the Holy Spirit, evangelical Christian groups whose faith is purely based upon the Bible opposed and contradicted them. Not only that, their own people felt drawbacks in their faith and principles. Contradictions between the book of Mormons and their faith in practice led to the splitting of the main L.D.S. Church and many different reformed groups were reorganized. All this goes to prove that those religious groups who are founded on the manmade principles, doctrines and misinterpretations of the word of God lack unity and oneness of faith and they are sure to split up and give rise to different denominations.

Note:

The Church of Jesus Christ of Latter Day Saints (Mormons) has been the object of criticism and opposition from the evangelical protestant Christians, the main reason of opposition being, the unacceptable and unbelievable doctrines and principles of this Church. No right minded Christian is ready to accept their theory about God, Jesus Christ and the Holy Spirit who constitute one God Head. Polygamy has been another issue. Even their ex-Mormon members like Sandra Tanners and Jeral Tanners are prominent who head Utah Light house ministry. There has been vast outpouring of Anti- Mormon literature. In spite of all the opposition, the literature on Mormonism is vast, and has been greatly increased by the Mormon history association.

References:

1. "What of Mormons?" by Gordon B. Hinckley, published by The Church of Jesus Christ of Latter Day Saints.
2. "A Guide to Cults and New Religions" by Ronald Enroth.
3. "Joseph Smith and the Beginning of Mormonism" by Richard L. Bushman, Urbana IL, University of Illinois Press 1984.
4. "Church History in the Fullness of Times" Published by Church of Jesus Christ of Latter Day Saints.1989
5. "Encyclopedia of American Religions"
6. "World religions" by Benson Y. Lanceis
7. "Story of American Religions" by Hartzell Spence Mormons Pp 198 -219.
8. "Our religions and Our neighbors" by M. G. Miller and S.D. Schwartzman Revised edition Pp 142, 145-7, 150.

Chapter Seventeen

The Salvation Army

(Protestant)

You must have seen in the United States, young and old men and women in red standing in front of stores in the Shopping Malls with a tripod stand and a red bucket/kettle hanging below the tripod and the men and women ringing the hand bell to appeal to the shoppers to put their change in the bucket to help the needy and the under privileged people. Especially you will see them during the Christmas season. Volunteers stand outside the stores braving the biting cold to bring some cheer at the Christmas time to the homeless and the less fortunate. These are the people working for the Salvation Army a protestant Christian organization whose massage is based upon the Bible. Salvation Army is a non-sectarian organization founded in London in 1865 to cater to the needs of the poor and suffering people in the society. It appears William Booth the founder was inspired by the life of Jesus Christ who cared for the poor and destitute in the human society. At His Second Advent when He will Judge the people, He will say to the righteous on His right hand, "I was hungry and you gave me food; I was naked you gave me clothing. I was sick or in prison you visited me. I was thirsty, you gave me drink…" Matt: 25:31-46. So Salvation Army's faith was based on the social gospel of Jesus Christ. This movement had phenomenal success within few years. Their ministries were inspired by the love of God. Their mission is to preach the good news of Jesus Christ to the world and meet the needs of the needy and suffering humanity without any discrimination. In the beginning their work was limited to England and the United States, but it rapidly spread to Canada, France, Switzerland, South Africa, Australia, India, Iceland, and all other countries of the world wherever poor and homeless needed their help. At present their work is spread over 122 countries of the world.

William Booth the Founder:

William Booth born on 10 April, 1829 and a Methodist Pastor in London started his ministerial career in 1852. He felt the need of preaching the good news of Jesus Christ to the lost multitudes in the streets of London. As the rich people are happy and feel satisfied in their worldly life, so he turned to the poor and the homeless to preach the gospel of Jesus Christ and help the hungry, helpless, and destitute people. He did not limit his message and preaching to the four walls of the church where people gathered once a week for some time, rather he went to the people outside the four walls of the church to preach the gospel. His enthusiasm and method of preaching was not accepted by the Church leaders of his time, especially the church organizations which preferred only the methodical and traditional methods of preaching. So he left the church and traveled throughout England taking the message to the needy masses through evangelistic meetings. In this crusade of preaching, his wife Catherine Booth was a major driving force. Very soon he was accepted as an independent religious leader. His enthusiasm and fervor inspired his followers also who made a dedicated group of warriors to save the souls of multitudes of lost men and women. As St. Paul writes Jesus chose the poor and destitute to shame the so called rich of the world, so his followers were thieves, gamblers, prostitutes, homeless, drunkards and the marginalized men and women of the society. They accepted Jesus Christ as their savior and formed his congregation of the poor and people rejected by the society.

"But God chose what is foolish in the world to shame the wise; God chose what is weak in the world to shame the strong. God chose what is low and despised in the world, the things that are not, to reduce to nothing that are, so that no one might boast in the presence of God." 1Corinthians 1:27-29

William Booth realized that as Christ came to save the lost and the sinners, so he and his wife also went to such people. He preached hope to the hopeless and salvation to the unsaved so that they may grow spiritually strong in Jesus and they may also work to save others. Thus who accepted his message followed him, preached the good news of salvation and became living testimony to the resurrected Christ and God. Initially this group served as "Christian Mission" and William Booth was declared as the General Superintendant. By his followers he was known as the 'General' and the whole group was known as, "The Hallelujah Army". In 1878 this group was called, "Christian Army" and then they changed the name to "Salvation Army".

Faith of Salvation Army:

1. Salvation Army believes that the Holy Scriptures of Old and the New Testaments were given directly by God through His prophets. These scriptures constitute the divine rules of Christian faith.
2. They believe in one God head having three persons The Father, The Son and the Holy Spirit undivided in essence and co-equal in power and glory.
3. There is only one God, who is almighty. Omnipresent, infinitely perfect, the creator and sustainer, Governor of all things and He is the only proper God of religious worship.
4. In the person of Jesus Christ the divine and human nature are united, so he is the true and proper image of God.
5. Jesus Christ is the Lord and he through His suffering and sacrificial death made the atonement for the sins of the whole world so that whosoever believes in Him may not perish but be saved.
6. For the salvation repentance from sins, faith in God, and His only son Lord Jesus Christ and regeneration by the Holy Spirit are essential.
7. God created our ancestors Adam and Eve in the sinless state of innocence, but by their disobedience of God's commandment they lost their purity and consequently because of their fall all human beings became sinners, totally depraved and will face the wrath of God unless they repent and trust in His son Jesus Christ and turn to God.
8. We are justified by grace through faith in our Lord Jesus Christ and he that believeth in Him hath the witness in himself.
9. They believe that continuance in the state of salvation depends upon continued obedience of faith in Christ.

10. It is the privilege of all believers to be wholly sanctified, so that their whole spirit and soul and body may be kept blameless till the second advent of our Lord and savior Jesus Christ.
11. Lastly they believe in the immortality of the soul; resurrection of the body; the judgment by Jesus at the end of the world; eternal happiness of the righteous; and in the endless punishment of the unrepentant wicked.

What they do not believe:

William Booth and his wife Catherine Booth excluded two main sacraments of water Baptism and Holy Communion from their faith with the argument that most of the Christian world totally relies on these sacraments and ignores other things which they shouldn't do. The Baptism and the Lord's Supper are outward signs of spiritual life, but grace of God is most important. They believe that Christian believers especially Salvation Army members should refrain from drinking alcohol (For this reason they do not celebrate Lord's Supper), taking illegal drugs, gambling, smoking, and other acts mentioned in the Bible, which take human beings away from God.

Their Work:

Initially the founder William Booth and his wife Catherine Booth embarked upon taking the message of the Bible and salvation to the down trodden, gamblers, prostitutes, and drunkards and helping the poor homeless and the marginalized people, but with time their main focus shifted to charity and the work among poor and suffering humanity. William Booth when realized the needs of the suffering people, he as a first General of the Salvation Army made this statement:

"While women weep, as they do now, I'll fight; while children go hungry as they do now, I'll fight; while men go to prison, in and out as they do now, I'll fight; while there is drunkard left. While there is poor lost girl upon the streets, while there remains one dark soul without the light of God, I'll fight to the very end."

Though William booth died in 1912, yet the work started by him in the streets of London, still continues all over the world. He laid the foundation of his movement on the unshakable rock Jesus Christ, so his death could not deter his ministry's march onward. The Salvation Army is a non-governmental relief agency. Whenever there are floods, tsunamis, earth quakes, poverty, drought, and famine, you will see the Salvation Army helping the people along with other agencies. They collect clothes, food, and money from the people and help the suffering humanity without caring for religion or country. They work to alleviate the suffering and help the people rebuild their lives after natural and manmade disasters. It has come to notice that people donate gold ornaments, gold coins, and even their diamond rings and drop in the red kettle anonymously.

Whatever aid and other stuff they get from people with that they run thrift stores and charity shops. Whatever money they earn through these stores they spend on helping the needy and building shelters for the homeless and taking care of the orphans.

Salvation Army Structure:

Salvation Army has its own flag which is a symbol of war against sin and social evils. The flag has red background which symbolizes the blood shed by Jesus Christ. In the center of the flag is a yellow star with 8 corners with the words 'Blood and Fire'. Yellow color of the star is fire of the Holy Spirit and blue border on the rectangular flag represents purity of God the father.

The official emblem of the Salvation Army is the Crest which has cross in the middle, which is cross of Lord Jesus Christ.

Around the cross is letter 'S' which means salvation from sins through Jesus Christ.

There is blue circle around the cross and S. Outside the circle are yellow rays representing the fire of the Holy Spirit.

There are seven dots in the lower part of the blue circle which represents truth of the gospel.

There are two swords making the sign X on the cross representing the salvation war. In the upper part of the circle are the words 'Blood and Fire'. The blood which was shed by Jesus to pay the price of our sins and the fire is of the Holy Spirit.

The Salvation Army Logo:

Red Shield with the words "Salvation Army" on it is their logo. This logo was introduced at the end of nineteenth century when British Army was fighting the Boer war in South Africa. Red shield league was constituted to help the British Army. The members of the Red Shield provided meals and refreshments to the soldiers in the trenches. They had ambulances to provide first aid to the wounded soldiers and also conducted Christian worship for the believers. This logo has become identity symbol of the Salvation Army all over the world. They use this Red Shield symbol along with the crest of the Salvation Army.

The Salvation Army has ranks just like the ranks of the Army of any country. These ranks are soldiers, Auxiliary Captains, Lieutenants, Sergeants, Majors, Colonels, and Generals. All these soldiers and officers constitute 'God's Army'. They wear Salvation Army uniform for meetings and ministry work. The three 'S's in the salvation Army mean soup, soap, and salvation which express the approach of the Salvation Army.

References:

1. Church History in Plain Language by Bruce Shelly Pp 432-436.
2. The Social Gospel in America. N.Y. Oxford press 1966 by Robert Ed. Handy.
3. The Social Gospel Ronald C. white Jr. and Hopkins C. Howard temple University Press 1976.
4. Christianity for Dummies by Richard Wagner Wiley Publishing Inc.
5. World Religions from Ancient History to the present by Geoffrey Parrinder facts on file publications N.Y.
6. Wikipedia free Encyclopedia

Chapter Eighteen

Congregationalists

(Protestant)

When Queen Elizabeth came to power in 1558, the Anglican Church was facing many problems and opposition; especially the Puritan Christians were having hard time. England was at war with France and the Church after being separated from Roman Catholicism queen was facing opposition not only from Roman Catholics, but also from other Protestants. On the other hand Queen Mary who was Roman Catholic had brought turmoil during her six years reign. Though English Church had thrown away the yoke of Pope and Catholicism, yet rituals and way of worship was the same. They still observed the seven sacraments as observed by the Roman Catholic Church. There were many dissenters and non-conformists who wanted to get away with Roman Catholic influence on the Anglican Church regarding rituals. Presbyterians wanted that Church should be administrated under the Presbyters and Synods instead of Bishops, but the queen was not ready to compromise on any issue regarding the Church matters. So it gave birth to two different groups, the Congregationalists and the Unitarians. Those who wanted independence of each local congregation were called Congregationalists. Robert Browne, a student of Cambridge University was their leader. Queen dismissed the supporters of Congregationalism from Cambridge University and then Robert Browne took over the leadership. Finally in 1581 Congregationalist Church was organized. They wanted rituals in the Church according to their own interpretations of the Bible and not according to the Anglican Church.

Their worship was simple without any instrumental music, reading from the Bible and discussions after the sermon.

Congregationalist Churches are protestant Churches separated from the mainline Presbyterian, Anglican and Reformed Churches. Congregationalism came into existence during the Puritan reformation of Church of England. Who considered themselves to be more pure and holy and hence called 'Puritans'. As the Congregationalists separated from the Presbyterian and Anglican Church and were running Churches independently, hence they were called 'Independents' or 'Separatists'. Their history goes back to the time of reformation when there was turmoil in the Roman Catholic Church and Martin Luther, John Calvin, John Wycliffe, John Huss, and other reformers were leaving Roman Catholic Church and formed Protestant Churches. Since Roman Catholic Church was dominated by Pope, Bishops, and Priests, so reformers thought of the power of Christian believers without the different categories of priests. Christian believers could not speak against or challenge the decisions made by the clergy. People thought there is no need of intercessory between them and God. They were fed up of the Roman Catholic Church abuses and distortion in the interpretation of the Bible. They believed that authenticity and the true beliefs are described in the message preached by the Lord and Savior Jesus Christ. So the Congregationalists that believed in the power of congregation advocated for the autonomy of the local congregation. Actually this idea was given by John Wycliffe who was a Roman Catholic priest and because of this idea; he was removed from the Roman Catholic Church. Congregationalists were very much influenced by the Baptist theology and so they wanted to have an ideal Church which should be pure in faith, character and deeds. In the Reformed Churches even the little children were baptized but Congregationalists believed that it is necessary for the person to repent before he comes into full membership of the Church after the baptism.

With time even in Congregationalists there were differences, so many independent Churches were established by John Penry, Thomas Jolie, Henry Barrow, John Robinson, and William Brewster. Congregationalists faced lot of opposition from the Church of England and other protestant Churches, so they fled to other countries. At that time many people were moving to various colonies in America. Since Congregationalists were struggling to separate from Anglican Church and facing hard time, so many Congregationalists traveled by ship in 1620. Those who came to New England Colony of America among those pilgrims was William wroth. He in 1639 established Congregationalist Church called "The Tabernacle United Reformed Church". With time Congregationalism spread its roots in various other countries like Ottoman Empire, Argentina, Canada, Australia, Samoa and South Africa.

Their Faith and Beliefs:

1. They are Lords' free people who have joined in the fellowship of the gospel to walk in all His ways and make known according to their best efforts, whatever it may cost with Lords' help and guidance.
2. Congregational Church is a Free Church and it is not Creedal Church. They work and build their life and Church upon the Bible, but they trust the guidance from conscience of the individual which helps to understand and implement Christ's command to love the neighbor and the God. They are committed to one another as they travel their life's common journey.
3. They are not totally dependent upon the priest's guidance, but each member is responsible individually to discover what God expects from them to live by their faith every day. There is complete religious freedom without any Creedal barriers. They believe service to humanity, the love of God and discipleship of Christ binds their members together. Their members have freedom to express if they disagree on certain religious beliefs. They believe that their Congregational Church is independent in self-governing and in decision making they are democratic. Their Churches operate by the established byelaws, elected boards and committees and thus make decisions by democratic vote.
4. There are fellowship activities which bind members at all levels. These activities are within the Church and local community. They are proud of their programs, group within the Church, service to the community, country, and the world. They participate and co-operate with other congregations to support the cause of Congregationalism.
5. They strictly abide by the teachings of Christ. They lay strong emphasis on evangelism.

6. They celebrate Holy Communion and baptism as part of their faith because it is commandment of our Lord.

The ideals of Congregationalism are not limited only to Christian Congregations but they have been adopted by the Unitarian Universalist Church of America and Canada, Jewish Synagogues and most of the Islamic mosques as well. Some Congregational Associations have joined other conventions like Southern Baptist Convention, The National Baptism Convention, and American Baptist Church of U.S.A. There are many non-denominational congregations that run on the Congregationalist lines. In these Congregations there are officers other than the priest and they are called elders, deacons, session and vestry. These terms have been borrowed from the Presbyterian and Anglican Churches.

They do not believe in the concentration of decisive power in the hands of one ruling man or body. It is such a system where whole congregation is involved in decision making and running the Church. They have union with other Churches, but there is independence within the union.

Churches of Christ are Congregational. They do not have central head quarters where there is ruling group, councils or conferences other than the local Church government. Yet there is network of independent Churches with each congregation working independently. Each congregation is overseen by the various committees of the elders, deacons and the priest. Elders are responsible for the spiritual uplift and needs of the congregation. Deacons take care of unspiritual needs and they work under the supervision of Elders. A successful deacon may be promoted to the position of Elder. Elders are supposed to be mature and to have good understanding of the word of God which is not essential in Presbyterian Churches. Elders in the Congregational Churches are expected to supervise the priest, perform governance functions and teach. They believe there is no difference between clergy and laity. Rather every member of the congregation has the responsibility and gift to accomplish the work of the Church. The other congregations who believe in Congregationalism are Southern Michigan Conference of Congregational Churches, National Association of Congregational Christian Churches and An International Congregational Fellowship.

With the passage of time when the believers have come to realize that we have one supreme savior congregations are merging with other denominations. In India and elsewhere they are merging with other like minded denominations. In Australia the most congregations of the Congregational Union of Australia in 1977 merged with the Methodist Church of Australia and Presbyterian Churches and have formed United Church of Australia.

In Bulgaria that was under Ottoman Empire they were called Evangelicals. They faced lot of opposition as they tried to convert Orthodox Christians to Congregationalism. Congregational missionaries were the first to arrive in Bulgaria when it was under Ottomans. Ottomans were Moslems and they had imposed death penalty on Moslems who will convert to Christianity, but this did not deter their determination to spread the Good News. When American missionaries came to Bulgaria they were supported by the Congregationalists. Between 1840-1878 many Congregational Churches were established. By 1909 there were 1456 congregations in Bulgaria. Not only that all evangelical Churches in Bulgaria formed United Evangelical Association in 1909.

Congregational and other missionaries played a laudable role in Bulgaria in bringing National Revival Movement. These Missionaries established Schools, Colleges, and Bible Colleges for training Pastors.

Congregationalists when migrated to United States they settled in New England, Massachusetts and Connecticut. Most of the Unitarians also migrated to New England. Since they were like minded so Congregationalists and Unitarians were unified in 1648. John Cotton their very influential leader persuaded John Owen a Calvinist theologian to accept Congregationalism and he became influential leader in developing Congregational theology. Most of the congregations joined Presbyterian Churches. Congregationalists in America founded many Colleges and Universities. Out of these important Universities are Harvard, Yale, Dartmouth, Williams, Bowdoin, Amherst, Middlebury, and Carleton.

As they were supporters of freedom they brought Civil Rights, fought the war of Independence and steered the movement against slavery. Initially they were very strict in observing Sunday as the Holy Sabbath, but with time they too became very liberal. Since the Congregational Churches were operating independently without any centralized power they started leaning towards Unitarianism, Deism and Transdentalism. By 1750 many congregational preachers were preaching the theology of Universal salvation and this created stir among the hard liners. Though Harvard University was founded by the Congregationalists, yet it became center of Unitarian training. Because of the differences in Congregational and Unitarian theology in 1825 Unitarian Churches separated from Congregationalists. These days Congregationalists are used to more formal and less evangelistic form of worship than the evangelical Churches. In 1957 General Council of Congregational Churches merged with Evangelical and Reformed Churches to form United Church of Christ.

From the study of Congregational Churches we find believers were satisfied with the original theology of Congregationalism. With time there has been difference of opinion among the independent Congregational Churches, so they have been merging with other denominations and those who did not agree they still kept their separate Congregational identity.

References:

1. Encyclopedia of Religions by Samuel Hill, Charles H. Lippy ; Charles Reagan Wilson Mercer University press 2005.
2. The complete guide to Christian denominations. Harvest House Publishers2005.
3. The Encyclopedia of the Stone- Campbell Movement. Wm B. Eerdmans publishing 2004.
4. World Religions: From Ancient History to the present Geoffrey Parrinder Pp 443-452 Facts on file Publications.
5. Church History in plain language by Bruce L. Shelly—World Publishers 1982.
6. Wikipedia free Encyclopedia

Chapter Nineteen

Worldwide Church of God

Worldwide Church of God with conflicting views and controversial beliefs was founded by Herbert W. Armstrong (1892-1986) in Pasadena California in late 1933 as "The Radio Church of God". Later on in 1968 its name was changed to "Worldwide Church of God". In the beginning it had large following and it aired / broadcast a program "The World Tomorrow" through 446 television and radio stations. It also published its magazine 'The Plain Truth' to propagate its beliefs and views. In the mid seventies Armstrong declared himself as the apostle of God and called himself "Elijah of end times". Whatever he wrote or broadcast, he claimed that all this is from God and he declared that God is using me. With time, because of controversial views and beliefs following of WCG started declining and followers started drifting away and many splinter groups with liberal views came into existence.

It has 51 acres of land and 72 buildings and now because of less following and low income the entire property is on sale. Following were the beliefs of this Worldwide Church of God:

Armstrong said that Hebrew word for God is Elohim which means a family, so God is not Trinity, but is a divine family. God and Jesus Christ are separate and different persons. Also Holy Spirit is not a person, but is an active force emanating from God. According to the Bible The Holy Spirit is poured out, so it cannot be a person because a person cannot be poured out. According to the Bible this is false doctrine.

According to Armstrong Jesus was not son of God before He was conceived by Mary. So He is not equal to God. He became son of God by His sacrificial death and after resurrection from the dead on the third day. Blood of Jesus Christ does not save anyone, but it saves from the death penalty of sin. It is Satan inspired doctrine that Jesus was not a human and He did not have normal human characteristics, so this is a doctrine of antichrist (Plain Truth January 1955 page-7).

Armstrong believed in theory of good deeds and actions, so he claimed that salvation is not only by faith, but it requires good works and water baptism by immersion is essential for salvation. He stated that six steps are necessary for salvation that is: repentance, faith, water baptism by immersion, receiving of the Holy Spirit, obedience and new birth (i.e. resurrection from the sinful life). He also claimed that true gospel was lost in A.D 70 when Jerusalem was attacked and Solomon's temple was demolished and it was restored by God through Herbert W. Armstrong in 1934. He also contradicted that work of salvation was completed by Christ on the cross rather it was begun there. He stated that salvation is not by just believing in Christ rather by believing his commandment of water baptism which is precondition for being saved.

1. Sabbath. Jewish Sabbath (that is Saturday) must be observed to maintain salvation; also other Old Testament feasts should be celebrated as per God's commandment.

2. Born again. The idea of born again as Jesus told Nicodemus does not mean the spiritual rebirth rather it refers to physical resurrection as Jesus was born again after resurrection from the dead.

3. Another opportunity for salvation: As the Roman Catholics believe that there is another chance for repentance and be saved when in purgatory likewise Armstrong said those who missed the opportunity to have salvation in this physical life still there is another chance in the second life. When they get resurrected at the end of millennium they will have another opportunity to believe the gospel and be saved. (Romans 2:12-15; 2Cor. 6:2; Heb. 9:27; Rev. 20:11-15)

4. Concept of Heaven and Hell: Armstrong refutes the promise of heaven for the righteous and the faithful, rather true believers will spend eternity with Christ on earth. Wicked will be annihilated and Satan and demons will go to hell for eternal punishment.

5. Soul is mortal: Worldwide Church of God claims that human soul is mortal; it dies as the human beings die. This is the same doctrine as Jehovah Witnesses and Seventh Day Adventists believe.

6. Tithing: According to Armstrong Tithing is mandatory and on special occasions the followers must give tithe of the tithe of the tithe (this is three tier system of the tithe i.e. 30 %).

7. Lost tribes of Israel: He claimed that Judah and Israel are two separate nations. Inhabitants of Britain are the tribe of Ephraim and the Americans are the descendants of the tribe of Manasseh. Whereas the white Anglo Saxons are the chosen people of God.

8. Divorce and Marriage: According to this doctrine of Worldwide Church of God (WCG) if you want to become member of WCG, you must divorce your mate if you are already married no matter how many children you have from the previous marriage. Because of this controversial rule many families were ruined and because of the fear of losing salvation many lives went through serious mental and emotional problems. Yet Herbert W. Armstrong did not stick himself to this rule. When his first wife died he married a divorced woman of half of his age.

It is because of the above noted controversial and conflicting views this Church was termed as a 'Cult'. So due to the self proclaimed authority from heaven and authoritarian law and prohibitions against the use of cosmetics, celebrating birthdays and holidays, seeking medical treatment and inter racial marriage followers rebelled against this doctrine. There being disillusionment and followers being frustrated started drifting away from this cultic Church and many splinter groups were formed. Some of these are listed below:

1. United Church of God.
2. Intercontinental Church of God.

3. Living Church of God.
4. Philadelphia Church of God.
5. Restored Church of God.
6. Church of God's Faithful.
7. Christian Biblical Church of God.
8. Church of God an International Community.
9. Independent Church of God.
10. Redeemed Christians Church of God (City of Faith)

There are many more splinter groups that have made changes in the original doctrine of Armstrong, so that they may not be called Cult.

Just before the death of Herbert W. Armstrong in 1986 Joseph W. Tkach Sr. became Pastor General of Worldwide Church of God. He realized the drawbacks in the doctrine of WCG and made 40 changes in the Armstrong's doctrine to make it Biblical but did not change the concept of mortality of human soul and kept other points with slight changes.

Modern day Church of God has made tremendous changes in the original doctrine to make it biblically based. Some of the important points of their doctrine are:

1. Church of God believes that Bible is the spiritually inspired word of God.

2. Jesus Christ the Messiah is the only begotten son of God conceived by the Holy Spirit and born of Virgin Mary. After His sacrificial death on the cross, he was buried and rose from the dead on the third day. He ascended into heaven and is seated at the right hand of God Almighty as the advocate and intercessor for His believers.

3. They believe in the Holy Trinity, The father, the Son Jesus Christ and the Holy Spirit.

4. That all has sinned and fall short of the glory of God. (Romans 3:23). So for forgiveness of sins repentance is essential as the commandment of God.

5. Justification, sanctification and New Birth are brought about by faith in the Holy blood of Jesus Christ shed on the cross.

6. Holiness is the only standard of living for believers, because scriptures say, "You should be holy because I am holy" (Eph. 1:4; 1Pet. 1:15,16.)

7. Believe in the baptism of Holy Spirit.

8. After New Birth and baptism of Holy Spirit a person is blessed with the gift of speaking tongues as an evidence of baptism of the Holy Spirit.

9. Baptism of water by immersion is the only right kind of baptism in the name of The Father, The Son Jesus Christ and the Holy Spirit.

10. Believe in the Lord's Supper and washing of feet of the saints as Christ instituted this rite at the time of last supper.

11. Worldwide Church of God believes in the Second Advent of Jesus Christ. Before the 1,000 years reign of Christ begins the righteous and saints will be resurrected first and catch up in air to meet their Lord and saints and reign with Christ for 1,000 years.

12. They believe in the bodily resurrection of all the dead after the millennium rule of Jesus. There will be eternal life for the righteous and eternal punishment for the wicked, Satan and demons.

United Church of God:

Though they made many changes in the original doctrine of Herbert W. Armstrong which was influenced by the Seventh day Adventists, Jehovah Witnesses, and Pentecostals, yet they kept some of the old beliefs of Armstrong. Their beliefs in brief are:

1. God the Father and Jesus Christ is the Messiah.

2. They believe in both the Old and New Testaments as the inspired word of God and it is the revelation of the will of God for the whole humanity.

3. Believe that Satan is the Devil and adversary of God and His believers.

4. That Adam was created in the image of God and so all the humanity. But Adam and Eve when tempted by Satan sinned by disobedience. Since then after Satan's fall it has been deceiving and misleading the whole humanity.

5. Sin. That sin is the transgression of the spiritual law of God which is based upon the commandments given to Israelites through Moses. Obedience to spiritual law of God is the only way to peace and happiness.

6. That, "God so loved the world that He gave His only begotten son, so that whosoever believeth in Him may not perish, but may have eternal life." Jesus' sacrificial death and His Holy Blood is sufficient to pay the price of our sins and save the whole humanity. Those who believe in His sacrificial death are forgiven and are released from the second death.

7. Repentance is precondition for the forgiveness of sins. Complete surrender and obedience to the will of God is essential for forgiveness and receiving God's grace.

8. Believe in the resurrection of Jesus on the third day.

9. Baptism by immersion. Water baptism by immersion is obeying commandment of Jesus as He commanded to His disciples.

10. The Sabbath. They do not consider Sunday as the Sabbath rather Saturday the seventh day of the week is the real Sabbath. God commanded to observe the seventh day as the true Sabbath. Jehovah Witnesses and Seventh Day Adventists believe the same.

11. They celebrate the Jewish Passover on the night of 14th of Jewish month Abib.

12. They observe all the seven annual Holy Days as God commanded to the Israelites, because Jesus and His disciples did so.

13. Biblical food laws. Like Seventh Day Adventists and Jews they only eat those foods that are defined clean in the Holy Bible.

14. Serving the Military. Like Jehovah Witnesses, adherents of United Church of God are forbidden to join the army and fight the war.

15. To be Holy. God said be holy as I am holy. So the followers of United Church of God are expected to lead righteous life and become holy by being born of the Holy Spirit.

16. Tithing is essential because by tithing we honor God.

17. Second Advent of our Lord and resurrection. They believe in the eternal life for believers after resurrection from the dead at the Second Advent of Jesus. All believers will be resurrected to the spirit life. They also believe that when at the Second Advent Christ has ruled 1,000 years rest of the dead will be raised to physical life. Those who did not repent in earlier life will have an opportunity to repent, believe in Jesus and get converted will receive eternal life.

18. Jesus King Of kings. At the Second Advent of Jesus His righteous believers will be raised and will live with Christ who will rule as the king for 1,000 years.

References:

1. "Worldwide Church of God" Phillip Arnn Watchman fellowship Profile 1996.
2. Hand Book of Denomination the United States. Abingdon Press 2001
3. The Kingdom of Cults Revised and updated Edition Walter Martin Bethany House 2003.
4. "The Armstrong Churches" The Edges of Seventh Day Adventism (1840-1980) Lowell R. Tarling 1981) Galilee Publications
5. Wikipedia Free Encyclopedia
6. The Essential Teachings of Herbert Armstrong Writers Club Press.
7. The True History of Worldwide Church of God. The daughter of Babylon Bruce Renehan. 1993

Chapter Twenty

Unitarian Universalists

The other group who refused to tolerate imposition of Roman Catholic rituals in the Church Worship was the Unitarians. They denied the belief in Trinity. They did not recognize Jesus as God, rather a great religious teacher. For their faith they are not accepted as members of the National Council of Churches. Michael Servetus is considered to be the founder of Unitarian Church. Servetus refuted the concept of Trinity and said Jesus is not God, rather He is the manifestation of God and the Faustus Socinus an Italian declared Jesus only a man filled with the wisdom of God, he was resurrected and after His ascension is seated at the right hand of God. Unitarians believe only in one God and Jesus as human being. Unitarians believe in the dignity and goodness of man. They believe that salvation can be earned by abiding by the principles laid by Jesus. Unitarian covenant states, "In the love of truth and in the spirit of Jesus, we unite for worship of God and the service of man." So this is a liberal Christian Church. They believe that Christians should not be rigid, but should exercise tolerance towards other religions and other forms of worship that is why they have accepted ideas into their worship from other non-Christian faiths.

Unitarian faith started in 16th century from Hungry and Poland and then came to England. When people were migrating to the United States of America the migrants brought this faith in 18th century to New England Colony. Their other component is the Universal Church which emerged in the United States in New England Colony as a non conformist Church. Its founder was Hosea Ballou. They argued that God is all merciful, all powerful and loving. He loves both the righteous and the sinners, so He will redeem every evil and the good person both at the personal level and the society as a whole. So God will save both the Christian believers and the non-Christians. But the main line Christian denominations do not accept this idea because of what Jesus Said.

"All the nations will be gathered before Him (Jesus), then He will separate people one from another as a shepherd separates sheep from the goats, and He will put the sheep at His right hand and goats at the left. Then the king will say to those at His right hand 'come ye that are blessed by my father, inherit the kingdom prepared for you from the foundation of the world……then He will say to those at His left hand 'you that are accursed, depart from me into the eternal fire prepared for the devil and his angels and these will go away into the eternal punishment, but the righteous into the eternal life". So that is God's judgment for the righteous and the evil ones who do not repent and believe and accept Jesus Christ as their savior and act upon His commandments. Matt: 25: 31-46.

Since the Unitarians and Universalists both have liberal faith so in 1961 they merged and formed Unitarian Universal association and are so called Unitarian Universal Church.

They do not believe in the virgin birth of Jesus, and the original sin inherited by the descendants of Adam and Eve. They celebrate Baptism as an act of dedication to the ethics of Jesus. Sometimes it seems that their faith is more centered on man rather than God. Jews feel Unitarians are very close to Judaism.

Since Unitarians have been very liberal, strong supporters of social justice, peace and freedom, so this group had tremendous influence on the American society. Important members of Unitarian sect have been American Presidents like John Quincy Adams, William Howard Taft, Thomson Jefferson, Millard Fillmore and also important personalities like H.W. Longfellow, Nathaniel Haw throne. James Russell Lowell, R.W. Emerson, Julia Ward were members of this group.

Unitarians have no common belief about God, but they have diverse views. Some believe in atheism thus denying existence of any God, and others believe there are many gods and goddesses. Some believe that if there is any God we are not certain about it also we cannot know it. Some believe that God has manifested through nature. Some Unitarians deny the existence of any God, but believe that there is spirit of life that binds all lives on earth. Since they do not have any official creed they are all bound by the principles and purpose suggested by the Unitarian Universalist association. These are the principles they affirm and promote:

1. The inherent worth and dignity of every person.
2. Justice, Equality, and compassion in human relations.
3. Accepting one another and encouragement to spiritual growth in the Unitarian Congregation.
4. A free and responsible search for truth and its meaning.
5. The right of conscience and the use of democratic process within the Congregation and in the society at large.
6. The goal of world community with peace, liberty and justice for all.

Recently adopted principle in 1995 called the seventh principle is, "Respect for the independent web of all existence of which we are a part. Their approach to sacred writings (Bible) is summed up in their Unitarian Universalist faith which says, "We do not however hold the Bible or any other account of human experience, to be infallible guide or the exclusive source of truth. Much of the Biblical material is mythical or legendary. For that reason it should not be discarded, rather it should be treasured for what it is. We should read the Bible as we read other books, with imagination and critical eye. We also respect the sacred literature of other religions. We also value contemporary works of science, art, and social commentary. We hold in the words of an old liberal formulation, that revelation is not sealed. Unitarian Universalists aspire to truth as wide as the world. We look to find the truth anywhere universally.

Worship:

As discussed above Unitarian Universalists worship according to their own theology and rituals are often a combination of elements derived from other faith traditions alongside original practices and symbols. In form, Church service might be difficult to distinguish from those of protestant Churches, but they vary widely among the congregations. They hold their services on Sundays. The service includes hymn singing accompanied by organ and musical instruments led by a song leader or Choir. They have their own song book having hymns from variety of sources. They do not celebrate Christian sacraments like Baptism, Holy Communion and confirmation ritual.

Symbol:

The most common symbol of Unitarian Universalism is the flaming Chalice, often framed by two overlapping rings which represent Unitarianism and Universalism. Chalice is a symbol of liberal religion. This symbol was created by Austrian artist Hans Deutsch. The holy oil burning in it is symbol of happiness, and sacrifice. This symbol can be seen outside their Church on the sign board indicating about their Church.

Chapter Twenty One

Pentecostals

Whenever some people realize that drawbacks have crept in the faith they are following, they become restless and start thinking of ways and means to bring changes in that faith and that gives rise to a new movement. When some believers realized that no miracles are happening, no spirit baptism and no speaking of tongues after the water baptism as it was in the first century apostolic church that laid the foundation of Pentecostalism. They knew that when the disciples were gathered and praying after the ascension of our Lord into heaven they according to the promise in John:14 received the spirit baptism and started speaking in tongues and the disciples received the power of divine healing and that was the day of Pentecost(21.1). Inspired by that, movement of Pentecostalism was started as a renewal movement within Christianity, because of the drawbacks in the Roman Catholic Church. Even the denominations like Anglicans, Presbyterians, Lutherans and Methodists which broke away from Roman Catholic Church who had adopted methods of baptism other than by immersion were lacking the things which founders of Pentecostalism expected. These believers felt that these denominations have gone away from the true apostolic faith whose foundation was laid by Jesus Christ and apostles like Peter, John, James, and St. Paul had built the true Catholic Church. Pentecostals have derived their name from the event pouring of Holy Spirit on the disciples on the day of Pentecost which was the Jewish feast of weeks. It was on the day of Pentecost when the disciples were together at one place and the Holy Spirit descended upon the believers in the form of divided tongues of fire from heaven with the sound like the rush of violent wind and they started speaking in different tongues and glorifying God. This was fulfillment of the promise Jesus had made in John:14.

In 1900 Charles Parham who strongly believed in divine healing, Spirit baptism and speaking of tongues was an American Evangelist and a faith healer was teaching the people about the spiritual gifts and evangelization of the whole world. Most of the believers felt that this is period of end times and Christ's Second Advent is very near. Charles Parham was one of those evangelists who preached about the Holy Spirit baptism after the water baptism by immersion and then receiving of the Holy Spirit gifts as preached by St. Paul and speaking of tongues was one of those spiritual gifts as the disciples and believers started speaking when they received the Holy Spirit in the form of divided tongues of fire, but he himself received these gifts sometime later. It was for the first time on January 1, 1901 that his students of the Topeka Kansas School while praying received the Holy Spirit baptism. There were many revival movements going on at that time to prepare the people to receive Jesus Christ at His Second Advent. Charles Parham preached for three years in Azusa Street revival in Los Angeles, California stressing upon Spirit baptism and speaking of different tongues as a proof of Spirit baptism and this was the basis of Pentecostalism. This resulted in the spread of Pentecostal faith throughout the United States and then throughout the world through their missionaries. The crowds of people started worshiping at the Azusa Street. William J. Seymour a black preacher and a student of Charles Parham in 1906 started preaching in Los Angeles and held much revival meeting thereby attracted thousands of followers for Pentecostal Movement.

Like other denominations and faiths Pentecostalism also experienced many divisions and controversies. They got divided into Trinitarians and non-Trinitarians resulting in over 700 denominations and large number of independent Churches. Like the Roman Catholics, Presbyterians, Lutherans, Methodists, and Baptist Churches there is no central governing authority of Pentecostalism, but in spite of all this there is World Pentecostal Fellowship which has many Pentecostal denominations affiliated with it. There are about 300 million Pentecostals and the movement is growing rapidly all over the world. Pentecostal movement is gaining acceptance mainly in South East Asia, Latin America because of the faith healing, Spirit baptism. Even non-Pentecostal denominations like Roman Catholic,

Protestant and orthodox Churches have started realizing the need for spiritual gifts and Spirit baptism and they have started Charismatic Movement. Though Pentecostals attribute their beginning from Azusa street mission where Charles Parham was holding revival meetings yet The Church of God which is also Pentecostal Church claim that their Church was founded 10 years before the Azusa Street Revival with 8 or 9 men and they experienced the Spirit baptism and received the gift of speaking in tongues but some of their own historians are doubtful about this claim.

Pentecostal Beliefs:

1. Pentecostal Movement is entirely evangelical faith. They believe:
2. In transformation of believer's life through faith in Jesus Christ.
3. They believe in Trinity.
4. In the inerrancy of the Bible because it is inspired word of God.
5. That the word of God the Bible written in the original tongues is infallible and the teachings of Christ in the four gospels are the fundamental belief of the Pentecostals.
6. Jesus Christ is the 'Word' and the Son of God the savior and baptizer of the Holy Spirit baptism after one has been baptized in the name of Holy Trinity.
7. Jesus Christ is the healer when we put our faith in Him.
8. At His Second Advent He will come to receive His saved believers.

Salvation through Jesus Christ:

They believe that believers are saved through the sacrificial death and the holy blood of Jesus Christ shed on the cross. He paid the price of our sins, so our sins are forgiven and we are reconciled with God through Jesus Christ our Lord and intercessor. To achieve salvation one must be born again as Jesus told Nicodemus (John 3: 3-5). Jesus answered Nicodemus, "Very truly, I tell you no one can see the kingdom of God without being born from above …….very truly I tell you no one can enter the Kingdom of God (Salvation) without being born of water and Spirit".

Pentecostals believe that this new birth is received by the grace of God through faith in Jesus Christ and accepting Him as the personal savior and the Lord. To receive the grace of God faith and repentance are mandatory preconditions for salvation and then remaining firm in that faith. They also believe literally in hell and heaven. Heaven is for those who receive Jesus Christ as their Lord and savior and receive the gift of salvation through the grace of our Lord and hell is for those who reject Lordship of Jesus Christ. Most of the Pentecostals believe that water baptism and the Spirit baptism are the main requirements for salvation. Jesus Christ and His redemptive work is the corner stone of their faith. They believe when a person surrenders to Christ and redemptive work has been done by the forgiveness of sins at that moment person is born again and the believer has the presence of Holy Spirit in his life. When the Holy Spirit is poured upon the believer, that is called anointing of the believer. With the anointing or baptism with the Holy Spirit believer is now prepared for the Christian service. He becomes ready for the spiritual warfare when he can fight against the spiritual enemies. He can make use of the spiritual gifts for the edification of the Church of Christ and to glorify his Lord's name not only that he can face persecution for Jesus' sake smilingly. Pentecostals believe that the requirement for salvation is repentance, baptism with Holy Spirit and the grace of God and that happens only when a believer has totally surrendered to Christ. They believe that spiritual gifts and the gift of salvation is given to the believer when he has a persistent faith in God and His son Jesus Christ.

Not all but some Pentecostals believe that speaking of tongues is God's gift which may or may not be immediate, but it is the physical evidence of born again and baptism of Holy Ghost. They believe that once the believer has the Holy Spirit baptism his life becomes purpose filled life to glorify God, passion for souls, witness to others, lead effective prayer life and use the gifts of Holy Spirit.

Faith Healing:

Pentecostals believe in faith healing because their Lord gave the gift of healing through prayer and in the name of Jesus Christ. Divine healing is one of the spiritual gifts and is part of salvation. Healing ministry is one of the main parts of Pentecostalism. One of the Pentecostal Scholars Vernon L. Purdy believed in spiritual and physical healing, because sin leads to human suffering and healing comes through faith and in the name of Jesus Christ. Pentecostals believe everyone may not receive healing through prayer because He may or may not grant healing. If a person does not receive healing it may be because God wants to teach the person through suffering or lack of faith may be another reason. Even St. Paul had some physical problem for which he fervently prayed and he received the answer from God who said, "My grace is sufficient for you". Even if we do not get healing we should continue to trust and have firm faith in Him as Job did. Prayer and fasting is central in Christian faith.

Second Advent of Jesus:

They believe in the Second Advent of Jesus Christ. Pentecostals believe that every day and every hour is eschatological. As Christ can come any moment at an unexpected hour so we should be ready and lead life of personal holiness. They believe in pre-tribulation rapture, so we should not be slack in worship, Christian service and evangelism.

Spiritual Gifts:

Pentecostals literally believe in all spiritual gifts including faith healing and miracles. St. Paul clearly stated in his epistles about the spiritual gifts. Romans 12: 3-8; 1 Corinthians 12: 4-11; Ephesians 4:7-16 which are also known as the fruits of the Spirit. Fruits of the Spirit exhibit the spiritual life of the believer and proof of the new birth in Christ. These fruits should be evident in the life of every believer in Christ irrespective of his denomination. Gift of prophecy and discerning of the Holy Spirit from the evil or human spirit is also spiritual gift. Even the vocal gifts like prophecy, speaking of tongues and interpretation of tongues is the gift of Holy Spirit.

Pentecostal Worship:

In traditional Pentecostal worship they have singing; sharing of spirit gifts, alter intercession, prayers, announcements, testimonies, music, scripture reading and sometimes Lord's Supper. Prayer has important role in Pentecostal worship. Prayer may be collective oral prayer in local language or different tongues if the person is inspired by the Holy Spirit. Most of the Pentecostals during prayer raise hands uttering Hallelujah. Even while singing they may raise hands and shout Hallelujah. If anyone needs special prayer people lay hands on the head of the person and pray for his healing or for any special need. Sometimes while the person who is being prayed over faints and falls backward. In their worship while praying it seems they experience the presence of God and are overwhelmed. Some times while singing if a person is overwhelmed by the presence of Holy Spirit may start dancing and this is very common in black churches. Pentecostals believe when Holy Spirit takes control of the physical and spiritual emotions the worshipper spontaneously starts dancing. This is what happened with David while taking the Ark of God; he was so overwhelmed the he started dancing without caring for anyone. Sometimes other worshippers also join with the loud shouts of Hallelujah and praise the Lord. This specially takes place in revival or special prayer meetings.

Sacraments/Ordinances:

There are two Biblical sacraments or Ordinances which Pentecostals celebrate. They believe in the Ordinance of water baptism by immersion and it is mandatory because it is commandment of our Lord. Water baptism only by immersion is an outward symbol that person has repented and inner conversion has already taken place, but this is not true in the case of a person getting baptized with some selfish motive. Most of the Pentecostals like other Pentecostals Churches do not view baptism essential for salvation and grace of God. Even then water baptism is necessary part of salvation and grace. Pentecostals are generally Trinitarians. Pentecostal celebrate Holy Communion like other denominations because it is commandment of our Lord, but they do not use wine instead they use grape juice. As Jesus did and commanded before the institution of Eucharist, they celebrate foot washing as an ordinance of humility. John 13:14-17. Some Pentecostal denominations do not consider foot washing as an ordinance but they recognize its spiritual value of humility and serving others.

Their Statistics:

According to 2011 survey it is estimated that there are 280 million Pentecostals which is 12.8 % of the world's Christian population. There are independent Pentecostal Churches so this number may be different. Large numbers of Pentecostals is found in Africa and then in America and about 16% are found in Asia and Pacific countries. Large number of people is accepting Pentecostalism in Asia and Latin America. Though the number of Pentecostal denominations is more than 700 but there are many independent Pentecostal Churches who do not have any affiliation. In the early 20th century Pentecostralism was Wesleyan. They believed in personal cleansing before water and Holy Spirit baptism. Churches of God and Church of God in Christ are Pentecostal. There are many Pentecostal denominations with slight difference in belief but all believe in Trinity, water baptism, Spirit baptism and grace of God and Jesus Christ as the corner stone of their faith. There is one Pentecostal denomination known as Oneness Pentecostals who do not believe in Trinity that is God as three persons but three manifestations of one living God. They baptize in the name of Jesus Christ only and then the Spirit baptism, grace of God through faith in Christ and then the Salvation. On this issue of baptism and speaking of tongues they criticize other protestant denominations like Methodists, Presbyterians, Lutherans, and the Roman Catholics and compel them to get re-baptized like the Mennonites/Anabaptists and sometimes they try to steal sheep from the fold of other denominations. The main figures who played prominent leading role in this movement other than the founders were Edward Irving, William Boardman, Albert Benjamin, and John Alexander Dowie.

American Pentecostal Church:

When Charles F. Parham started his Bible School in 1905 in Houston Texas many whites got influenced by his preaching about Spirit Baptism and speaking of tongues. That was a time when blacks were racially discriminated. William J. Seymor son of a black slave (He was blinded in one eye by small pox) also got influenced by his teaching. He wanted to attend Parham's school, but he was not permitted to sit with the white students inside the room, but he could sit outside in the hallway and listen to Parham's lectures. He was so much influenced that being convinced of Spirit baptism and speaking of tongues he moved to Los Angeles and started his own revival meetings where he attracted many blacks and whites, so his congregation became multiracial, but certain racial people scandalized multiracial thought. Though certain people advocated that racism has no place in Christianity and blood of Jesus has washed away the color and all are equal before God. Even Parham realized that in Pentecostalism racialism has no place but because of his white followers he could not oppose it. In 1906 when he saw a large following of blacks and whites in William J. Seymour's congregation he was not happy on mixing of blacks and whites. So after that they got separated and even Pentecostals got divided into Church of God in Christ having black members and assemblies of God with white congregation and then emerged other denominations like the Church of God and the Pentecostal holiness Church. Assemblies of God make world's largest denomination with about 65 million adherents. Later on with the passage of time they realized that racism is not good in Christian faith so in 1965 they passed a resolution to discourage discriminatory practices in Pentecostalism and after that they declared that racism is a sin against God who does not discriminate human beings on the basis of color. Now most of the Pentecostal Churches have mixed congregation of blacks and whites. In America Mr. Charles F.

Parham and William J. Seymour are considered forefathers of American Pentecostalism. The wave of Pentecostalism influenced many main line protestant Churches and especially the Lutheran Church. In 1967 Missouri Synod of Lutherans was called and this movement was dubbed as neo- Pentecostalism. Many Lutheran pastors stated they have found new dimensions because of this faith. So the Missouri Synod defrocked many of its pastors on this issue. Even the United Presbyterian Church of America was influenced by this Charismatic movement, so ten thousand to fifteen thousand members of United Presbyterian Church and the Presbyterian Church of U.S.A. received the Pentecostal baptism by1975. Yet in spite of the controversies Pentecostalism is still on the rise.

Ceylon Pentecostals:

Ceylon Pentecostal Mission (CPM) or Ceylon Pentecostal denomination was founded in Colombo Sri Lanka (Ceylon) by a Hindu convert Raman Kutty who was later on known as Pastor Paul. Raman Kutty was child of Kerala Hindu parents who migrated to Sri Lanka. He got converted at the age of 18 and in1923 he founded the Pentecostal Church. Now it has about two and a half million followers worldwide in 65 nations. Since it has largest following in India so it has its head quarters in Chennai Tamil Nadu. As many Tamilians and Keralites have moved to Far East countries so it has Churches in Singa pore, Malaysia, Nepal, Australia, Hongkong, New Zealand, U.S.A, Canada, Europe, Africa, and Caribbean Islands. Ceylon Pentecostal mission also have branches in Latin American countries like Brazil, Ecuador, Guinea, Rwanda, Zambia, Zimbabwe, Cameroon, Jamaica, Haiti, Mauritius, Seychelles, South Africa, Ivory Cost, Honduras, and Dubai.

Many Ceylon Pentecostal Churches are now functioning in North India and because of healing ministry and casting out of demons people in cities and rural areas are adopting Pentecostal faith. These churches are led by a chief pastor, with the help of deputy chief pastor, and associate Deputy Chief Pastor.

Faith:

1. They are Trinitarian
2. Bible is the inspired word of God and it is not mythology.
3. Jesus Christ is the only begotten son of God the father, conceived of the Holy Spirit and born of Virgin Mary. He was crucified, buried and third day rose from the dead. He ascended into heaven and is seated at the right hand of the father as an intercessor for the believers.
4. Believer's new birth and born again.
5. Water baptism by immersion only in the name of the Father, and the son and the Holy Spirit.
6. Spirit baptism and speaking of tongues as a proof of baptism by Holy Spirit.
7. Divine healing.
8. Sanctification of body, mind, soul and the spirit.
9. Resurrection of the body.
10. All are sinners and come short of the glory of God.
11. After being born again, justification wrought by faith and Holy blood of Jesus Christ.
12. Second Advent of the Lord (Rapture and tribulation).
13. They are millenarians, because they believe in 1,000 years reign of Jesus Christ and then the judgment.
14. Eternal life.
15. Preaching of the gospel for which they have Mission Education Fund, Tract Ministry and many publications.
16. Ordinance of washing the saint's feet.

Note:

21.1. Pentecost.

Pentecost (fiftieth) is the Greek name for festival of weeks. Originally it was a prominent Jewish feast of harvest and was celebrated 50 days after the Passover. Jews also attached importance to this, because of the giving of Mosaic Law on Mount Sinai 50 days after they left Egypt. Later they named this feast of Pentecost as Shavout (Ex: 34:22; Deut. 16:10; Lev. 23. 15, 16.). After the ascension of Jesus and pouring of the Holy Spirit on this day Christians adopted it to celebrate the birth of 'Christian Church'. On this day Holy Spirit descended upon the Apostles and the other believers in the form of divided tongues of fire. This is now celebrated seven weeks (50 days) after the Easter Sunday. It falls on the 10th day after ascension Thursday. Jews celebrated as Shavout the Thanksgiving to Adoni (Jehovah God). According to Jewish belief king David's birth and death took place on this day of Pentecost (Shavout).

References:

Universal Pentecostal Church Brixton

The Pentecostal Mission Media.

Pentecostal Mission – Wikipedia, the free encyclopedia.

Assemblies of God U.S.A. Website our History.

International Pentecostal Holiness Church Website.

Assemblies of God U.S.A. Website –beliefs.

Story of American Pentecostalism (The Assemblies of God)Vol 1 1941 by L Edith Blumhofer, Gospel Publishing House 1989.

Theological roots of Pentecostalism—Donald W, Dayton.

'Later Rain' falling in the East—Twentieth century Pentecostalism in India Church History by Gary B, McGee.

World Religions Pages 452, 513 Geoffrey Parrinder.

Church History in Plain Language - Bruce L. Shelly.

Our Religions and our Neighbors (Revised Edition) by Milton and Miller.

World Religions by Michael D. Coogan Oxford University Press 1998.

The Last Word

After reading about the starting of Christianity, Roman Catholicism, and emergence of different denomination mentioned in this dissertation, we find the cause behind the formation of all these denominations has been difference of opinion about the same God. In the olden times people worshipped forces of nature like wind, water, sun, animals and they respected and worshipped them as their gods and goddesses. In Greek mythology and Egyptian religion there were many gods and goddesses. In Asian religion like Hinduism and Chinese religion they too worshipped gods, goddesses, trees and their ancestors and there have been millions of gods and goddesses. Guru Nanak Dev realizing the drawbacks in the religions around him at that time started reformation movement. He preached about one God. He preached against the fanaticism existed in two major religions of his times and it gave rise to Sikhism. Islam came into being because of the drawbacks in Roman Catholicism and Judaism. Original Christian faith was Catholic in the real sense and Christ laid its foundation and the brick work on that was done by the disciples like Peter, John, James, Stephen, St. Paul, Philip, Thomas and others, who were witnesses to the sacrificial death of Christ. They walked on the dusty and hilly roads of Palestine they were real heroes. They did not have properties, palatial church buildings and crowns studded with expensive diamonds. They did not enjoy royal luxurious life. While on the preaching trips they did not stay in the five star hotels, now with the spread of education, changing cultures has changed the thinking of human beings; People cannot be suppressed and made to follow one religion. Wherever people find irrelevant rules, policies and dogmatic views they look for alternatives and that gives rise to different denominations. In Christianity there are more than 400 denominations and sub denominations. In Islam there are more than 100 denominations and some of them do not recognize each other and are deadly against each other and they are Ahmediyas, Sunnis and Shias There was a time when Catholics have been warring with their Protestant counterparts. In Sikhism and Hinduism there are so many denominations and these denominations have been hating each other. In some cases lower castes were not permitted to listen to the Holy Scripture. Only members of the high caste could listen to those scriptures, so they were killed and tortured. All these social, political and religious differences compelled the people to have different denominations and have their own worship places. This is almost in all the major religions of the world. Low caste people cannot attend the worship in the worship place, which belonged to the high caste people. Even they could not draw water from the source, which belonged to high caste community. Even now in south India there are high caste and low caste Christians, whereas the Bible says, "For in the one spirit we were all baptized into one body Jews or Greeks, slaves or free and we were all made to drink of one spirit." I Cor: 12:13. In spite of all this, different denominations are being formed and they are having different doctrines.

So I will say different interpretation about God, His word, selfish motives and dogmas have given birth to different denominations. As I have said somewhere in this dissertation it is only God the true Judge who will decide between the wrong and the right. God does not want anymore denominations because He himself did not belong to any denomination. He wants warriors who believe and trust in Him and fight against the evil forces of darkness and bring the lost unbelievers to Him so that more and more people may be saved before the Second Advent of Jesus Christ.

Catholic Daily Prayer

Our Father

Our Father, who art in Heaven, hallowed be thy name;
Thy kingdom come; Thy will be done on earth as it is in Heaven.
Give us this day our daily bread; and forgive us our trespasses
As we forgive those who trespass against us;
And lead us not into – temptation,
But deliver us from evil...
Amen

Hail Mary

Hail Mary, full of grace; the Lord is with you.
Blessed are you among women, and blessed is the fruit of your womb, Jesus.
Holy Mary, mother of God, pray for us sinners, now and at the hour of our deaths. Amen

Litany to all saints

God the Father, God the Son, God the Holy Spirit......
your image is found in your saints
All you Angels --- pray for us
All you patriarchs
All you matriarchs
All you prophets
All you holy kings, and judges
All you keepers of the law......
All you apostles......
All you disciples......
All you martyrs:...-..
All you desert Fathers.
All you holy women......
All you priests and religious.....
All you souls in purgatory.....
All you holy innocents......
All you holy people......
All you saints......
Pray for us and for those in most need...
Amen

> 2000 years ago, prayer joined to sacrifice constituted force the most powerful in human history

Prayers for the souls of purgatory

Eternal rest grant to them, O Lord, let perpetual light shine upon them. May they rest in peace... Amen.

Eternal Father, I offer you the precious blood of your divine Son, Jesus, in union with the Masses said throughout the world today for all the holy souls in purgatory. Amen

Novena to the Holy Spirit (recite for nine days)
Most Holy Spirit; God; breath of life, virtue, and all creation
You breathe where you will... How much more on those who ask.

Grant me fullness of your gifts; I will walk the path on which they are found.
In your goodness, Holy Spirit, I also ask that you grant…..

Litany of the Blessed Virgin Mary

Lord, have mercy on us;
Christ, have mercy on us;
Lord, have mercy on us;
Christ, hear us;
Christ, graciously hear us;

God the Father of Heaven,
……*have mercy on us*
God the Son, Redeemer of the world
……*have mercy on us*
God the Holy Spirit
……*have mercy on us*
Holy Trinity, one God,
……*have mercy on us*

Holy Mary…..*pray for us* Holy Mother of God…..
Holy Virgin of virgins…..
Mother of Christ…..
Mother of Divine Grace…..
Mother most pure…..
Mother most chaste…
Mother inviolate…..
Mother undefiled…..
Mother most amiable…..
Mother most admirable…..
Mother of good counsel…..
Mother of our Creator…..
Mother of our Savior…'.
Virgin most prudent…..
Virgin most venerable…..
Virgin most renowned…..
Virgin most powerful…..

Virgin most merciful.....
Virgin most faithful.....
Mirror of justice.....
Seat of wisdom.....
Cause of our joy.....
Spiritual vessel.....
Vessel of honor.....
Singular vessel of devotion.....
Mystical Rose......
Tower of David.....
Tower of Ivory.....
House of gold.....
Ark of the covenant.....
Gate of Heaven.....
Morning star...-..
Health of the sick.....
Refuge of sinners.....
Comforter of the afflicted.....
Help of Christians.....
Queen of Angels.....
Queen of Patriarchs.....
Queen of Prophets.....
Queen of Apostles.....
Queen of Martyrs.....
Queen of Confessors....
Queen of Virgins.....
Queen of all Saints.....
Queen conceived without original sin.....
Queen assumed into Heaven.....
Queen of the most holy Rosary...-..
Queen of peace.....

Lamb of God, who takes away the sins of the world
.......*spare us* 0 *Lord*
Lamb of God, who takes away the sins of the world,
.......*graciously hear us* 0 *Lord*
Lamb of God, who takes away the sins of the world
.......*have mercy on* us

Litany against moral corruption

O God, our Father, hear our plea.
On those who dress immodestly
..........*grant modesty*
On those who view immodest, and violent books and videos
..........*grant reform*
On those tempted to adultery
..........*grant chastity*
On those in anger and despair
..........*grant peace*
On those who deny and blaspheme God
..........*grant contrition*
On those addicted and obsessed
..........*grant relief*
On those tempted to sin
..........*grant strength*
On those of power and influence
..........*grant* a *holy conscience*
On those who have no moral example or upbringing
..........*grant moral Knowledge*
On those who give a worthy example
..........*grant wider influence*
On those suffering purgatory because of moral ignorance
..........*grant mercy*
On those dying in mortal sin
..........*grant mercy and salvation*
On our families
..........*grant your blessing*

God most holy, grant the Holy Spirit to breathe on us always, forming our conscience in your image...

Amen

For the salvation of souls

God most merciful, hear me.
I ask mercy for all who are far from you, (especially_).
Out of ignorance they do not seek to share in your life.
Father, they alone are not responsible; they carry the burden of the sins of others.
Inspire me to make reparation, which your Spirit may breathe on them.
In doing so I become more like you, who is love in its highest form… sacrificial love.

Spiritual Communion
(Authorized form)

"O Jesus I turn toward the holy tabernacle where You live hidden for love of me. I love you, O my God. I cannot receive you in Holy Communion-.
Come nevertheless and visit me with Your grace.
Come spiritually into my heart.
Purify it. Sanctify it.
Render it like your own ….
Amen

Prayer for Priests

Jesus,
I pray for all your priests;
Those faithful and fervent;
Those unfaithful and tepid;
Those lonely and old;
Those sick and dying;
Those in purgatory.
Sustain and guide your
Priests on earth and lead
Them to the everlasting life of the resurrection…Amen

> We live our daily life as Christ would; Our spiritual life is then our entire life.

Christian Denominations

The Ten Commandments
I am the Lord your God.
You shall have no other gods.
You shall not use the name of the Lord in vain.
Keep holy the Lord's day.
Honor your father and mother
You shall not kill.
You shall not commit adultery
You shall not steal
You shall not bear false witness.
You shall not covet your neighbor's wife
You shall not covet your neighbor's goods.

Gifts of the Holy Spirit
Wisdom
Fortitude
Understanding
Piety
Knowledge
Counsel Fear of the Lord

Fruits of the Holy Spirit

Charity
Generosity
Gentleness
Peace
Fidelity
Patience
Modesty
Kindness
Self Control
Goodness
Chastity

Seven Capitol Sins

Pride
Covetousness
Anger
Gluttony
Envy
Sloth
Lust

The Cardinal Virtues

Prudence
Fortitude
Justice
Temperance

> We live our daily life as Christ would; Our spiritual life is then our entire life.

Commandments of the Church

Assist (attend) at Mass on Sundays and holy days of obligation.
To confess sins at least once a year
To receive Holy Communion during Easter
To keep holy the holy days of obligation
To fast and abstain on the appointed days
To contribute to the support of the Church

Corporal Works of Mercy

Feed the hungry
Give drink to the thirsty
Clothe the naked
Shelter the homeless
Visit the sick
Visit the imprisoned
Bury the dead

Spiritual Works of Mercy

Instruct the ignorant
Counsel the doubtful
Admonish the sinner
Comfort the sorrowful
Forgive Injuries
Bear Wrongs Patiently

Sacraments

Baptism
Conformation
Eucharist
Penance
Anointing the Sick
Matrimony
Holy Orders

Reconciliation (confession)

Phone or check parish bulletin for times,
Enter the confessional booth, kneel and say "Bless me father for I have sinned, it has been months/years since my last confession".
The priest gives a brief blessing and you continue "these are my sins".
Tell your sins and end with "this is my confession father".
The priest will give you absolution (God's forgiveness) and ask you to say an act of contrition:
"My God I am sorry for having offended you, who I should love above all else.
I resolve, with your help to avoid sin,
and whatever leads me into sin."
The priest will assign you an act of penance·(prayer usually) and dismiss you. The sacrament of reconciliation is completed when you perform your assigned penance.. All past sins not remembered and not confessed are forgiven; the confession is invalid if we deliberately fail to confess a sin.

HAVE I

--denied God, made success, status, or things the focus of my life
--cursed in any way or used God's name in a frivolous manner
--conducted the Lord's Day (Sunday) as an ordinary, or work day
--dishonored or disobeyed father or mother, abandoned aged parents
--unjustly killed, aborted a child, hurt, threatened, or endangered anyone
--committed adultery or homosexuality, dressed immodestly, used pornography, masturbated, had unmarried sex, misused sex in any way
--stolen damaged, defrauded, been neglected been or deceitful in work
--lied or helped others in deceit
--consented to lustful desires. Watched unwholesome or violent television
--engaged in greedy or envious thought or action, disregarded charity
--failed to attend mass on Sunday or holy days, or disregard church laws
--used artificial birth control, obtained a civil divorce
--used fortune telling, psychics, horoscopes, or similar devices
--failed in my duty in the spiritual and moral upbringing of my children
--been impatient, angry, hateful, revengeful
--misused food, alcohol, drugs, been immoderate
--given bad example, judged others, or talked idly or poorly of others

--Married outside the Church, failed to be remarried in the Church
--failed to help, defend, respect, or forgive others
Note: This is not a complete list, and advising others to act sinfully, or permitting sin (according to position) is also a sin.
(Courtesy Roman Catholic Church)

Printed in Great Britain
by Amazon